VOGUE KNITTING

NORAH GAUGHAN

40 TIMELESS KNITS

VOGUE KNITTING

NORAH GAUGHAN

40 TIMELESS KNITS

JACK DEUTSCH

 sixth&springbooks   104 W 27th St, 3rd Floor, New York, NY 10001
www.sixthandspring.com

Editor
JACOB SEIFERT

Vice President/Editorial Director
TRISHA MALCOLM

Art Director
JOE VIOR

Chief Operating Officer
CAROLINE KILMER

Yarn Editor
JACLENE SINI

Production Manager
DAVID JOINNIDES

Supervising Patterns Editor
CARLA SCOTT

President
ART JOINNIDES

Technical Illustrator
LORETTA DACHMAN

Chairman
JAY STEIN

Library of Congress Cataloging-in-Publication Data is available upon request

Manufactured in China

3 5 7 9 10 8 6 4

First Edition

ACKNOWLEDGMENTS

This book could not have been possible without all of the **Vogue Knitting** editors I've worked with over the years. Lola Ehrlich gave me my start, and I still marvel at the lush pages produced under her editorship. Margery Winter was, and still is, much more than an editor to me. Her mentorship lasted at least twenty years while our friendship endures to this day. The editor who always knew how to bring out my quirky side was Adina Klein. Many thanks to Trisha Malcolm, my co-author for this volume, who has skillfully guided me through the past twenty years of designing for **Vogue Knitting**. Thanks also to Joe Vior for his amazing art direction and to Jacob Seifert who skillfully handled the organization of this volume. Thanks to all of the staff from the past thirty years. It does, indeed, take a village! Lastly, I cannot be thankful enough for the expert work of Carla Patrick Scott's technical expertise, a constant throughout my thirty-year relationship with **Vogue Knitting**.

DEDICATION

To my mom, Phoebe Adams Gaughan, who was
the most devoted fan and best mom anyone could ask for.

CONTENTS

PAUL AMATO

FOREWORD

By Trisha Malcolm

Long before I came to **Vogue Knitting**, I was in awe of Norah Gaughan. I read the article naming her a Master Knitter of the Nineties (reproduced on pages 45-47) and was incredibly impressed with her story and her talent. Then, when I first became Editor in Chief, I had the pleasure of finally meeting Norah in person (and then working with her since). I will never forget opening the envelope containing her sketches for the first issue I worked on and loving them all! I chose two for that issue (see pages 74-84), one of which I was lucky enough to wear for several years after.

Selecting the garments to include in this volume was both immensely enjoyable and incredibly challenging. We chose from more than 120 pieces, a tremendous body of work, editing down to the 40 you find here. Norah and I went over each piece, considering whether to include it. We discussed if the older designs had stood the test of time and would still appeal to knitters today. As we reviewed, many personal experiences came into play—designs we both had very fond memories of, the beginnings of an exploration of a new technique, or various milestones, such as anniversary issues. Some yarns are still available, but others don't have suitable replacements on the market right now, so that helped cull as well. (Every effort has been made to find suitable yarn substitutions, and we have included the original yarns used in case your stash still contains some of these gems.)

Norah's career has included time working as the head designer for a yarn company, first for Reynolds/JCA and then later for Berroco. This explains why you will see so many designs originally worked in yarns from those companies. While most of the pieces she has designed for us carry her name, there was a considerable number created by Norah published under the Adrienne Vittadini yarn label. We have not included those pieces in this collection.

For several years now Norah has been keeping busy as an independent hand-knit designer. Her designs continue to show up in **Vogue Knitting** and in collaboration with various yarn companies and publishers. Most notably, Norah works with the Brooklyn Tweed design team, has created a collection with The Fibre Co., and designed a book of linen patterns with Quince & Co. Her recent book, **Norah Gaughan's Knitted Cable Sourcebook**, is considered one of the most definitive titles on the subject. You can find Norah traveling around the country teaching at **Vogue Knitting LIVE!** and at other events and retreats around the world. Learn from her videos on CreativeBug, follow her on Ravelry, and stay up to date with all of her work at her website, norahgaughan.net.

———————————————

Norah's mother, Phoebe, to whom this book is dedicated, was a longtime contributor to **Vogue Knitting**. Phoebe was an incredible illustrator, and many of our hand-illustrated how-tos over the years were impeccably drawn by her. She is greatly missed.

INTRODUCTION

Stunning photography, an eye for trends, and a deep understanding of a knitter's need for knowledge have been the hallmarks of **Vogue Knitting**'s success and longevity. Thirty years ago, I was immensely thrilled to be published in this magazine for the first time. While I have gotten more used to the excitement, I am, to this day, very proud to be included in its pages along with an ever-evolving cadre of talented designers.

This family of editors and designers has been an integral influence throughout my career, especially at the start. Whenever I have occasion to talk about my creative process, I rarely fail to credit **Vogue Knitting** with seeding my love of pattern stitch development. During one of the early-era design meetings, while we were all immersed in a stimulating slide show of themes and textures, an image became lodged in my head. Back home, I sought to replicate what was in my memory, with nothing but my quick sketch for reference. The twisted stitch pattern of the Zigzag Turtleneck from Fall/Winter 1987 (pages 15-17) was the immediate result. Whether I "unvented" it (as Elizabeth Zimmermann might have said) or whether the pattern was truly something new, the act of making the idea work and recording it on paper triggered an outpouring of twisted-stitch patterns from my brain, pencil, and needles. As I knit one idea, two or three more would spring to mind. At first, invention came while knitting. Soon I understood the knitted structure enough to be able to make up new ideas with pencil and paper prior to having the needles in my hands. In my heart, I know this burst of creativity led to my larger love of making up cabled stitches, and my creative method remains similar to this day.

Clearly, many of the designs in this volume display my perennial obsession with cables. Studying the cabled designs we've included here, I see they also illustrate my love of working in series, revisiting my previously established cable vocabulary. One of my favorites, the Trellis Cardigan from Fall 1997 (pages 80-84), has intertwined figures made with my favorite slanted O motif. Almost twenty years later, the motif shows up in the yoke of the Funnel-Neck Pullover from Fall 2014 (pages 141-145) and once again in the diagonal cables of my Cabled Cardigan from Spring/Summer 2017 (pages 162-167). I'm sure this is not the last time you'll see this motif from me.

Knitters cannot live by cables alone. I hope you will be happily surprised to see my forays into other techniques over the years as well. I've dabbled in colorwork, worked a lot with knit/purl textures, and repeated myself (yet again) by building multiple garments and accessories from polygons.

With colorwork I try to keep things simple, even when the finished result may look complicated. If there are more than two colors in a row, the additional colors are laid in with duplicate stitch (see the Southwest Band Cardigan from Winter Special 1989/90 on pages 26-29, the Plaid Pullover from Winter 2014/15 on pages 150-155, and the Persian Yoke Pullover from Winter 2017/18 on pages 170-173). Or, in the case of the oversized Tiled Colorwork Cardigan from Spring/Summer 1992 (pages 52-54), an easy-to-learn combo of Fair Isle-like stranding and intarsia forms tile-like motifs and enables the use of multiple colors across the row without much bother.

Menswear is a love of mine, and I think it's because the fabric comes first. The shapes are quite simple, and the fun is in the texture. When designing for men, my goal is to create sweaters that men I know would really wear, so they are classic and don't go out of style—as seen in The Textured Plaid Pullover from Winter Special 1989/90 (pages 30-32) and the Gridded Pullover from Spring/Summer 1999 (pages 91-93). Knit/purl textures like these may personally be my favorite thing to knit. I like to learn the pattern quickly so I can ignore the chart or pattern text while indulging in my favorite movies or binging a TV series.

My polygon obsession stems from an idea I read in a nineteenth-century book about the process of creating surface patterns for architecture. I'll paraphrase, but the idea is that by repeating a simple element you create something that appears more complicated while remaining elegantly simple. Taking that to heart, I designed the Cabled Bolero for Winter 2006/07 (pages 120-123), otherwise known as the Capecho, which is comprised of pentagons, each made with five identical simple rib-and-cable triangles. Likewise, the Kaleidoscopic Cables Coat from Fall 2007 (pages 124-127) is built around large triangles with a cabled lattice in each center and a simple lace pattern is repeated six times per hexagon in the Medallion Shawl from Winter 2007/08 (pages 128-129).

Don't hesitate to make these patterns your own. I think most of us knit for two reasons; The first is to learn, and the second is to have something great to wear. My philosophy is that my pattern is just a starting point. Change the color, change the length, leave out the details that don't suit you, and put in your own special touches to achieve a finished garment that brings you joy in the process and pride in the wearing.

— *Norah Gaughan*

CABLED VEST

A sleeveless pullover with a crew neck and three-button back neck opening, this was my debut design for **Vogue Knitting.** I was unimaginably thrilled to see my work published, and this gorgeous photo bathed in amber light made it all the sweeter. The classic design of cables and ladders still looks fresh today. Stay with the longer length or abbreviate it to fit your personal style.

■■■▭

SIZES
X-Small (Small/Medium, Large/X-Large). Shown in size Small/Medium.

KNITTED MEASUREMENTS
Bust 33½ (38½, 42½)"/84 (96,106)cm
Length 26 (27, 28)"/65.5 (68,70.5)cm

MATERIALS
• Original Yarn
14 (15, 16) 1¾oz/50g balls (each approx 70yd/63m) of **Classic Elite Yarns** Newport (cotton) in #2344 Bronze (4)
• Substitute Yarn
5 (6, 6) 3½oz/100g hanks (each approx 205yd/187m) of **Berroco** Weekend (acrylic/Peruvian cotton) in 5988 Redwood (4)
• One pair each sizes 5 and 7 (3.75 and 4.5mm) needles, OR SIZE TO OBTAIN GAUGE
• Three ⅝"/15mm buttons
• Cable needle (cn)
• Removable stitch markers

GAUGE
22 sts and 28 rows to 4"/10cm over charts 1 and 2 (see note section) with larger needles.
TAKE TIME TO CHECK GAUGE.

NOTE
To work gauge swatch, cast on 25 sts. P2, work chart 1 over 5 sts, chart 2 over 11 sts, chart 1 over 5 sts, p2. Cont in pat for 28 rows. Bind off. Measure piece over charts.

STITCH GLOSSARY
4-st RC Sl 2 sts to cn and hold to back, k2, k2 from cn.

BACK
With smaller needles, cast on 88 (96, 106) sts.
Work in k1, p1 rib for 1"/2.5cm, inc 7 (9, 11) sts evenly across last row—95 (105, 117) sts. Change to larger needles.
Row 1 (RS) P2, work first 11 (0, 6) sts of chart 2, [work 5 sts of chart 1, work 11 sts of chart 2] 5 (6, 6) times, work 0 (5, 5) sts of chart 1, work last 0 (0, 6) sts of chart 2, p2.
Cont in this manner, working first and last 2 sts in rev St st (p on RS, k on WS) until piece measures 16½ (17, 17½)"/42 (43, 44.5)cm from beg, end with a WS row.

Armhole Shaping
Bind off 4 (5, 5) sts at beg of next 2 rows, bind off 2 sts at beg of next 6 (8, 8) rows, then dec 1 st each end of every other row 2 (3, 4) times—71 (73, 83) sts.
Cont in pat as established until armhole measures 2¾ (3, 3¼)"/6.5 (7.5, 8)cm.

Back Placket Opening
Next row Work 34 (35, 40) sts, join 2nd ball of yarn, bind off center 3 sts, work to end.
Working both sides at once, cont in pat until armhole measures 8¼ (8¾, 9¼)"/20.5 (22, 23)cm.

Neck and Shoulder Shaping
Bind off from each neck edge 11 (12, 13) sts once, 4 sts twice, 3 (3, 4) sts once, AT THE SAME TIME, when armhole measures 8½ (9, 9½)"/21.5 (23, 24)cm, bind off from each armhole edge 4 (4, 5) sts 3 times.

FRONT
Work as for back (omitting back placket opening) until armhole measures 7 (7½, 8)"/17 (18.5, 19.5)cm.

Neck and Shoulder Shaping
Work 23 (23, 27) sts, join 2nd ball of yarn, bind off center 25 (27, 29) sts, work to end.
Working both sides at once, bind off from each neck edge

4 sts twice, 3 (3, 4) sts once, AT THE SAME TIME, when same length as back to shoulder, shape shoulder as for back.

FINISHING
Block pieces to measurements. Sew shoulder seams.

Armhole Bands
With RS facing and smaller needles, pick up and k 85 (89, 93) sts evenly along front and back armhole edge.
Knit 2 rows. Work in k1, p1 rib for 1"/2.5cm. Bind off in rib.

Neckband
With RS facing and smaller needles, pick up and k 18 (19, 21) sts along left back neck edge, 44 (46, 50) sts along front neck, and 18 (19, 21) sts along right back neck edge −80 (84, 92) sts.
Knit 2 rows. Work in k1, p1 rib for 1"/2.5cm. Bind off in rib.

Right Back Placket
With RS facing and smaller needles, pick up and k 34 (36, 38) sts along right back placket edge.
Knit 2 rows. Work in k1, p1 rib for 1"/2.5cm. Bind off in rib. Place markers on placket for 3 buttons, first marker in 8th st from lower edge, last marker in 4th st from top edge, and 1 evenly between.

Left Back Placket
Pick up sts as for right back placket. Knit 2 rows. Work in k1, p1 rib for 1 row.
Work buttonholes on next row opposite markers by binding off 2 sts for each buttonhole. On next row, cast on 2 sts over bound-off sts. Complete as for right placket. Sew side edges of placket, left over right, along 3 center bound-off sts.
Sew on buttons. Sew side seams, including armhole bands. ●

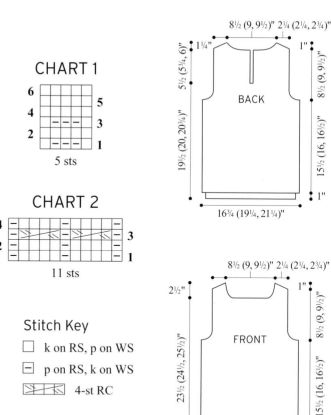

CHART 1

5 sts

CHART 2

11 sts

Stitch Key
☐ k on RS, p on WS
– p on RS, k on WS
4-st RC

8½ (9, 9½)" 2¼ (2¼, 2¾)"

1¼" 1"

5½ (5¾, 6)"

BACK

19½ (20, 20¾)"

15½ (16, 16½)" 8½ (9, 9½)"

1"

16¾ (19¼, 21¼)"

8½ (9, 9½)" 2¼ (2¼, 2¾)"

2½" 1"

FRONT

23½ (24½, 25½)"

15½ (16, 16½)" 8½ (9, 9½)"

1"

16¾ (19¼, 21¼)"

ZIGZAG TURTLENECK

This turtleneck represents a turning point in my career. After soaking in inspiration at an annual **Vogue Knitting** design meeting, I hurried home to reimagine what I had seen using twisted stitches. This marked the beginning of my obsession with inventing textural pattern stitches and cables.

SIZES
2X-Small (X-Small, Small, Medium, Large, X-Large).
Shown in size Medium.

KNITTED MEASUREMENTS
Bust 38 (40, 42, 44, 46, 48)"/97 (103, 107, 111, 117, 121)cm
Length 27 (28, 28½, 29, 29½, 30)"/68.5 (71, 72, 73, 74.5, 76)cm
Upper Arm 18 (19, 20, 20, 21, 21)"/46 (48, 50, 50, 53, 53)cm

MATERIALS
• Original Yarn
13 (14, 14, 15, 15, 16) 1¾oz/50g balls (each approx 110yd/100m) of **Reynolds** Andean Alpaca Classic 4-Ply (alpaca) in #21 Beige (4)
• Substitute Yarn
13 (14, 14, 15, 15, 16) 1¾oz/50g hanks (each approx 109yd/100m) of **Classic Elite Yarns** Inca Alpaca (baby alpaca) in 1116 Natural (4)
• One pair each sizes 6 and 7 (4 and 4.5mm) needles, OR SIZE TO OBTAIN GAUGES
• One each sizes 5 and 6 (3.75 and 4mm) circular needles, 16"/40cm long
• Stitch markers

GAUGES
• 20 sts and 28 rows to 4"/10cm over St st using size 7 (4.5mm) needles.
• 78 sts to 12½"/32.5cm over chart 1 using size 7 (4.5mm) needles.
TAKE TIME TO CHECK GAUGES.

TWISTED RIB
(multiple of 4 sts plus 2)
Row 1 (RS) K2 tbl, *p2 tbl, k2 tbl; rep from * to end.
Row 2 P2 tbl, *k2 tbl, p2 tbl; rep from * to end.
Rep rows 1 and 2 for twisted rib.

STITCH GLOSSARY
RT (right twist) K2tog leaving sts on LH needle, k first st again, sl both sts from needle.

LT (left twist) With RH needle behind LH needle, skip first st and k 2nd st tbl, insert RH needle into backs of both sts and k2tog tbl.

BACK
With smaller needles, cast on 94 (98, 102, 106, 110, 114) sts. Work in twisted rib for 2"/5cm, inc 16 (18, 18, 18, 20, 20) sts evenly across last WS row—110 (116, 120, 124, 130, 134) sts. Change to larger needles.

Begin Chart 1
Row 1 (RS) K16 (19, 21, 23, 26, 28), pm, work row 1 of chart 1 over 78 sts, pm, k16 (19, 21, 23, 26, 28).
Cont in this manner, working chart 1 over center 78 sts and rem sts in St st (k on RS, p on WS) until piece measures 17 (17½, 17½, 18, 18, 18½)"/43 (44.5, 44.5, 45.5, 45.5, 47)cm from beg.

Armhole Shaping
Dec 1 st each end every other row 5 times—100 (106, 110, 114, 120, 124) sts.
Cont in pat until armhole measures 9 (9½, 10, 10, 10½, 10½)"/23 (24, 25, 25, 26.5, 26.5)cm.

Shoulder and Neck Shaping
Bind off 8 (9, 9, 9, 10, 10) sts at beg of next 6 (8, 6, 2, 6, 4) rows, then 9 (0, 10, 10, 11, 11) sts at beg of next 2 (0, 2, 6, 2, 4) rows, AT THE SAME TIME, bind off center 14 (14, 16, 16, 18, 20) sts for neck, and working both sides at once, bind off 5 sts from each neck edge twice.

FRONT
Work as for back until armhole measures 7½ (8, 8½, 8½, 9, 9)"/19.5 (20.5, 21.5, 21.5, 23, 23)cm, end with a WS row.

Neck and Shoulder Shaping
Next row (RS) Work 45 (48, 50, 52, 54, 56) sts, join 2nd ball of yarn and bind off center 10 (10, 10, 10, 12, 12) sts, work to end. Working both sides at once, bind off from each neck edge 3 sts 1 (1, 2, 2, 2, 3) times, bind off 2 sts 3 (3, 2, 2, 2, 1) times,

then dec 1 st each neck edge every other row 3 times, AT THE SAME TIME, when same length as back to shoulder, work shoulder shaping as for back.

SLEEVES
With smaller needles, cast on 38 (38, 42, 42, 46, 46) sts. Work in twisted rib for 2"/5cm, inc 6 (6, 6, 6, 4, 6) sts evenly across last WS row—44 (44, 48, 48, 50, 52) sts. Change to larger needles.

Begin Chart 2
Row 1 (RS) K8 (8, 10, 10, 11, 12), pm, work row 1 of chart 2 over 28 sts, pm, k8 (8, 10, 10, 11, 12).
Cont in this manner, working chart 2 over center 28 sts and rem sts in St st, AT THE SAME TIME, inc 1 st each end (working inc sts into St st) every other row 2 (6, 6, 6, 8, 6) times, then every 4th row 23 (22, 22, 22, 22, 23) times—94 (100, 104, 104, 110, 110) sts.
Work even until piece measures 16½ (17, 17½, 17½, 18, 18)"/41 (42.5, 43.5, 43.5, 45, 45)cm from beg.

Cap Shaping
Dec 1 st each end every other row 5 times. Bind off rem sts.

FINISHING
Block pieces to measurements. Sew shoulder seams.

Turtleneck
With RS facing and smaller circular needle, beg at right shoulder, pick up and k 80 (80, 84, 84, 88, 92) sts evenly around neck edge. Join and pm to mark beg of rnd.
Rnd 1 *K2 tbl, p2 tbl; rep from * around.
Rep rnd 1 for 4"/10cm. Change to larger circular needle. Rep rnd 1 until turtleneck measures 8"/20cm. Bind off in rib.

Sew top of sleeve to straight edge of armhole, then sew dec armhole sts of front and back to dec sts of sleeve. Sew side and sleeve seams. ●

CHART 1

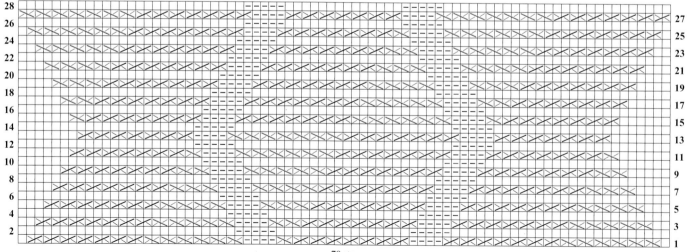

78 sts

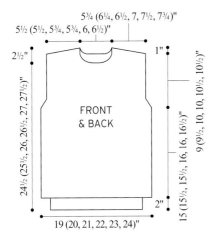

5¾ (6¼, 6½, 7, 7½, 7¾)"

5½ (5½, 5¾, 5¾, 6, 6½)"

2½"

1"

FRONT
& BACK

9 (9½, 10, 10, 10½, 10½)"

24½ (25½, 26, 26½, 27, 27½)"

15 (15½, 15½, 16, 16, 16½)"

2"

19 (20, 21, 22, 23, 24)"

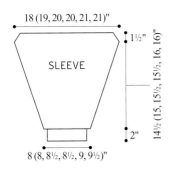

18 (19, 20, 20, 21, 21)"

1½"

SLEEVE

14½ (15, 15½, 15½, 16, 16½)"

2"

8 (8, 8½, 8½, 9, 9½)"

Stitch Key

☐ k on RS, p on WS

⊟ p on RS, k on WS

⊠ RT

⊠ LT

CHART 2

28 sts

CHEVRON PULLOVER

A simple combination of knits and purls creates a striking embossed effect, distinguishing this comfortable, oversized pullover. Ridged borders along the ribbed edges and buttons embellishing the left shoulder add a few extra touches that make all the difference.

■■■■

SIZES
Small (Medium, Large, X-Large, 2X-Large). Shown in size X-Large.

KNITTED MEASUREMENTS
Bust 39½ (42, 45½, 48, 51½)"/98 (106, 113, 121, 128)cm
Length 24½ (25, 25½, 26, 26½)"/62 (63.5, 64.5, 65.5, 67)cm
Upper Arm 18 (19, 19, 20, 20)"/45 (48, 48, 50, 50)cm

MATERIALS
• Original Yarn
23 (23, 24, 24, 25) 1¾oz/50g balls (each approx 80yd/73m) of **Melrose** Memory Eight (cotton/stretch fiber) in #821 Purple (4)
• Substitute Yarn
17 (17, 18, 18, 19) 1¾oz/50g skeins (each approx 110yd/100m) of **Plymouth Yarn Company** Jeannee (cotton/acrylic) in 0025 (4)
• One pair each sizes 5 and 8 (3.75 and 5mm) needles, OR SIZE TO OBTAIN GAUGE
• Removable stitch markers
• Five ⅝"/15mm buttons

GAUGE
24 sts and 28 rows to 4"/10cm over chart using larger needles.
TAKE TIME TO CHECK GAUGE.

BACK
With smaller needles, cast on 102 (110, 118, 126, 134) sts.
Work in k2, p2 rib for 3"/7.5cm.
Knit 1 row on RS, purl 2 rows, then knit 2 rows.
Purl next row, inc 16 (17, 18, 19, 20) sts evenly across—118 (127, 136, 145, 154) sts.
Change to larger needles.

Begin Chart
Row 1 (RS) Work first st of chart, work 18-st rep 6 (7, 7, 8, 8) times, then work last 9 sts of chart 1 (0, 1, 0, 1) times.
Cont in pat until piece measures 14½ (14½, 15, 15, 15½)"/37 (37, 38, 38, 39.5)cm from beg.

Armhole Shaping
Bind off 9 sts at beg of next 2 rows—100 (109, 118, 127, 136) sts. Work even until armhole measures 9 (9½, 9½, 10, 10)/22.5 (24, 24, 25, 25)cm.

Shoulder and Neck Shaping
Bind off 7 (8, 9, 10, 11) sts at beg of next 8 rows, AT THE SAME TIME, bind off center 12 (13, 14, 15, 16) sts for neck and working both sides at once and cont in pat, bind off from each neck edge 4 sts once, then 6 sts twice.

FRONT
Work as for back until armhole measures 6½ (7, 7, 7½, 7½)"/16 (17.5, 17.5, 18.5, 18.5)cm, end with a WS row.

Neck shaping
Next row (RS) Work 43 (47, 51, 55, 59) sts, join 2nd ball of yarn and bind off center 14 (15, 16, 17, 18) sts, work to end. Working both sides at once and cont in pat, bind off from each neck edge 4 sts once, bind off 3 sts once, bind off 2 sts twice, then dec 1 st every other row 4 times, AT THE SAME TIME, when armhole measures 8 (8½, 8½, 9, 9)"/20 (21.5, 21.5, 22.5, 22.5)cm, work shoulder shaping at left front only (beg of RS rows) as for back, working right front even. When right front is same length as back to shoulder, work shoulder shaping as for back.

SLEEVES

With smaller needles, cast on 46 (46, 46, 50, 50) sts.
Work in k2, p2 rib for 2"/5cm.
Knit 1 row on RS, purl 2 rows, then knit 2 rows.
Purl next row, inc 22 (26, 26, 26, 26) sts evenly across—68 (72, 72, 76, 76) sts.
Change to larger needles.

Begin Chart

Work chart, beg with first st of row 1, as foll: inc 1 st each end (working inc sts into pat) every 4th row 15 (16, 16, 17, 17) times, then every 6th row 5 times—108 (114, 114, 120, 120) sts.
Work even in pat until piece measures 15½ (16, 16, 16½, 16½)"/39.5 (40.5, 40.5, 42, 42)cm from beg, end with a WS row.
Knit next row, dec 12 sts evenly across—96 (102, 102, 108, 108) sts.
Knit 1 row, purl 2 rows, knit 2 rows, then purl 2 rows. Bind off knitwise.

FINISHING

Block pieces to measurements. Sew right shoulder seam.

Neckband

With RS facing and smaller needles, beg at left front neck edge, pick up and k 62 (62, 64, 64, 66) sts to the right shoulder and 48 (48, 50, 50, 52) sts along back neck—110 (110, 114, 114, 118) sts.
Purl 2 rows, knit 2 rows, then purl 1 row.
Work in k2, p2 rib for 3"/7.5cm. Bind off in rib.

Back Shoulder Band

With RS facing and smaller needles, beg at left back neckband edge, pick up and k 37 (41, 45, 49, 53) sts along back shoulder edge. Purl 1 row. Work in k1, p1 rib for 1¼"/3cm. Bind off knitwise.
Place markers on band for 5 buttons, first ½"/1.5cm from neckband edge, last ½"/1.5cm from shoulder edge, and rem 3 evenly between.

Front Shoulder Band

Beg at left front shoulder edge, work as for back shoulder band for 3 rows. Work buttonholes opposite markers on next row by binding off 2 sts for each buttonhole. On next row, cast on 2 sts over bound-off sts.
Complete as for back shoulder band.

Place front band over back band and sew sides at shoulder edge. Sew top of sleeves to straight edge of armholes, sewing last 1½"/4cm of sleeve to bound-off armhole sts. Sew side and sleeve seams. Sew on buttons. ●

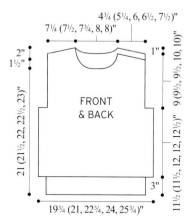

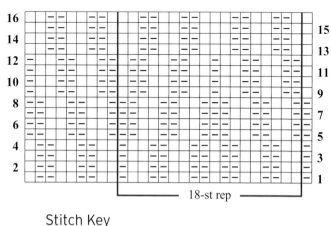

Stitch Key

☐ k on RS, p on WS   ⊟ p on RS, k on WS

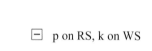

CLOCKWORK PULLOVER

The central decorative motif was borrowed from a Bavarian sock pattern. Knit from the top down, the pattern on the front of this pullover widens as the sweater widens, creating a comfortable and flattering A-line silhouette perfect for keeping warm while on the go or cozying up at home.

■■■■

SIZES
Small (Medium/Large, X-Large).
Shown in size Medium/Large.

KNITTED MEASUREMENTS
Bust 40 (43, 46)"/100 (108, 115)cm
Length 25 (26, 27)"/63 (66, 68.5)cm
Upper Arm 15½ (16, 16½)"/39 (40, 41.5)cm

MATERIALS
• Original Yarn
12 (13, 14) 1¾oz/50g balls (each approx 92yd/84m) of **Bernat** Rusticale (wool/mohair) in #14042 Off-white (**5**)
• Substitute Yarn
6 (7, 7) 3½oz/100g hanks (each approx 191yd/175m) of **HiKoo/Skacel** Oh! in #144 Heavens (**5**)
• Two size 9 (5.5mm) circular needles, 16"/40cm and 29"/80cm long, OR SIZE TO OBTAIN GAUGE
• Two size 7 (4.5mm) circular needles, 16"/40cm and 29"/80cm long
• Cable needle (cn)
• Stitch markers
• Stitch holders

GAUGE
16 sts and 24 rows to 4"/10cm over St st using larger needles.
TAKE TIME TO CHECK GAUGE.

STITCH GLOSSARY
M1 Insert LH needle from front to back under strand between last st worked and next st on LH needle, knit strand through back loop.
M1 p-st Insert LH needle from front to back under strand between last st worked and next st on LH needle, purl strand through back loop.
2-st RC Sl 1 st to cn and hold to back, k1 tbl, k1 from cn.
2-st LC Sl 1 st to cn and hold to front, k1, k1 tbl from cn.
2-st twisted RC Sl 1 st to cn and hold to back, k1 tbl, k1 tbl from cn.
2-st twisted LC Sl 1 st to cn and hold to front, k1 tbl, k1 tbl from cn.
2-st RPC Sl 1 st to cn and hold to back, k1 tbl, p1 from cn.
2-st LPC Sl 1 st to cn and hold to front, p1, k1 tbl from cn.
3-st RC Sl 1 st to cn and hold to back, k2 tbl, k1 from cn.
3-st LC Sl 2 sts to cn and hold to front, kl, k2 tbl from cn.
3-st twisted RC Sl 1 st to cn and hold to back, k2 tbl, k1 tbl from cn.
3-st twisted LC Sl 2 sts to cn and hold to front, k1 tbl, k2 tbl from cn.
3-st RPC Sl 1 st to cn and hold to back, k2 tbl, p1 from cn.
3-st LPC Sl 2 sts to cn and hold to front, p1, k2 tbl from cn.
4-st RC Sl 2 sts to cn and hold to back, k2 tbl, k2 tbl from cn.

NOTES
1) Pullover is knit in one piece from the neck down.
2) Work chart 1 on center front only through row 29. Mark center 4 sts on front. On row 30, work 4-st cable in center of chart 2 on these sts and 13 sts each side in chart 1. Rep rows 31–50 of chart 1 and cont working chart 2 in center (except for the first and last p st on chart).
3) On back, work row 1 of chart 2 over center 6 sts. After row 26 of chart 2, cont to inc 1 st inside of twisted side sts every 4th row, alternating inc between left side and right side as established in chart 2.
4) For ease in working, use different color markers to denote raglan and dart incs and for chart sts.
5) Begin with a 16"/40cm circular needle, then change to 29"/80cm when enough sts have been inc'd.

BODY

With smaller 16"/40cm needle, beg at top of highneck, cast on 76 (80, 84) sts. Join, taking care not to twist sts, and pm for beg of rnd.

Knit 4 rnds.

Next rnd *K1 tbl, p1; rep from * around.

Rep last rnd for twisted rib for 3"/7.5cm.

Change to larger 16"/40cm needle.

Knit 1 rnd, dec 8 sts evenly around—68 (72, 76) sts.

Note Read the next section carefully before continuing. Keep careful track of rows and increases.

Next rnd K22 (24, 24) for front, place raglan marker; k6 (6, 7), place sleeve dart marker; k6 (6, 7) for sleeve, place raglan marker; k22 (24, 24) for back, place raglan marker; k6 (6, 7), place sleeve dart marker; k6 (6, 7) for sleeve, change beg of rnd marker to raglan marker.

Work inc each side of markers as foll: work to 1 st before marker, M1, k1, sm, k1, M1.

Work inc and charts as foll:

On body sides of raglan markers, inc 1 st on next rnd, then every other rnd 24 (26, 29) times more, then every 4th rnd 1 (1, 0) times; on sleeve sides of raglan markers, inc 1 st every

4th rnd 12 (10, 9) times, then every 6th rnd 1 (3, 4) times; on each side of sleeve dart markers, inc 1 st every other rnd 9 times, AT THE SAME TIME, work St st (k every rnd) on all sts for 4 rnds, then mark center 2 sts on front to correspond to center 2 sts on chart 1, and work chart 1 on center front only, through rnd 29 and rem sts in St st.

Begin Chart 2

Mark center 6 sts on back and center 4 sts on front and work chart 2 on back and center front (between chart 1) and rem sts in St st (review notes 2 and 3 before proceeding).

After all inc have been worked, work until piece measures 9½ (10, 10½)"/24 (25.5, 26.5)cm from highneck rib—there are 83 (90, 95) sts on front, 79 (86, 91) sts on back, and 56 (58, 58) sts on each sleeve.

Divide for Back, Front, and Sleeves

Cast on 3 (3, 4) sts, work to raglan marker, remove marker, place sts of sleeve on holder, cast on 3 (3, 4) sts, pm for side seam, cast on 3 (3, 4) sts, work to raglan marker, remove marker, place sts of sleeve on holder, cast on 3 (3, 4) sts, sm (2nd side seam).

Cont in pats, inc 1 st each side of each side seam marker every 8th row 9 times. Work even until piece measures 13½ (14, 14½)"/34 (35.5, 37)cm from dividing point.

Lower Edge Rib

Change to smaller needle.

Next rnd Inc 1 st in every 4th st to front chart, then dec 1 st, k12 sts instead of chart 1, work chart 2 as established, k12 sts instead of chart 1, dec 1 st, inc 1 st in every 4th st to back chart, work chart 2, inc 1 st in every 4th st to end of rnd.

Work in twisted rib for 2"/5cm. Bind off in rib.

SLEEVES

With larger 16"/40cm circular needle, work across sts of sleeve as foll:

Cast on 3 (3, 4) sts, k sts from holder, cast on 3 (3, 4) sts, place marker for sleeve seam—62 (64, 66) sts. Join and work in rnds of St st, dec 1 st each side of marker every 6th rnd 12 (11, 10) times, then every 8th rnd 0 (1, 2) times—38 (40, 42) sts.

Work even until sleeve measures 12½ (13, 13½)"/31.5 (33, 34)cm.

Change to smaller needle. Work in twisted rib for 3"/7.5cm. Work 4 rows in St st. Bind off.

FINISHING

Sew underarm and sleeve seams. Block to measurements. ●

CHART 1

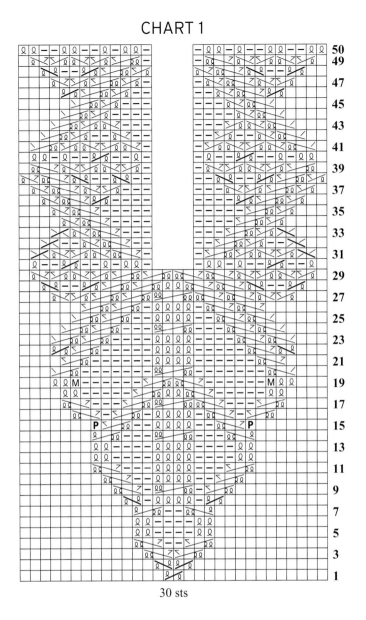

30 sts

CHART 2

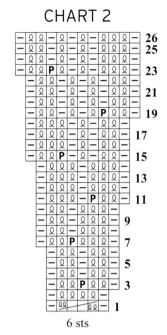

6 sts

Stitch Key

☐	knit	2-st RPC
−	purl	2-st LPC
ℚ	k1 tbl	3-st RC
M	M1	3-st LC
P	M1 p-st	3-st twisted RC
	2-st RC	3-st twisted LC
	2-st LC	3-st RPC
	2-st twisted RC	3-st LPC
	2-st twisted LC	4-st RC

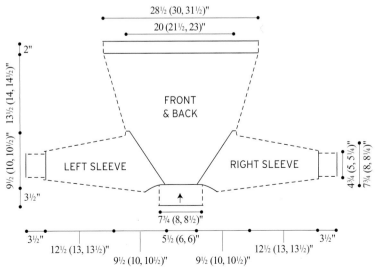

↑ = Direction of work

SOUTHWESTERN CARDIGAN

With motifs borrowed from Southwest Indian textiles, the oversized body of this cardigan is balanced by narrow sleeves and a high V-neck. Though it uses a combination of intarsia and stranded colorwork in the vivid border, duplicate stitch adds the final flourish of color, so it's easier than it may look. I had fun with my button collection by using a variety of colors and materials.

SIZE
Oversized to fit most.

KNITTED MEASUREMENTS
Bust (buttoned) 57"/142.5cm
Length 28"/71cm
Upper Arm 17"/43cm

MATERIALS
• Original Yarn
11 1¾oz/50g balls (each approx 95yd/87m) of **Classic Elite Yarns** Paisley (wool/viscose rayon) in #1775 Mushroom (MC) (4)
8 balls in #1752 Dark Purple (A)
2 balls in #1772 Aqua (B)
1 ball each in #1753 Cranberry (C), #1704 Peacock (D), and #1784 Gold (E)
• Substitute Yarn
9 1¾oz/50g balls (each approx 122yd/112m) of **Classic Elite Yarns** Liberty Wool (washable wool) in 7836 Taupe (MC) (4)
7 balls in 78196 Root Beer (A)
2 balls each in 7814 Mallard (B)
1 ball each in 7853 Crimson (C), 7849 Lapis (D), and 7881 Patina (E)
• One pair each sizes 6 and 8 (4 and 5mm) needles, OR SIZE TO OBTAIN GAUGE
• Eight ¾"/20mm assorted buttons
• Removable stitch markers

GAUGE
20 sts and 22 rows to 4"/10cm over colorwork using larger needles.
TAKE TIME TO CHECK GAUGE.

NOTES
1) When changing colors, twist yarns on WS to prevent holes in work.
2) If desired, work small areas on chart 1 in duplicate st after pieces are done.

BACK
With smaller needles and MC, cast on 140 sts.
Row 1 (RS) *K1 tbl, p1; rep from * to end.
Rep last row for twisted rib for 2"/5cm, end with a WS row. Change to larger needles. Work in St st (k on RS, p on WS) for 2 rows.

Begin Chart 1
Cont in St st as foll:
Row 1 (RS) Work the first 4 sts of chart, work 33-st rep 4 times, then work the last 4 sts of chart.
Cont in chart 1 as established through row 43.

Begin Chart 2
Row 1 (WS) Reading chart from left to right, work the first 10 sts of chart, work 30-st rep 4 times, then work last 10 sts of chart.
Cont in chart 2 as established through row 30, then rep rows 1–30 until piece measures 28"/71cm from beg. Bind off.

LEFT FRONT
With smaller needles and MC, cast on 70 sts. Work in twisted rib as for back. Change to larger needles. Work in St st for 2 rows. Cont in St st as foll:
Chart 1: Row 1 (RS) Work the first 4 sts of chart, then work 33-st rep twice.
Cont in chart 1 as established through row 43.
Chart 2: Row 1 (WS) Reading chart from left to right, work 30-st rep of chart twice, then work the last 10 sts of chart.
Cont in chart 2 as established through row 30, then rep rows 1–30 until piece measures 20½"/52cm from beg, end with a WS row.

Neck Shaping
Cont in chart 2 as established, dec 1 st at end of next RS

row and rep dec [every 2nd row once, every 4th row once] 3 times, then every 2nd row 9 times—54 sts.
Work even until same length as back. Bind off.

RIGHT FRONT

With smaller needles and MC, cast on 70 sts. Work in twisted rib as for back. Change to larger needles. Work in St st for 2 rows. Cont in St st as foll:
Chart 1: Row 1 (RS) Work 33-st rep of chart twice, then work the last 4 sts of chart.
Cont chart 1 as established through row 43.
Chart 2: Row 1 (WS) Reading chart from left to right, work the first 10 sts of chart, then work 30-st rep twice.
Cont chart 2 as established through row 30, then rep rows 1–30 until piece measures 20½"/52cm from beg, end with a WS row.

Neck Shaping

Cont in chart 2 as established, dec 1 st at beg of next RS row and rep dec [every 2nd row once, every 4th row once] 3 times, then every 2nd row 9 times—54 sts.
Work even until same length as back. Bind off.

SLEEVES

With smaller needles and A, cast on 44 sts. Work in twisted rib for 1"/2.5cm.
Knit next row on RS, inc 1 st—45 sts. Change to larger needles. Beg with a WS row, work 2 rows St st with C.

Begin Chart 2

Row 1 (WS) Reading chart from left to right, beg with 4th st of chart, work to rep, work 30-st rep once, then work next 8 sts after rep.
Cont in chart 2 as established, inc 1 st each side (working inc sts into chart 2) every 4th row 19 times, then every other row once—85 sts.
Work even until piece measures 16"/40cm from beg. Bind off.

FINISHING

Block pieces to measurements. Sew shoulder seams.

Left Front Band and Neckband

With smaller needles and MC, cast on 9 sts. Work in twisted rib with first st in garter st (k every row) until band fits along front edge to center back neck. Place sts on a holder.
Sew band in place. Place markers on band for 8 buttons with first ½"/5cm from lower edge, the last at first neck dec and 6 others evenly between.

Right Front Band and Neckband

Work to correspond to left front band and neckband, working buttonholes opposite markers by binding off 2 sts for each buttonhole. On next row, cast on 2 sts over bound-off sts.
Sew band in place. Weave sts tog with left front band at center back neck.

Place markers 8½"/21.5cm down from shoulders on front and back for armholes. Sew top of sleeves between markers.
Sew side and sleeve seams. Sew on buttons. ●

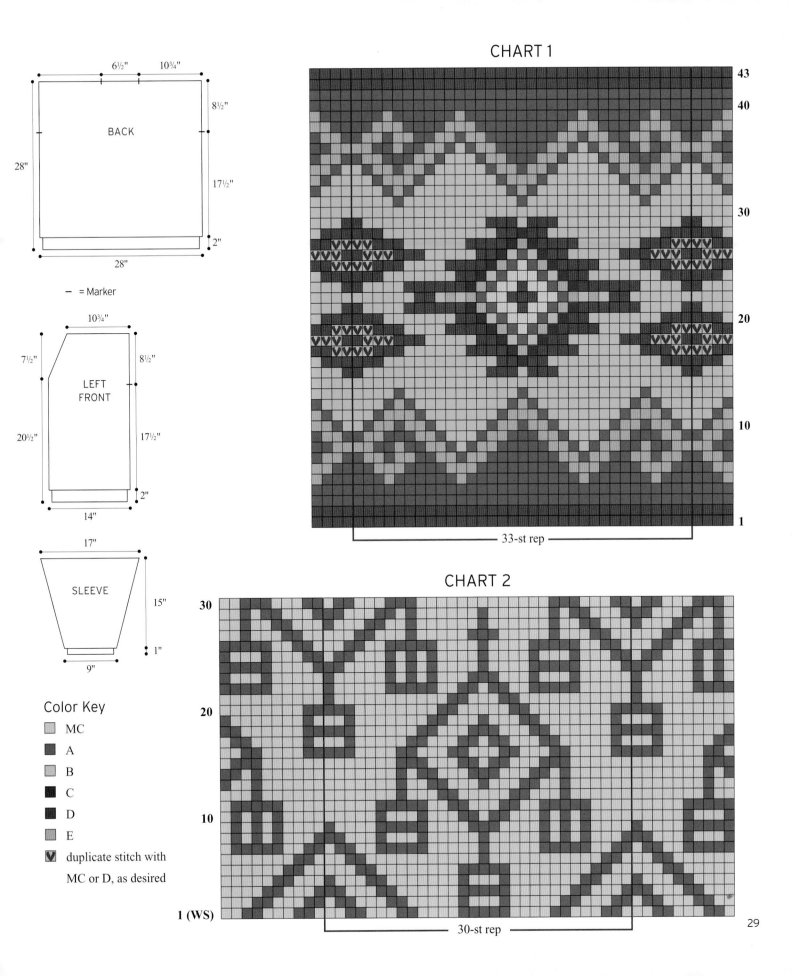

CHART 1

43
40

30

20

10

1

33-st rep

CHART 2

30

20

10

1 (WS)

30-st rep

BACK

6½" 10¾"

8½"

28" 17½"

2"

28"

— = Marker

LEFT
FRONT

10¾"

7½" 8½"

20½" 17½"

2"

14"

SLEEVE

17"

15"

1"

9"

Color Key

MC
A
B
C
D
E
duplicate stitch with
MC or D, as desired

TEXTURED PLAID PULLOVER

The bold pattern of this men's pullover is from a Buffalo Plaid, but here I reinterpreted it as a mixture of textures created from nothing more than humble knit and purl stitches. Combining rich textures with a doubled crewneck and cozy drop shoulders makes what could have been a basic pullover anything but.

■■□□

Sizes
Small (Medium, Large). Shown in size Medium.

KNITTED MEASUREMENTS
Chest 43 (47, 51)"/108 (118, 127)cm
Length 27 (28, 29)"/68.5 (71, 73.5)cm
Upper Arm 21 (23, 23)"/53 (58, 58)cm

MATERIALS
• Original Yarn
9 (10, 10) 3½oz/100g balls (each approx 164yd/150m) of **Rowan/ Westminster Trading Corp.** Magpie (wool) in #102 Beige (**4**)
• Substitute Yarn
8 (9, 9) 3½oz/100g skeins (each approx 200yd/201m) of **Harrisville Designs** Highland (virgin wool) in Sand (**4**)
• One pair each sizes 5 and 7 (3.75 and 4.5mm) needles, OR SIZE TO OBTAIN GAUGE
• One size 5 (3.75mm) circular needle, 16"/40cm long
• Stitch markers

GAUGE
17 sts and 24 rows to 4"/10cm over St st using larger needles.
TAKE TIME TO CHECK GAUGE.

BROKEN RIB
(even number of sts)
Row 1 (RS) Knit.
Row 2 *P1, k1; rep from * to end.
Row 3 Rep row 2.
Row 4 Purl.
Row 5 *K1, p1; rep from * to end.
Row 6 Rep row 5.
Rows 7–24 Rep rows 1–6 three times more.
Rows 25 and 26 Rep rows 1 and 2.

RIB AND WELT
(multiple of 8 sts)
Row 1 (RS) *K1, p1, k1, p5; rep from * to end.
Row 2 and all WS rows K the knit sts and p the purl sts.

Row 3 K1, p1, *k5, p1, k1, p1; rep from * to last 6 sts, k5, p1.
Row 5 K1, *p5, k1, p1, k1; rep from * to last 7 sts, p5, k1, p1.
Row 7 *K5, p1, k1, p1; rep from * to end.
Row 9 P4, *k1, p1, k1, p5; rep from * to last 4 sts, [k1, p1] twice.
Row 11 K3, *p1, k1, p1, k5; rep from * to last 5 sts, p1, k1, p1, k2.
Row 13 P2, *k1, p1, k1, p5; rep from * to last 6 sts, k1, p1, k1, p3.
Row 15 K1, *p1, k1, p1, k5; rep from * to last 7 sts, p1, k1, p1, k4.
Row 17 Rep row 1.
Row 19 Rep row 3.
Row 21 Rep row 5.
Row 23 Rep row 7.
Row 25 Rep row 9.
Row 26 Rep row 2.

BACK

With smaller needles, cast on 82 (90, 98) sts.
Row 1 *K1, p1; rep from * to end.
Rep row 1 for k1, p1 rib for 2½"/6.5cm, end with a RS row.
Purl next row on WS, inc 10 sts evenly across—92 (100, 108) sts.
Change to larger needles.

Begin Patterns

Row 1 (RS) Work St st (k on RS, p on WS) over 6 (10, 14) sts, [pm, work row 1 of broken rib over 16 sts, pm, work St st over 16 sts] twice, pm, work row 1 of broken rib over 16 sts, pm, work St st over 6 (10, 14) sts.
Cont in pat for a total of 6 (10, 12) rows. *Knit 1 row, purl 1 row.
Next row (RS) Work row 1 of broken rib over 6 (10, 14) sts, [sm, work row 1 of rib and welt over 16 sts, sm, work row 1 of broken rib over 16 sts] twice, sm, work row 1 of rib and welt over 16 sts, sm, work row 1 of broken rib over 6 (10, 14) sts.
Cont in pat for 25 rows more. Knit 1 row, purl 1 row.
Next row (RS) Work St st over 6 (10, 14) sts, [sm, work row 1 of broken rib over 16 sts, sm, work St st over 16 sts] twice, sm, work row 1 of broken rib over 16 sts, sm, work St st over 6 (10, 14) sts.
Cont in pat for 25 rows more.
Rep from * (56 rows) until piece measures 27 (28, 29)"/68.5 (71, 73.5)cm from beg. Bind off.

FRONT

Work as for back until piece measures 24 (25, 26)"/61 (63.5, 66)cm from beg, end with a WS row.

Neck Shaping

Cont in pat, work as foll:
Next row (RS) Work 39 (42, 46) sts, join 2nd ball of yarn, bind off 14 (16, 16) sts, work to end.
Working both sides at once, bind off from each neck edge 3 sts once, bind off 2 sts twice, then dec 1 st every other row 3 times—29 (32, 36) sts.
Cont in pat and when same length as back, bind off.

SLEEVES

With smaller needles, cast on 40 (42, 42) sts. Work in k1, p1 rib for 2"/5cm, end with a RS row. Purl next row on WS, inc 6 sts evenly across—46 (48, 48) sts. Change to larger needles.

Begin Patterns

Work pat and inc at same time as foll:
Row 1 (RS) Work St st over 15 (16, 16) sts, pm, work row 1 of broken rib over 16 sts, pm, work St st over 15 (16, 16) sts.
Cont in pat as for back, AT THE SAME TIME, inc 1 st each side (working inc sts into pat) every 4th row 10 (15, 15) times, then every 6th row 12 (10, 10) times—90 (98, 98) sts.
Work even in pat until piece measures 21 (22, 22)"/53 (56, 56)cm from beg. Bind off.

FINISHING

Block pieces to measurements. Sew shoulder seams.

Neckband

With RS facing and circular needle, pick up and k 88 (92, 92) sts evenly around neck edge. Join and work in k1, p1 rib for 3½"/9cm. Bind off in rib. Fold band in half to WS, sew in place.

Place markers 10½ (11½, 11½)"/26.5 (29, 29)cm down from shoulders on front and back for armholes. Sew top of sleeves between markers. Sew side and sleeve seams. ●

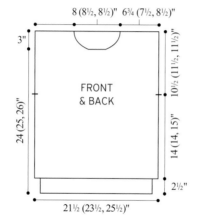

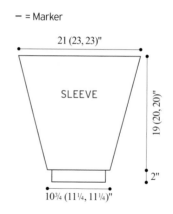

− = Marker

DIAMOND PULLOVER

This cabled yoke, crowned with a folded funnel neck, is shaped by tapering alternating columns of tight braids amid the luscious texture of twisted ribbing. Fields of knit/purl diamonds across the body and sleeves perfectly align with the yoke pattern to unify both striking textures.

SIZE
Oversized to fit Small, Medium, Large.

KNITTED MEASUREMENTS
Bust 48"/120cm
Length 28"/71cm
Upper Arm 16½"/41cm

MATERIALS
• Original Yarn
12 3½oz/100g skeins (each approx 110yd/100m) of **Crystal Palace** Carnival (wool) in #854 Celadon (5)
• Substitute Yarn
11 3½oz/100g hanks (each approx 130yd/119m) of **Classic Elite Yarns** Mystique (wool/alpaca) in #1502 Spearmint (5)
• One each sizes 7 and 9 (4.5 and 5.5mm) circular needles, 24"/60cm long, OR SIZE TO OBTAIN GAUGE
• One size 9 (5.5mm) circular needle, 16"/40cm long
• Cable needle (cn)
• Stitch holders
• Stitch markers

GAUGE
16 sts and 24 rows to 4"/10cm over chart 1 using larger needle.
TAKE TIME TO CHECK GAUGE.

NOTES
1) As gauge may differ between working row and in rnds, check work after a few inches (cm) and adjust needle size if necessary.
2) Body of sweater is knit in one circular piece to underarm, then joined with sleeves at yoke. Sleeves are knit back and forth to underarm.

STITCH GLOSSARY
4-st RC Sl 2 sts to cn and hold to back, k2, k2 from cn.
4-st LC Sl 2 sts to cn and hold to front, k2, k2 from cn.
4-st RCbdec (with back cross dec) Sl 2 sts to cn and hold to back, k2, k2tog from cn.
4-st RCfdec (with front cross dec) Sl 2 sts to cn and hold to back, k2tog, k2 from cn.
4-st LCdec (with decs) Sl 2 sts to cn and hold to front, k2tog, k2tog from cn.
6-st LCdec (with decs) Sl 3 sts to cn and hold to front, k2tog, k1, then k2tog, k1 from cn.

BODY

With smaller needle, cast on 192 sts. Join, taking care not to twist sts, and pm for beg of rnd.

Rnd 1 (RS) *K1 tbl, p1; rep from * around.

Rep rnd 1 for twisted rib for 3½"/9cm.

Change to larger 24"/60cm needle. Knit 1 rnd.

Begin Chart 1

Beg with first st, work chart 1 (reading all chart rnds from right to left) until 73 rnds have been worked in chart pat, piece measures approx 16"/40cm from beg.

Divide for Front and Back

Next rnd Cont in chart pat, bind off 8 sts (underarm), work until there are 80 sts from bind-off and sl sts to holder (front), bind off next 16 sts (underarm), work until there are 80 sts from bind-off and sl sts to holder (back), bind off rem 8 sts (underarm).

SLEEVES

With smaller needle, cast on 46 sts. Do not join. Work each sleeve back and forth in rows.

Row 1 (RS) *K1 tbl, p1 tbl; rep from * to end.

Rep row 1 for twisted rib for 3"/7.5cm, end with a WS row. Change to larger needle. Knit 1 row.

Begin Chart 1

Beg with row 24, work chart 1 as foll:

Row 24 (WS) Beg with st 7, work chart from left to right to st 1, work sts 16–1 twice, then work sts 16–10.

Cont in chart pat, (read RS rows from right to left and WS rows from left to right), inc 1 st each side (working inc sts into pat) every 6th row 5 times, then every 8th row 5 times—66 sts. Work even until 74 rows have been worked, end with chart row 1, piece measures approx 15½"/38.5cm from beg.

Next row (WS) Bind off 9 sts, work to last 9 sts, bind off last 9 sts. Sl rem 48 sts to holder.

CHART 1

(chart grid with rows numbered 1–24; bottom axis labeled 16, 10, 7, 1)

16-st rep

CHART 2

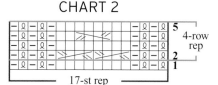

5
4-row rep
2
1

17-st rep

CHART 3

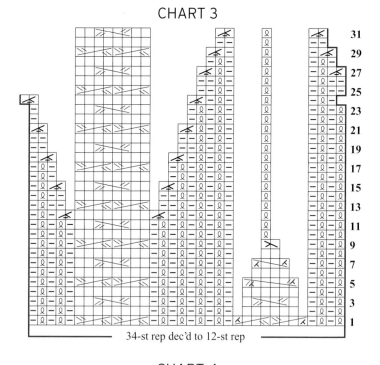

(chart grid with rows numbered 1–31)

34-st rep dec'd to 12-st rep

CHART 4

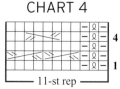

4

1

11-st rep

Stitch Key

☐ k on RS, p on WS

⊟ p on RS, k on WS

Ⴍ k1 tbl

⟋ p2tog

⟍ ssk

4-st RC

4-st LC

4-st RCbdec

4-st RCfdec

4-st LCdec

6-st LCdec

YOKE

Note Change to larger 16"/40cm needle as necessary.

Joining rnd Beg with rnd 2 of chart 1, work sts from holders in pat as foll: 48 sts of one sleeve, 80 sts of front, 48 sts of 2nd sleeve, and 80 sts of back—256 sts.

Join and pm for beg of rnd.

Cont in chart 1 for 12 rnds more, end with rnd 13.

Inc rnd *K16, M1; rep from * around—272 sts.

Work rnds 1–5 of chart 2 once, then rep rnds 2–5 five times more.

Work rnds 1–31 of chart 3—88 sts.

FINISHING

Neckband

Work chart 4 over rem 88 sts for 5"/12.5cm.

Bind off loosely. Fold band in half to WS and sew in place.

Sew underarm and sleeve seams. Block to measurements. ●

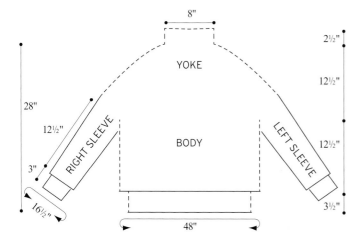

SHAWL-COLLAR CARDIGAN

Folded hems, a generous shawl collar, and the satisfying textured rib distinguish this cropped cardigan, which has drop shoulders and an easy fit. Style it a dozen ways—with leggings, layers, or dresses—to get you through the winter.

■■■■

SIZES
Small (Medium, Large). Shown in size Medium.

KNITTED MEASUREMENTS
Bust (buttoned) 41½ (46, 50½)"/102.5 (114.5, 126.5)cm
Length 20½ (21, 22)"/52 (53, 55.5)cm
Upper Arm 19 (20, 21)"/48 (50, 53)cm

MATERIALS
• Original Yarn
14 (15,16) 1¾oz/50g balls (each approx 92yd/84m) of **Bernat** Rusticale (wool/mohair) in #14058 Oatmeal (5)
• Substitute Yarns
9 (10, 10) 1¾oz/50g balls (each approx 153yd/140m) of **Rowan** Kid Classic (wool/mohair/polyamide) in 00888 Pumice (4)
6 (7, 7) .88oz/25g balls (each approx 230yd/210m) of **Rowan** Kid Silk Haze (mohair/silk) in 00590 Pearl (2)
• One pair each sizes 7 and 9 (4.5 and 5.5mm) needles, OR SIZE TO OBTAIN GAUGE
• Four 2"/5cm long horn buttons
• Stitch markers

GAUGE
17 sts and 24 rows to 4"/10cm over pat st using larger needles and 1 strand of original yarn or 1 strand of each substitute yarn held together. TAKE TIME TO CHECK GAUGE.

NOTE
Hold together 1 strand of each substitute yarn throughout.

PATTERN STITCH
(multiple of 5 sts plus 7)
Row 1 (RS) K3, *p1, k4; rep from * to last 4 sts, p1, k3.
Row 2 *P2, k3; rep from * to last 2 sts, p2.
Rep rows 1 and 2 for pat st.

BACK
With smaller needles, cast on 86 (94, 106) sts.
Work in k2, p2 rib for 3"/7.5cm, inc 1 (3, 1) sts on last row—87 (97, 107) sts. Change to larger needles.
Work in pat st until piece measures 22 (22½, 23½)"/56 (57, 59.5)cm from beg. Bind off.

LEFT FRONT
With smaller needles, cast on 42 (46, 50) sts.
Work in k2, p2 rib for 3"/7.5cm, inc 0 (1, 2) sts on last row —42 (47, 52) sts. Change to larger needles.
Work in pat st until piece measures 13 (13½, 14½)"/33 (34, 36.5)cm from beg, end with a WS row.

Neck Shaping
Dec 1 st at end of next RS row, rep dec every 4th row 9 (12, 12) times, then every 6th row 2 (0, 0) times—30 (34, 39) sts. Work even until same length as back. Bind off.

RIGHT FRONT
Work to correspond to left front, reversing neck shaping (dec at beg of RS rows).

SLEEVES
With smaller needles, cast on 46 (46, 50) sts.
Work in k2, p2 rib for 3"/7.5cm, inc 1 (1, 2) sts on last row— 47 (47, 52) sts. Change to larger needles.
Work in pat st, inc 1 st each side (working inc sts into pat st) every 4th row 6 (10, 10) times, then every 6th row 11 (9, 9) times—81 (85, 90) sts.
Work even until piece measures 19 (19½, 19½)"/47.5 (49, 49)cm from beg. Bind off.

FINISHING
Block pieces to measurements. Sew shoulder seams.

Place markers 9½ (10, 10½)"/24 (25, 26.5)cm down from shoulders on front and back for armholes. Sew side seams to markers. Fold lower edge rib in half to WS and sew in place. Sew hem sides.

Front Bands and Collar
Note When working band and collar, RS of collar becomes WS when sewn in place.
With smaller needles, cast on 5 sts.
Row 1 (RS) [P1, k1 tbl] twice, k1.
Row 2 K1, [p1, k1 tbl] twice.
Rep rows 1 and 2 for twisted rib until piece measures 9½ (10, 11)"/24 (25, 27.5)cm from beg, end with a WS row.
Change to larger needles.
Next row (RS) Cast on 2 sts (neck edge), p1, k1, pm, rib to end.
Next row Rib 5, sm, k2.
Next row Cast on 2 sts, k1, p2, k1, sm, rib 5.
Next row Rib 5, sm, k4.
Next row Cast on 2 sts, k3, p2, k1, sm, rib 5.
Next row (row 1 of pat) Rib 5, sm, k4, p1, k1.
Next row (row 2 of pat) Cast on 2 sts, p2, k3, p2, k1, sm, rib 5.
Cont to inc at neck edge (working inc sts into pat st as established), beg with a row 1 of pat and keeping 5 sts at front edge in established rib by casting on 2 sts 7 times more,

then inc 1 st at same edge every other row 6 times, then every 4th row twice—35 sts.
Work even in pat until straight edge measures 20½ (21, 22)"/52 (53, 55.5)cm from beg.
Work short rows as foll:
*__Next row (WS)__ Work 5 sts, w&t, work to end.
Next row (WS) Work 10 sts, w&t, work to end.
Cont in this manner, working 5 more sts at end of every WS row 3 times more, end with a RS row.
Work 6 rows even over all sts.*
Rep between *'s 7 times more.
Work even on 35 sts for 4"/10cm. Dec 1 st at end of RS rows on next row, then every 4th row twice, then every other row 5 times. Bind off at same edge 2 sts 11 times. Work in rib on rem 5 sts for 9½ (10, 11)"/24 (25, 27.5)cm. Bind off.
With WS of collar facing RS of body, baste bands and collar in place. Place markers on left front band for 4 buttons, first marker ½"/1.5cm from lower edge, last marker at first collar cast-on, and 2 others evenly between. Sew bands and collar in place, leaving unsewn openings on right front band opposite markers for buttonholes. Sew on buttons.

Sew top of sleeves between markers. Sew sleeve seams.
Fold rib at lower edge of cuffs in half and sew in place. •

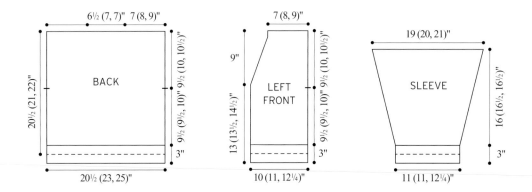

— = Marker

CABLE COMBO

Modern again, a duo of a generous, high-neck raglan tunic with syncopated lace and cable leggings makes a head-to-toe statement. A mid-weight yarn in the easy cable and seed stitch patterned top is coordinated with a lighter weight for the leggings.

TUNIC

■■■■

SIZES
Small (Medium, Large). Shown in size Medium.

KNITTED MEASUREMENTS
Bust 42 (47, 50½)"/105 (117, 127)cm
Length 31½ (32, 32¾)"/79.5 (81, 82.5)cm
Upper Arm 16 (16½, 17)"/40 (41, 43)cm

MATERIALS
• Original Yarn
20 (22, 24) 1¾oz/50g balls (each approx 85yd/76m) of **Classic Elite Yarns** Caravan (camelhair/wool) in #6144 Toffee (**4**)
• Substitute Yarns
10 (11, 12) 3½oz/100g hanks (each approx 170yd/155m) of **Quince & Co.** Osprey (American wool) in Gingerbread (**4**)
• One pair each sizes 7 and 9 (4.5 and 5.5mm) needles, OR SIZE TO OBTAIN GAUGE
• Cable needle (cn)
• Stitch holders
• Stitch markers

GAUGE
20½ sts and 26 rows to 4"/10cm over chart 2 using larger needles.
TAKE TIME TO CHECK GAUGE.

STITCH GLOSSARY
4-st RC Sl 2 sts to cn and hold to back, k2, k2 from cn.
Double dec Work 10 sts, sssk, work to last 13 sts, k3tog, work to end.
LT (left twist) With RH needle behind LH needle, skip first st and k 2nd st tbl, insert RH needle into backs of both sts and k2tog tbl.
Single dec Work 10 sts, ssk, work to last 12 sts, k2tog, work to end.
sssk (slip, slip, slip, knit) Sl next 3 sts knitwise, one at a time, to RH needle, insert tip of LH needle into fronts of these sts and k them tog.

BACK
With smaller needles, cast on 108 (120, 130) sts.
Beg and end as indicated, work chart 1 for 30 rows.
Change to larger needles.
Beg and end as indicated for chart 1, work chart 2 until piece measures 22"/55.5cm from beg, end with chart row 4.

Raglan Armhole Shaping
Cast on 11 sts at beg of next 2 rows—130 (142, 152) sts.
Next row (RS) Work chart 3 over first 11 sts, cont chart 2 to last 11 sts, work chart 4 over last 11 sts.
Cont in pats as established, AT THE SAME TIME, work raglan dec every RS row as foll: double dec 0 (0, 2) times, [double dec twice, single dec once] 4 (10, 10) times, [double dec once, single dec once] 9 (0, 0) times, double dec 0 (1, 1) times, single dec 0 (1, 1) times—36 (36, 38) sts.
Work even for 6"/15.5cm for funnel neck. Place sts on holder.

FRONT
Work as for back.

SLEEVES
With smaller needles, cast on 64 (68, 72) sts.
Beg and end as indicated, work chart 1 for 24 rows.
Change to larger needles.

Beg and end as indicated for chart 1, work chart 2, AT THE SAME TIME, inc 1 st each side (working inc into pat) every 6th row 2 (0, 0) times, every 8th row 7 (3, 0) times, then every 10th row 0 (5, 8) times—82 (84, 88) sts.
Work even until piece measures 15 (16, 16½)"/37.5 (40.5, 41)cm from beg, end with a WS row.

Raglan Cap Shaping
Note Work dec for sleeves as foll:
Double dec K2, sssk, work to last 5 sts, k3tog, k2.
Single dec K2, ssk, work to last 4 sts, k2tog, k2.
Cast on 3 sts at beg of next 2 rows—88 (90, 94) sts. Work cast-on sts in St st (k on RS, p on WS), AT THE SAME TIME, work raglan dec every RS row as foll: double dec 0 (0, 1) times, [double dec once, single dec 3 (4, 6) times] 7 (6, 4) times, double dec 0 (0, 1) times, single dec 2 (2, 4) times—14 sts. Work even until funnel neck is same length as back, then work 2 rows more. Place sts on holder.

FINISHING
Block pieces to measurements. Sew raglan sleeve caps to raglan armholes. Sew sides of funnel neck. Sew side and sleeve seams. Fold funnel neck in half and sew open sts from holders to WS. ●

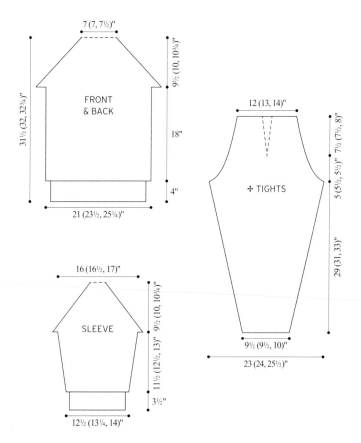

LEGGINGS

SIZES
X-Small (Small, Medium). Shown in size Small.

KNITTED MEASUREMENTS
Waist 24 (26, 28)"/60 (65, 71)cm
Hip 33½ (35½, 37)"/84 (89, 93)cm
Inseam 29 (31, 33)"/73.5 (78.5, 83.5)cm

MATERIALS
• Original Yarn
7 (8, 9) 1¾oz/50g balls (each approx 130yd/120m) of **Classic Elite Yarns** Caravan 2-Ply (camelhair/wool) in #6244 Toffee (Ⓘ)
• Substitute Yarn
6 (6, 7) 1¾oz/50g hanks (each approx 181yd/166m) of **Quince & Co.** Chickadee (American wool) in Gingerbread (Ⓘ)
• One pair each sizes 4 and 5 (3.5 and 3.75mm) needles, OR SIZE TO OBTAIN GAUGE
• 1yd/1m of ¾"/1.5cm waistband elastic
• Stitch holders
• Stitch markers

GAUGE
22 sts and 32 rows to 4"/10cm over chart 5 using larger needles.
TAKE TIME TO CHECK GAUGE.

STITCH GLOSSARY

LT (left twist) With RH needle behind LH needle, skip first st and k 2nd st tbl, insert RH needle into backs of both sts and k2tog tbl.

Rib Pattern
(multiple of 10 sts)
Row 1 (RS) *K2, p2, k2, p1, k2, p1; rep from * to end.
Row 2 K the knit sts and p the purl sts.
Rep row 2 for rib pat.

NOTE
Keep 2 sts at each side in St st (k on RS, p on WS) and work all inc and dec inside these sts.

LEGS
With larger needles, beg at ankle, cast on 52 (52, 54) sts. Beg and end as indicated, work chart 5, inc 1 st each side (working inc sts into pat) every 14th (12th, 12th) row 8 (10, 11) times, every 6th row 10 times, every 4th row 9 (10, 11) times, then every other row 10 (10, 11) times—126 (132, 140) sts.
Work even until piece measures 29 (31, 33)"/72.5 (77.5, 82.5) cm from beg, end with a WS row.

Crotch Shaping
Change to smaller needles. Working in rib pat, bind off 3 sts at beg of next 2 rows, then 2 sts at beg of next 4 (4, 6) rows.
Dec 1 st each side every other row 8 (8, 7) times, then every 4th row 2 (2, 3) times—92 (98, 102) sts.
Work even until piece measures 5 (5½, 5½)"/12.5 (14, 14)cm from beg of crotch shaping, end with a WS row.

Hip Shaping
Mark center 4 sts.
Next row (RS) Work to 2 sts before first marker, k2tog, sm, work center 4 sts, sm, ssk, work to end.
Cont to dec 1 st each side of center sts every 4th row 10 (10, 5) times, then every 6th row 2 (2, 6) times—66 (72, 78) sts.
Work even for 1"/2.5cm more. Bind off.

FINISHING
Block pieces to measurements. Sew crotch seams and inseam.

Cut elastic to fit waist. Place 4 pins equal distance apart on elastic and place pins around waistband in same way. Pin elastic to WS of waist, matching pins. Using yarn and needle, working from left to right, secure thread below the elastic. Insert the needle through a lp of st (3 sts to the right) above the elastic. *Insert needle down into the lp of st (3 sts to right) below the elastic, then up into lp of next st. Rep from * around. ●

CHART 1

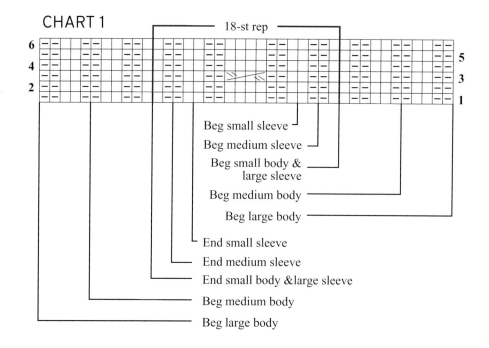

18-st rep

6   5
4   3
2   1

Beg small sleeve
Beg medium sleeve
Beg small body & large sleeve
Beg medium body
Beg large body

End small sleeve
End medium sleeve
End small body & large sleeve
Beg medium body
Beg large body

CHART 2

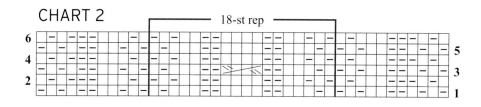

18-st rep

6   5
4   3
2   1

CHART 3

6   5
4   3
2   1

11 sts

CHART 4

6   5
4   3
2   1

11 sts

Stitch Key

☐ k on RS, p on WS

⊟ p on RS, k on WS

◿ k2tog on RS, p2tog on WS

⊡ yo

⧖ LT

⧓ 4-st RC

CHART 5

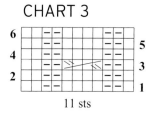

10-st rep

4
2   3
   1

End small & medium
Beg large

Beg small & medium
Beg large

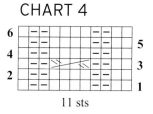

MASTER KNITTERS OF THE NINETIES

NORAH'S KNITTING EQUATIONS

An inventive young designer takes a fresh look at the craft

By John Birmingham

I don't know if I can flex it," says Norah Gaughan, pushing up the right sleeve of her blazer. "It definitely stands out, though."

Gaughan, who double-majored in biology and art at Brown University, is referring to her impressively pumped-up flexor carpi radialus, a forearm muscle that plays a crucial role in her knitting. Not all knitters develop this particular muscle, however. According to Gaughan, it depends largely on their style of knitting. "I knit Continental, which involves a simple sort of rocking motion," she says. "Right-handed knitters make this big throw-over motion, so I'm sure they exercise a different muscle altogether."

In any case, Gaughan recently has been getting quite a workout. At 29, she runs a thriving business from her apartment in a three-family house in Providence, Rhode Island, producing original sweaters for prominent yarn companies like Reynolds and Bernat, and for magazines from **Woman's World** to **Vogue Knitting**. On average, she turns out 60 sweaters a year. Only four years in business, she already has a considerable reputation as an inventive knitter with a keen eye for detail.

"She does the most unbelievable stitch work," says Kristin Nicholas, director of marketing at Classic Elite Yarns. "Instead of taking a pattern out of one of the Barbara Walker books, she makes up her own stitches—or she takes the basic idea, then changes it to make it her own. You can tell immediately when Norah knits something."

Not that she makes every sweater herself. While actually knitting about a dozen sweaters a year, Gaughan assigns the others to her team of four to eight knitters, which includes her downstairs neighbor Janet D'Alesandre, a multilingual teacher and former pattern-writer for Bernat. (Another member of the cadre is D'Alesandre's 15-year-old daughter, Claire.) Before giving the go-ahead to one of her knitters, Gaughan asks her to produce a swatch, "just to make sure the fabric looks the way I want it to—I find the stitches always vary a little from one knitter to another." After that, Gaughan writes instructions from the swatch, and the knitter knits the sweater in pieces. It is Gaughan who assumes the task of finishing the sweater.

Norah Gaughan, who grew up in rural Rifton, New York, learned to knit at the age of 14, during one of her traditional summer visits to a friend in Princeton, New Jersey. "It got incredibly hot, and all we could do was sit inside in the air conditioning," she recalls. "So my friend, Grace, taught me how to knit." Gaughan's first project, a hat in two colors, came off without a hitch. Buoyed by that success, she attempted a full-scale sweater soon after returning home. But she found the instructions exasperating. "Then my mother bought Elizabeth Zimmermann's book, **Knitting Without Tears**," she says, "and the rest is history."

Even before learning to knit, Gaughan showed talent for such crafts as embroidery and crochet, and she often entered sewing projects in 4-H competitions. In school, however, she focused on science and mathematics. Although she enjoyed studying biology, Gaughan finally decided against pursuing a career as a scientist. But she soon found a practical use for her math skills—applying them to her knitting.

How does your knowledge of mathematics help you in knitting?
I use algebra all the time—simple X-Y equations . . . stuff you learned in junior high school but later forgot, unless you took a lot more math. Since I took so much more math, algebra is still readily available to me. I also use geometry. For instance, I figured out a way to use the Pythagorean theorem for shaping sleeve caps.

How does that work?
It's not too complicated. Just picture the armhole as a triangle; it's actually a curve, but you can simplify it into a triangle. Then picture half of the sleeve cap as another triangle. Well, the hypotenuse of one—the distance from the underarm at the side seam to the tip of the shoulder—should about equal the hypotenuse of the other—the curve of the sleeve cap . . .

Now let's call the sides of the armhole triangle A, B, and C. Then the sides of the sleeve cap triangle are A' and B', which are different from the first triangle, and C, which is the same. What we're really looking for is A′, which is the depth of the sleeve cap.

From the Pythagorean theorem, we know that A squared plus B squared equals C squared. We also know that A′ squared plus B′ squared equals C squared. Therefore, A squared plus B squared equals A′ squared plus B′ squared. You can determine A′ from the equation; you don't even have to figure out what C is.

Do you consciously look for new ways to use math?
Sure. I keep thinking there must be a way to apply calculus to knitting. After all, calculus adds up all these infinitesimal things, and that's exactly what stitches are. But in the end, it always seems easier to figure it out on graph paper, by geometry, or by proportions. I think you really have to be math oriented to want to use calculus. It becomes just too complicated.

Yet you seem to enjoy complicated knitting projects.
That's always been true for me. When I was starting out, I tried to make each sweater more complicated than the last. The challenge was to do something that would have seemed impossible when I began the last sweater. I'll show you an example . . .

[Gaughan brings out a mounted and framed section of knitted fabric, illustrating about 10 different types of stitches, from rope cables to blackberry stitches.]

This was part of a ninth-grade social-studies project I did on Irish fishermen's sweaters. I picked all these stitches out of a stitch dictionary, and decided how they would go together. Then I had to keep track of all the patterns, which repeat on different rows. Right now I can look at it and say, "Oh, that's no big deal." But before trying it, the idea seemed impossible.

What was your first sweater like?
It was a fisherman's sweater, made with wool that I bought at the county fair, the week after I first learned to knit. While exploring the fair, I went into a barn. There was this man with his sheep, and he was selling the wool that came from the sheep. I thought that was great. So I bought some wool—it cost about $15. As it turned out, the sweater wasn't all that easy. Not only did I have trouble with the instructions, but I was very hard on myself. I felt I had to rip it out if it wasn't just perfect.

Are you still such a perfectionist?
Pretty much. I try not to go overboard, but craftsmanship is very important to me. I like sweaters that have a beautifully finished look. I guess that's why, in my business, I've become known for paying attention to detail.

What techniques do you use for finishing?
I weave the seams together. There are different kinds of weaving for different kinds of seams. But I always do it from the "right" side, so that I can see what I'm doing. Some other techniques for sewing seams require that you put the "right" sides together and sew from the inside. The trouble is, then you can't see. It's the most frustrating thing.

What about blocking? Do you prefer to wet-block or steam?
In the past, I would only steam, because it seemed more expedient. I would steam all the pieces before putting them together, and then steam the seams. And I still like that method, especially for colorwork—when the yarns stretch out, they become much flatter and nicer.

Recently I've discovered that, for some sweaters—those with a lot of rib for instance—wet-blocking on a "woolly board" is the most wonderful thing. Steaming flattens out ribs, whereas with a board, you can block the sweater to the size you want, and it still has all the depth. This has been a revelation to me.

Do you always use the continental method?
Most of the time. But I can do both methods, which comes in handy when you knit with two colors. Especially when you don't have much twisting to do. When the gap between the colors isn't very big—and I'm sure I learned this, like a lot of things, from Elizabeth Zimmermann—you can hold one color in one hand, and one color in the other hand, and just go. It's wonderful. And it's even better if you are knitting circular, because you never have to purl.

Why do you think so many knitters don't like to purl?
It's almost always harder, especially when you're using the knitting method that you don't normally use. Still, I have a friend, John, who loves to purl. He has a Ph.D. in theoretical physics, and I taught him how to knit. But he couldn't just do it; he had to analyze every motion. And he said he loved purling because it enabled him to see exactly what he was doing. "Why didn't you teach me this first?" he said. It was really funny.

How did you start your business?
It built up gradually. When I was about 17, my mother was doing illustrations for **Ladies Home Journal Needle & Craft**. On a lark, she took a sweater I had knit and showed it to the editor. That's how I got published for the first time. While in college, I published more pieces. After college, while working in a yarn shop, I sent some pieces to **Woman's World**, and started working for Elite and Bernat. Eventually I had more work than I could handle, so I began working with other knitters. They're not hard to find around here. I don't know if it's because of RISD [Rhode Island School of Design], but Providence is home to an amazing number of talented knitters. Some call it "the knitting capital of the world."

What special instruction do you give to your knitters?
Well, there are things that I like to be done a certain way. Like binding off the shoulders—there's a special way to make it slope gradually, rather than being "stepped." And I always tell my knitters not to end the yarn in the middle of the row. I actually don't mind it if the sweater is all cabled or complicated. But with stockinette—even if you weave in nicely on the "wrong" side—it pulls, and you can tell from the "right" side. So that's definitely unacceptable.

What's most important to you as a designer?
To me, the fabric itself comes first—knowing the drape and being creative

with the fabric. Many other designers start by sketching the silhouette, before they even know what they want the fabric to look like. My approach is exactly the opposite. I care about the silhouette, but it never comes first.

How do you go about designing the fabric?

I do a lot of sitting with my graph paper and just working things out. At the same time, I swatch the fabric—that's when I'm most creative. And I have a copy machine that helps me immeasurably. With that, I'm able to copy the pattern and paste it together, to see if I'm getting a good repeat. I don't have to redraw it a million times.

Do you prefer focusing on stitches or colors?

It goes in cycles. I think that's true for most knitters. You go along for a while, and you just love cables. Suddenly you can't stand the thought of doing another cable, and you start doing all colorwork. You explore one thing, then move on. Of course, in business, I have to bounce back and forth.

Last year I did lots of things with color, but this year it's definitely stitches. At one point, I did a series of twisted-stitch sweaters. I was making up new stitches, which was a good challenge. But I ended up knitting many myself, and it actually hurt my wrist to do them—it takes a special motion to do these stitches. By now I'm completely fed up with twisted stitches.

Where do you look for inspiration?

That's also cyclical. I have lots of books on rugs and textiles. And I try to keep files of fashion clippings. In many cases, though, I simply start by thinking about what I would like to be wearing this season. I usually end up with something quite different, but that's how the ideas start flowing.

Which is your favorite among the sweaters you designed for Vogue Knitting?

Probably this one. [Gaughan opens the Winter Special 1989/90 issue of VK to page 38.] It's based on two [Native American] rugs, but the colors are completely different. In designing this sweater, we started with an overall feeling of where we wanted to go, and then my editor

just set me loose. I'm very happy with the result. It's definitely something I would wear.

What do you enjoy most about your work?

Last year I took a course in fashion illustrating at RISD. So this year I've found drawing the most fun. I'm fascinated by my new ability to draw a sweater on a model. I love putting hats on them, and different skirts. Although I essentially design the fabric in advance, I work out details—such as what kind of ribbing I'm going to use, or whether there's a little welt somewhere—while I'm drawing.

Then there's the knitting itself. That's like the staff of life. Even when I'm feeling burned out after deadlines, I can't go more than a week without knitting.

What do you enjoy least?

The things that go wrong. And that happens all the time. Even working with good knitters, even in situations that seem simple and under control, all kinds of things can go wrong. Sometimes you get halfway through a sweater and discover a serious defect in the yarn. Then what do you do? I mean, three weeks is a moderately long deadline in this business, and when I'm busy, I have 10 to 20 projects going at once. All that juggling can be stressful.

What's your advice to beginning knitters?

Many people will disagree with me, but I don't think you should ever read instructions in their entirety before you start knitting. It will only scare you. I used to do that—read the whole pattern in advance—and as I did, I'd be thinking: "I don't know what that means . . . or that . . . or that." I felt panicked. But when you're knitting and you come to the shoulder shaping, it becomes fairly obvious what that means, because you have it in front of you. In cooking, you should always read a recipe through, and make sure you have all the ingredients. But with knitting, it's best not to let yourself get overwhelmed. Just face the problems as they arise.

Seen here is Lamont O'Neal's updated version of Norah's original illustration that appeared in the Special Winter 1990/91 issue of Vogue Knitting.

BARK PULLOVER

Inspired by tree bark, the undulating ribbed stitch pattern was carefully engineered to begin and end with the same number of stitches for ease of knitting. At the time, I was particularly proud of making up a pattern unlike any I had seen before. The silhouette is kept simple so the focus stays on the organic texture. The high neckline adds an extra touch of grace.

SIZES
Small (Medium, Large). Shown in size Medium.

KNITTED MEASUREMENTS
Bust 43 (46, 49)"/109 (117, 124.5)cm
Length 28"/72cm
Upper Arm 18 (19, 20)"/45.5 (48, 51)cm

MATERIALS
• 8 (8, 9) 3½oz/100g balls (each approx 245yd/221m) of **Brown Sheep Company** Nature Spun 3-Ply Worsted (wool) in #N-95 Light Yellow (4)
• One pair each sizes 5 and 7 (3.75 and 4.5mm) needles, OR SIZE TO OBTAIN GAUGES
• Removable stitch markers

GAUGES
• 20 sts and 27 rows to 4"/10cm over St st using larger needles.
• 38 sts to 5½/14cm and 60 rows to 9½"/24cm over chart, blocked and slightly stretched, using larger needles.
TAKE TIME TO CHECK GAUGES.

STITCH GLOSSARY
M1 Insert LH needle from front to back under strand between last st worked and next st on LH needle, knit strand through back loop.
M1 p-st Insert LH needle from front to back under strand between last st worked and next st on LH needle, purl strand through back loop.

TWISTED RIB
(an odd number of sts)
Row 1 (RS) P1, *k1 tbl, p1; rep from * to end.
Row 2 K1 tbl, *p1, k1 tbl; rep from * to end.
Rep rows 1 and 2 for twisted rib.

NOTE
Chart pattern is a repeat of 38 sts decreased to 32 sts then increased back to 38 sts.

BACK
With smaller needles, cast on 98 (106, 118) sts.
Work in k2, p2 rib for 4"/10cm, end with a RS row.
Change to larger needles.
Purl 1 row, inc 49 (53,53) sts evenly across—147 (159, 171)sts.

Begin Chart
Row 1 (RS) Beg as indicated, work 38-st rep 3 (4, 4) times, end as indicated.
Cont in chart pat as established, work rows 1–62 of chart once, rows 3–62 once, then rows 3–32 once, piece measures approx 28"/71cm from beg.

Neck and Shoulder Shaping
Working rows 33 and 34, bind off 51 (57, 60) sts at beg of next 2 rows—45 (45, 51) sts.
Rep rows 33 and 34 until neck measures 4"/10cm from bind-off row, end with a WS row.
Bind-off in pat.

FRONT
Work as for back.

SLEEVES

With smaller needles, cast on 54 (58, 62) sts.
Work in k2, p2 rib for 3"/7.5cm, end with a RS row.
Change to larger needles.
Purl 1 row, inc 25 sts evenly across—79 (83, 87) sts.

Begin Chart

Row 1 (RS) Beg as indicated, work 38-st rep 2 times, end as indicated.

Work rows 1–62 of chart pat once, then cont to work chart beg with row 3, AT THE SAME TIME, inc 1 st each side (working inc sts into twisted rib pat) every 4th row 12 (16, 19) times, then every 6th row 7 (4, 2) times—117 (123, 129) sts.
Work in pat until sleeve measures 18"/45.5cm from beg.
Bind off in pat.

FINISHING

Block pieces to measurements. Sew shoulder and neck seams.

Place markers 9 (9½, 10)"/23 (24, 25.5)cm down from shoulders on front and back for armholes.
Sew top of sleeves between markers.
Sew side and sleeve seams. ●

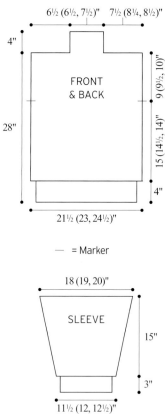

6½ (6½, 7½)"   7½ (8¼, 8½)"

4"

FRONT & BACK

9 (9½, 10)"

28"

15 (14½, 14)"

4"

21½ (23, 24½)"

— = Marker

18 (19, 20)"

SLEEVE

15"

3"

11½ (12, 12½)"

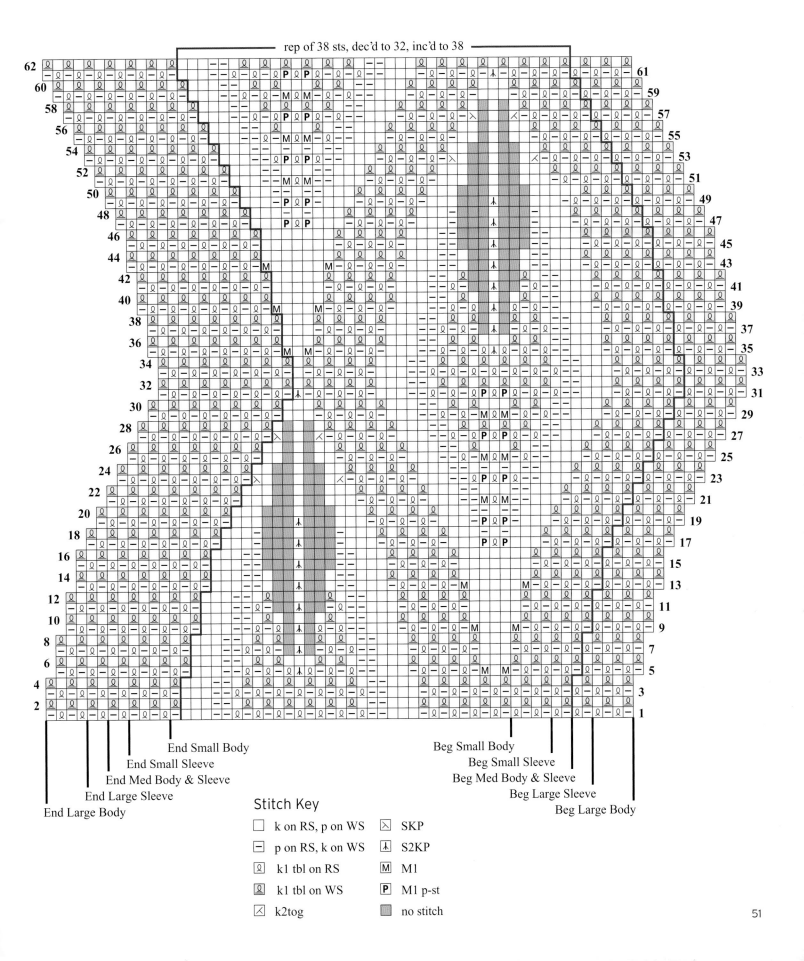

rep of 38 sts, dec'd to 32, inc'd to 38

End Small Body
End Small Sleeve
End Med Body & Sleeve
End Large Sleeve
End Large Body

Beg Small Body
Beg Small Sleeve
Beg Med Body & Sleeve
Beg Large Sleeve
Beg Large Body

Stitch Key

☐ k on RS, p on WS

— p on RS, k on WS

ℚ k1 tbl on RS

ℚ k1 tbl on WS

⟋ k2tog

⟍ SKP

⅄ S2KP

Ⓜ M1

🅿 M1 p-st

▨ no stitch

51

TILED COLORWORK CARDIGAN

Inspired by the decorative arts, this oversized cardigan boasts tile-patterned emblems that are knit with a combination of intarsia and stranded colorwork. The result is a luxuriously relaxed fit that is perfect for lounging at home or on a leisurely vacation stroll, as seen here shot on location in Puerta Vallarta, Mexico.

■■■▶

SIZES
Small (Medium, Large). Shown in size Medium.

KNITTED MEASUREMENTS
Bust (buttoned) 41 (49, 53½)"/104 (124.5, 136)cm
Length 28 (28, 29)"/71 (71, 73.5)cm
Upper Arm 18 (19, 20)"/45.5 (48, 51)cm

MATERIALS
• Original Yarn
6 (7, 8) 3½oz/100g balls (each approx 185yd/176m) of **Reynolds** Saucy (cotton) in #753 Beige (MC) (**3**)
2 (3, 3) balls each in #379 Burgundy (A) and #395 Rose (B)
• Substitute Yarn
6 (6, 7) 3½oz/100g hanks (each approx 219yd/200m) of **Berroco** Pima 100 (pima cotton) in 8408 Rye (MC) (**4**)
2 (3, 3) hanks each in 8444 Foxglove (A) and 8437 Bee Balm (B)
• One pair each sizes 6 and 8 (4 and 5mm) needles, OR SIZE TO OBTAIN GAUGE
• Six ¾"/20mm buttons
• Removable stitch markers
• Bobbins

GAUGE
22 sts and 25 rows to 4"/10cm over chart pat using larger needles.
TAKE TIME TO CHECK GAUGE.

NOTES
1) Use a separate bobbin for each large block of color.
2) When changing colors, twist yarns on WS to prevent holes. Carry yarn not in use loosely along WS of work.

SEED STITCH
(an even number of sts)
Row 1 (RS) *K1, p1; rep from * to end.
Row 2 K the purl sts and p the knit sts.
Rep row 2 for seed st.

BACK
With smaller needles and MC, cast on 108 (129, 144) sts. Work in seed st for 1½"/4cm, end with a WS row. Change to larger needles and cont in St st (k on RS, p on WS).

Begin Chart
Row 1 Beg with st 1 (26, 18), work chart through st 36, work 36-st rep 1 (3, 3) times, then work sts 1–36 (1–10, 1–17). Cont to work chart as established until piece measures 28 (28, 29)"/71 (71, 73.5)cm from beg, end with a WS row. Bind off.

LEFT FRONT
With smaller needles and MC, cast on 55 (66, 72) sts. Work in seed st for 1½"/4cm, end with a WS row. Change to larger needles and cont in St st.

Begin Chart
Row 1 Beg with st 1 (26, 20), work chart through st 36, work 36-st rep 0 (1, 1) times, then work sts 1–19. Cont to work chart as established until piece measures 17 (17, 18)"/43 (43, 45.5)cm from beg, end with a WS row.

Neck Shaping
Next row (RS) Work in pat to last 2 sts, k2tog (neck edge). Cont in pat, dec 1 st at neck edge every other row 2 (4, 2) times, then every 4th row 15 (14, 15) times. Work even until same length as back, bind off rem 37 (47, 54) sts.

RIGHT FRONT
Work as for left front, working chart as foll:
Beg with st 20, work through st 36, work 36-st rep once, then work sts 1–2 (1–13, 1–19).

Neck Shaping
Next row (RS) K2tog (neck edge), work in pat to end.

Cont in pat, dec 1 st at neck edge every other row 2 (4, 2) times, then every 4th row 15 (14, 15) times. Work even until same length as back, bind off rem 37 (47, 54) sts.

SLEEVES
With smaller needles and MC, cast on 46 (50, 56) sts. Work in St st for ½"/1.5cm. Work in seed st for 1"/2.5cm, inc 7 (9, 9) sts evenly across last WS row—53 (59, 65) sts.

Begin Chart
Row 1 (RS) Beg with st 28 (25, 22), work chart through st 36, work 36-st rep once, then work sts 1–8 (1–11, 1–14).
Cont to work in chart as established, AT THE THE SAME TIME, inc 1 st each side (working inc sts into chart pat) every 4th row 23 times—99 (105, 111) sts.
Work even until piece measures 17"/43cm from beg. Bind off.

FINISHING
Block pieces to measurements. Place markers to mark center 6 (6½, 6½)"/15 (16.5, 16.5)cm for back neck. Sew shoulder seams.

Left Front Band
With RS facing, using smaller needles and MC, beg at center

back neck, pick up and k 163 (163, 169) sts evenly along back neck and front edge to lower edge.
Work in seed st for 1"/2.5cm. Work in St st for 1"/2.5cm. Bind off loosely.

Place markers for 6 buttons in center of seed st section with first at beg of neck shaping, last at ½"/1.5cm from lower edge, and 4 evenly spaced between.

Right Front Band
With RS facing, using smaller needles and MC, pick up and k 163 (163, 169) sts evenly from front edge to back neck.
Work as for left front band, working buttonholes in seed st section opposite markers as foll:
Bind off 3 sts. On next row, cast on 3 sts above bound-off sts.

Sew seed st sections closed at back neck, leaving St st section free to roll naturally. Place markers 9 (9½, 10)"/23 (24, 25.5)cm down from shoulders on front and back for armholes.
Sew top of sleeves between markers.

Sew side and sleeve seams, leaving St st section free to roll naturally. Sew on buttons. ●

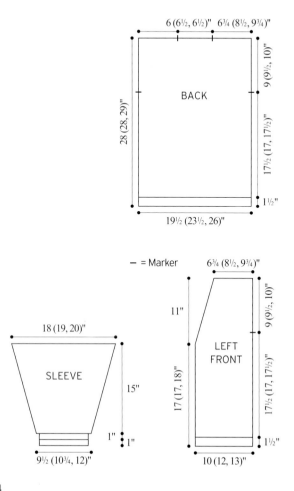

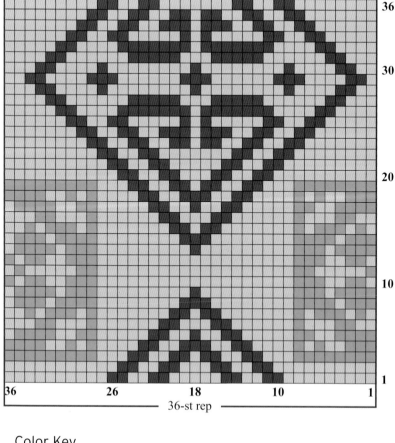

Color Key

□ MC   ■ A   ■ B

54

CABLED SHAWL-COLLAR VEST

Menswear-style is interpreted here in a richly textured sweater vest with a flattering shawl collar and bold cables. It is equally at home in the Maine woods as it is dressed up for a stroll in Paris, where these photos were taken. A rich, rustic wool adds dimension, warmth, and character.

◼◼◼◻

SIZES
X-Small (Small, Medium, Large/X-Large). Shown in size Small.

KNITTED MEASUREMENTS
Bust (buttoned) 36 (39¼, 43¼, 47)"/91.5 (99.5, 110, 119.5)cm
Length 18½ (20, 21½, 22½)"/47 (51, 54.5, 57)cm

MATERIALS
• Original Yarn
5 (5, 6, 6) 3½oz/100g balls (each approx 170yd/153m) of **Reynolds** Candide (wool) in #74 Charcoal (4)
• Substitute Yarn
5 (5, 5, 5) 4oz/113g skeins (each approx 215yd/197m) of **Briggs & Little** Heritage (wool) in 12 Medium Grey (4)
• One pair each sizes 7 and 9 (4.5 and 5.5mm) needles, OR SIZE TO OBTAIN GAUGE
• Cable needle (cn)
• Four ⅞"/22mm buttons
• Removable stitch markers

GAUGE
22 sts and 26 rows to 4"/10cm over charts 1 and 2 (see note section) using larger needles.
TAKE TIME TO CHECK GAUGE.

NOTE
To work gauge swatch, cast on 22 sts and work as foll: P1, work 4-st rep of chart 1 twice, 8 sts of chart 2, 5 sts of chart 1.

STITCH GLOSSARY
6-st LC Sl 3 sts to cn and hold to front, k3, k3 from cn.

BACK
With smaller needles, cast on 80 (90, 98, 106) sts.
Row 1 (RS) *K1, p1; rep from * to end.
Rep row 1 for k1, p1 rib for 2"/5cm, end with a RS row.
Purl 1 row, inc 3 (1, 1, 1) sts evenly across—83 (91, 99, 107) sts.
Change to larger needles

Begin Charts

Row 1 (RS) Work 4-st rep of chart 1 for 1 (2, 3, 4) times, work last st of chart 1, [work 8-st rep of chart 2, work 5 sts of chart 1] 5 times, work 8-st rep of chart 2, then 4-st rep of chart 1 for 1 (2, 3, 4) times, then work last st of chart 1.
Cont to work in pat as established, inc 1 st each side every 6th row 6 (7, 8, 9) times (working inc sts into chart 1)—95 (105, 115, 125) sts.
Work even in pat until piece measures 8½ (9, 10½, 11)"/21.5 (23, 26.5, 28)cm from beg, end with a WS row.

Armhole Shaping

Bind off 4 sts at beg of next 2 (2, 4, 4) rows, 3 sts at beg of next 4 (6, 6, 6) rows, then 2 sts at beg of next 4 (4, 2, 4) rows.
Dec 1 st each side every other row 2 (1, 2, 1) times, every 4th row once, every 6th row once, then every 8th row once—57 (63, 67, 75) sts.
Work even in pat until armhole measures 10 (11, 11, 11½)"/25.5 (28, 28, 29)cm. Bind off.

LEFT FRONT

With smaller needles, cast on 42 (46, 50, 54) sts.
Work in k1, p1 rib for 2"/5cm, end with a RS row. Purl 1 row. Change to larger needles.

Begin Charts

Row 1 (RS) Work 4-st rep of chart 1 for 1 (2, 3, 4) times, work last st of chart, [work 8-st rep of chart 2, work 5 sts of chart 1] twice, work 8-st rep of chart 2, work sts 1–3 of chart 1.
Cont in pat as established, inc 1 st at beg of RS rows (side edge) every 6th row 6 (7, 8, 9) times—48 (53, 58, 63) sts.
Work even in pat until same length as back to armhole, end with a WS row.

Armhole and Neck Shaping

Shape armhole at side edge only (beg of RS rows) as for back, AT THE SAME TIME, when piece measures 9 (10, 11½, 11½)"/23 (25.5, 29, 29)cm, work neck shaping as foll:
Cont to work armhole shaping, dec 1 st at end of every other RS row (neck edge) twice, then every 4th row 13 (14, 14, 16) times.
Work even in pat until same length as back, bind off rem 14 (16, 18, 20) sts for shoulder.

RIGHT FRONT

Work k1, p1 rib same as for left front.

Begin Charts

Row 1 (RS) Work sts 3–5 of chart 1, [work 8-st rep of chart 2, work 5 sts of chart 1] twice, work 8-st rep of chart 2, work 4-st rep of chart 1 for 1 (2, 3, 4) times, work last st of chart 1.
Cont as for left front, reversing all shaping.

FINISHING

Block pieces to measurements. Place markers to mark center

5½ (5¾, 5¾, 6½)"/14 (14.5, 14.5, 16.5)cm for back neck.
Sew shoulder seams.

Armhole Bands

With smaller needles, cast on 7 sts.
Row 1 K2, p1, k1, p1, k2.
Row 2 K1, [p1, k1] 3 times.
Rep rows 1 and 2 until rib measures 21 (23, 23, 24)"/53 (58.5, 58.5, 61)cm from beg. Bind off. Sew armhole band around armhole, easing to fit.
Sew side seams.

Front Bands and Collar

Note When working band and collar, RS of collar becomes WS when sewn in place.
With smaller needles, cast on 8 sts (for lower left front edge).
Row 1 [P1, k1] 3 times, k2.
Row 2 K2, [p1, k1] 3 times.
Rep last 2 rows until piece measures 9 (10, 11½, 11½)"/23 (25.5, 29, 29)cm from beg, end with row 2.
Change to larger needles.
Next row Cast on 2 sts (neck edge), work to end.
Next row Cont in rib on 8 sts, pm, beg with row 9 and st 2 of chart 2, work sts 2–3.
Cont to work in pats, casting on 2 sts at neck edge every other row 7 times more, then inc 1 st at neck edge every other row 15 times (working inc sts in pat as foll: 7 sts of chart 2, 5 sts of chart 1, 8 sts of chart 2, [4-st rep of chart 1] twice, then sts 1–3 of chart 1.
Cont in pats on 39 sts for 7 (7, 7½, 8½)"/18 (18, 19, 21.5)cm more.

Dart shaping

Cont in pat, AT THE SAME TIME, bind off 2 sts at neck edge 13 times—13 sts.
Next row Pick up 2 sts in 2 bound-off sts, work to end.
Cont to pick up 2 sts in each bound-off sts 12 times more (working picked up sts in pat rows to mirror bound-off sts)—39 sts.
Work even for 7 (7, 7½, 8½)"/18 (18, 19, 21.5)cm from dart shaping.

Right Collar

Cont to work in pat, dec 1 st at neck edge every other row 15 times, then bind off 2 sts at neck edge 8 times—8 sts.
Place markers on left front band for 4 buttons with first 1"/2.5cm from lower edge, the last 1"/2.5cm below beg of collar shaping and 2 evenly spaced between.
Change to smaller needles.
Cont in rib pat, working buttonholes opposite markers as foll: K2, p1, k1, bind off 2 sts, work to end. On next row, cast on 2 sts over bound-off sts. Work even until same length as left front band.
Sew collar and bands around front and neck edges, easing to fit around neck.
Sew on buttons. ●

CHART 1

2
5 4 3 2 1
1
4-st
rep

CHART 2

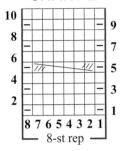

10
9
8
7
6
5
4
3
2
1
8 7 6 5 4 3 2 1
8-st rep

Stitch Key

☐ k on RS, p on WS

⊟ p on RS, k on WS

▨ 6-st LC

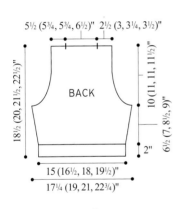

5½ (5¾, 5¾, 6½)" 2½ (3, 3¼, 3½)"

BACK

18½ (20, 21½, 22½)"

10 (11, 11, 11½)"

6½ (7, 8½, 9)"

2"

15 (16½, 18, 19½)"

17¼ (19, 21, 22¾)"

— = Marker

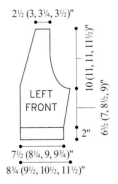

2½ (3, 3¼, 3½)"

10 (11, 11, 11½)"

LEFT
FRONT

6½ (7, 8½, 9)"

2"

7½ (8¼, 9, 9¾)"

8¾ (9½, 10½, 11½)"

TANGLED TEXTURES PULLOVER

Generously sized ladder cables create an unusual stand-out texture with the addition of garter stitch. Slim bands of fresh pinks and corals gild the cast-on edges and highlight the sandy main shade—an ideal complement to a chilly stroll on the beach in Montauk, New York, where these shots were taken.

■■■▭

SIZES
Small (Medium, Large). Shown in size Medium.

KNITTED MEASUREMENTS
Bust 44 (48, 52)"/112 (122, 132)cm
Length 24 (25, 26)"/61 (63.5, 66)cm
Upper Arm 16 (17, 18)"/41 (43.5, 46)cm

MATERIALS
• Original Yarn
12 (13, 14) 3½oz/100g balls (each approx 132yd/121m) of **Cascade Yarns** Pastaza (llama/wool) in #003 Sand (MC) (4)
1 ball each in #022 Pink (A) and #011 Coral (B)
• Substitute Yarn
4 8⁴/₅oz/250g hanks (each approx 478yd/437m) of **Cascade Yarns** Ecological Wool (natural Peruvian wool) in 8016 Beige (MC) (4)
1 8⁴/₅oz/250g hank (approx 478yd/437m) of **Cascade Yarns** Eco+ (Peruvian highland wool) in 3113 Ginger Spice (A & B) (4)
• One pair each sizes 7 and 9 (4.5 and 5.5mm) needles, OR SIZE TO OBTAIN GAUGES
• One size 7 (4.5mm) circular needle, 16"/40cm long
• Cable needle (cn)
• Stitch markers

GAUGES
• 16 sts and 32 rows to 4"/10cm over garter st using larger needles.
• 20 sts and 28 rows to 4"/10cm over chart pat using larger needles.
TAKE TIME TO CHECK GAUGES.

NOTE
If using substitute yarn, use only one color for A and B.

STITCH GLOSSARY
8-st Back Garter Cable Sl 4 sts to cn and hold to back, k4, work 4 sts from cn as foll: k1, sl 2 wyif, k1.
8-st Front Garter Cable Sl 4 sts to cn and hold to front, k1, sl 2 wyif, k1, k4 from cn.
8-st Back Slip Cable Sl 4 sts to cn and hold to back, k1, sl 2 wyif, k1, k4 from cn.
8-st Front Slip Cable Sl 4 sts to cn and hold to front, k4, work 4 sts from cn as foll: k1, sl 2 wyif, k1.

BACK
With smaller needles and A, cast on 112 (122, 132) sts. Knit 1 row. Change to B. Knit 2 rows. Change to larger needles and MC.
Set-up row (WS) K2, [k4, p4, k6, p4, k2] 5 (6, 6) times, k4 (0, 4), p4 (0, 4), k2 (0, 2).

Begin Chart
Row 1 (RS) Beg with st 11 (0, 11), work to end of rep, then work 20-st rep 5 (6, 6) times, work sts 1–2.
Row 2 (WS) Reading chart from left to right, work sts 2–1, work 20-st rep 5 (6, 6) times, then work sts 20–11 (0, 20–11). Cont to work in pat as established through chart row 32, then rep rows 1–32 until piece measures 15½ (16, 16½)"/39.5 (41, 42)cm from beg, end with a WS row.

Armhole Shaping
Bind off 3 sts at beg of next 2 rows, bind off 2 sts at beg of next 4 rows, then dec 1 st each side every other row 3 times—92 (102, 112) sts.
Work even in pat until armhole measures 8½ (9, 9½)"/21.5 (23, 24.5)cm, end with a WS row. Bind off.

FRONT
With smaller needles and A, cast on 112 (122, 132) sts. Knit 1 row. Change to B. Knit 2 rows. Change to larger needles and MC.
Set-up row (WS) K6 (2, 6), p4 (0, 4), k2 (0, 2), [k4, p4, k6, p4, k2] 5 (6, 6) times.

Begin Chart

Row 1 (RS) Beg with st 1, work 20-st st rep 5 (6, 6) times, work sts 1–12 (1–2, 1–12).

Row 2 (WS) Reading chart from left to right, work sts 12–1 (2–1, 12–1), work 20-st rep 5 (6, 6) times.

Cont to work in pat as established and work armhole shaping as for back. When armhole measures 5 (5, 5½)/13 (13, 14)cm, end with a WS row.

Neck Shaping

Next row (RS) Cont in pat, work 40 (44, 48) sts, join 2nd ball of yarn and bind off center 12 (14, 16) sts, work to end. Working both sides at once, bind off from each neck edge 3 sts twice, bind off 2 sts twice, then dec 1 st each side every other row twice.

Work even in pat until armhole measures same as back, then bind off rem 28 (32, 36) sts each side.

SLEEVES

With smaller needles and A, cast on 62 sts. Knit 1 row. Change to B. Knit 2 rows. Change to MC.

Next row (WS) P2, *k3, p3; rep from * to end.

Next row (RS) *K3, p3; rep from * to last 2 sts, k2.

Rep last 2 rows until piece measures 1½"/4cm from beg, end with a RS row. Change to larger needles.

Set-up row (WS) K2, [k4, p4, k6, p4, k2] 3 times.

Begin Chart

Row 1 (RS) Work 20-st rep 3 times, work sts 1–2.

Row 2 (WS) Reading chart from left to right, work sts 2–1, work 20-st rep 3 times.

Cont to rep 32 rows of chart as established, AT THE SAME TIME, inc 1 st each side (working inc sts into garter st) every 6th row 0 (0, 8) times, every 8th row 0 (10, 4) times, then every 10th row 8 (0, 0) times—78 (82, 86) sts.

Work even until piece measures 15½"/39.5cm from beg, end with a WS row.

Cap Shaping

Cont in pat, bind off 3 sts at beg of next 2 rows, 2 sts at beg of next 14 (12, 10) rows, then 3 sts at beg of next 2 (4, 6) rows. Bind off rem 38 (40, 42) sts.

FINISHING

Block pieces lightly to measurements. Sew shoulder seams.

Turtleneck

With RS facing, using circular needle and MC, pick up and k 84 (90, 90) sts evenly around neck edge. Place marker and join.

Rnd 1 *K3, p3; rep from * around.

Rep rnd 1 for k3, k3 rib for 4"/10cm. Bind off loosely in pat.

Set in sleeves, easing to fit. Sew side and sleeve seams. ●

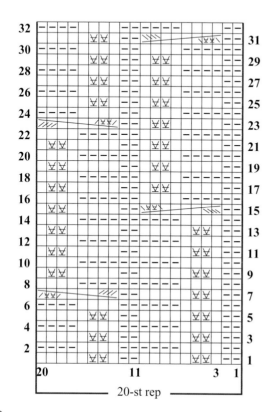

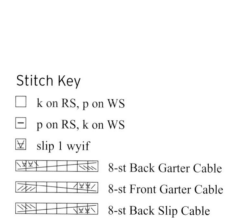

Stitch Key

☐ k on RS, p on WS

⊟ p on RS, k on WS

⊻ slip 1 wyif

8-st Back Garter Cable

8-st Front Garter Cable

8-st Back Slip Cable

8-st Front Slip Cable

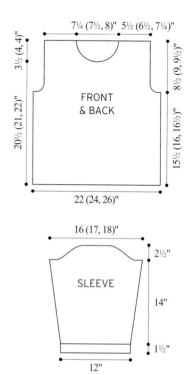

THREE-QUARTER COAT

A three-quarter length coat travels easily from city streets to country shores, flaunting a patchwork of mock cables for texture. A dark ribbed collar and deep cuffs add jolts of contrasting color, and you can go all buttoned up or just do a few, depending on your mood.

■■■■◗

SIZES
Small (Medium, Large). Shown in size Medium.

KNITTED MEASURES
Bust (buttoned) 48 (52½, 56¾)"/124.5 (133, 144)cm
Length 33½ (36, 37½)"/85 (91.5, 95)cm
Upper Arm 17 (17, 18)"/43 (43, 46)cm

MATERIALS
• Original Yarn
23 (26, 30) 1¾oz/50g balls (each approx 68yd/63m) of **Tahki Yarns** Cottage Chunky Knit (wool) in #585 Gray (MC) ⑤
2 (2, 3) 3½oz/100g balls (each approx 129yd/119m) of **Tahki Yarns** Lana (wool) in #7021 Black (CC) ⑤
• Substitute Yarn
15 (17, 19) 3½oz/100g skeins (each approx 109yd/100m) of **Ístex** Álafosslopi (wool) in 9974 Light Grey Tweed (MC) ⑤
2 (3, 3) 3½oz/100g hanks (each approx 131yd/120m) of **Berroco** Ultra Alpaca Chunky (super fine alpaca/Peruvian wool) in 7245 Pitch Black ⑤
• One pair each sizes 7 and 9 (4.5 and 5.5mm) needles, OR SIZE TO OBTAIN GAUGES
• Six 1⅝"/40mm buttons
• Stitch markers

GAUGES
• 18 sts and 20 rows to 4"/10cm over chart 1 using larger needles and MC.
• 19 sts and 20 rows to 4"/10cm over chart 2 using larger needles and MC.
TAKE TIME TO CHECK GAUGES.

STITCH GLOSSARY
2-st RC (on RS rows) Sl 1 st to cn and hold to back, k1, k1 from cn.
2-st RC (on WS rows) Sl 1 st to cn and hold to back, p1, p1 from cn.
2-st LC Sl 1 st to cn and hold to front, k1, k1 from cn.
3-st RC Sl 1 st to cn and hold to back, k2, k1 from cn.
3-st LC Sl 2 sts to cn and hold to front, k1, k2 from cn.

BACK
With larger needles and MC, cast on 102 (114, 126) sts. Work chart 1 for 36 (42, 48) rows. Knit 1 row. Purl 1 row, inc 1 (0, 0) sts—103 (114, 126) sts.

Begin Charts
Next row (RS) Work row 1 of chart 2 over 33 (39, 39) sts, pm, row 1 of chart 3 over 37 (37, 49) sts, pm, row 1 of chart 4 over rem 33 (38, 38) sts.
Cont in pats as established until 42 rows of charts 2 and 4 have been completed.
Next row (RS) K to marker, sm, cont chart 3 over sts between markers, sm, k to end.
Next row P to marker, inc 0 (1, 1) st to 33 (39, 39) sts, sm, cont chart 3 over sts between markers, sm, p to end, inc 1 (dec 1, dec 1) st to 34 (38, 38) sts—104 (114, 126) sts.
Next row (RS) Work row 1 of chart 1 to marker, cont chart 3 over sts between markers, work row 1 of chart 2 to end.
Cont in pats as established until 32 (38, 38) rows of charts 1 and 2 have been completed and piece measures approx 22¾ (25¼, 26½)"/58 (64, 67)cm from beg, end with a WS row.

Armhole Shaping
Cont in pats, bind off 3 sts at beg of next 4 rows, bind off 2 sts at beg of next 4 rows, dec 1 st each side on next row, then dec 1 st each side every other row once more, AT THE SAME TIME, after 42 rows of charts 1 and 2 have been completed, work as foll:
Next row (RS) Cont armhole shaping, k to marker, cont chart 3 over sts between markers, k to end.
Next row P to marker, inc 1 (dec 1, dec 1) st, sm, cont chart 3 over sts between markers, sm, p to end, inc 1 (2, 2) sts across.

Next row Work row 1 of chart 4 to marker (counting back from marker, if armhole shaping is not complete, in order to beg pat at correct point), sm, cont chart 3 over sts between markers, sm, work row 1 of chart 1 to end.

After armhole shaping has been completed and there are 82 (91, 103) sts, work even until armhole measures 9¾ (9¾, 10)"/24 (24, 25.5)cm, end with a WS row.

Shoulder Shaping

Bind off 9 (10, 11) sts at beg of next 4 (6, 2) rows, then 8 (0, 12) sts at beg of next 2 (0, 4) rows. Bind off rem 30 (31, 33) sts for back neck.

LEFT FRONT

With larger needles and MC, cast on 54 (58, 62) sts. Work chart 1 for 36 (42, 48) rows. Knit 1 row. Purl 1 row, dec 2 (0, inc 2) sts across—52 (58, 64) sts.

Begin Charts

Next row (RS) Work row 1 of chart 2 over 33 (39, 39) sts, pm, row 1 of chart 3 over 19 (19, 25) sts.
Cont in pats as established until 42 rows have been completed.
Next row (RS) K to marker, sm, cont chart 3 over rem sts.
Next row Work chart 3 to marker, sm, p to end, inc 1 (dec 1, dec 1) st to 34 (38, 38) sts.
Next row (RS) Work row 1 of chart 1 to marker, sm, cont chart 3 over rem sts.
Cont in pats as established until piece measures same length as back to armhole, end with a WS row.

Armhole Shaping

Shape armhole at beg of RS rows as for back, AT THE SAME TIME, work until 42 rows of chart 1 have been completed.
Next row (RS) K to marker, sm, cont chart 3 over rem sts.
Next row Work chart 3 to marker, sm, p to end, inc 1 (2, 2) sts across.
Next row Work row 1 of chart 4 to marker (beg pat as for back), sm, cont chart 3 over rem sts.
After armhole shaping is complete and there are 42 (47, 53) sts, work even until armhole measures 8¾ (8¾, 9)"/21.5 (21.5, 23)cm, end with a RS row.

Neck and Shoulder Shaping

Next row (WS) Bind off 5 (6, 6) sts (neck edge), work to end. Cont to bind off at neck edge 4 (4, 5) sts once, 3 sts once, then 2 sts twice, AT THE SAME TIME, when piece measures same length as back to shoulder, shape shoulder at beg of RS rows as for back.

RIGHT FRONT

Work as for left front for 36 (42, 48) rows of chart 1. Knit 1 row. Purl 1 row, dec 2 (dec 1, inc 1) sts across—52 (57, 63) sts.

Begin Charts

Next row (RS) Work row 1 of chart 3 over 19 (19, 25) sts, pm, row 1 of chart 4 over 33 (38, 38) sts.
Cont in pats as established until 42 rows have been completed.
Next row (RS) Cont chart 3 over 19 (19, 25) sts, sm, k to end.
Next row P to marker, inc 0 (1, 1) st to 33 (39, 39) sts, sm, work chart 3 to end.
Next row (RS) Work chart 3 to marker, sm, work row 1 of chart 2 over rem sts.
Cont in pats as established until piece measures same length as back to armhole, end with a RS row.

Shape Armhole

Shape armhole at beg of WS rows and end of RS rows as for back, AT THE SAME TIME, after 42 rows of chart 2 have been completed, work as foll:
Next row (RS) Work chart 3 to marker, sm, k to end.
Next row P to marker, inc 1 (dec 1, dec 1) st across, sm, work chart 3 to end.
Next row Work chart 3 to marker, sm, work row 1 of chart 1 to end.
After armhole shaping has been completed and there are 41 (45, 51) sts, work even in pats until 1 row less than left front to neck shaping, end with a WS row.

Neck and Shoulder Shaping

Next row (RS) Bind off 4 (4, 5) sts (neck edge), work to end.
Bind off at neck edge 4 sts once, 3 sts once, then 2 sts twice, AT THE SAME TIME, when piece measures same length as back to shoulder, shape shoulder at beg of WS rows as for back.

SLEEVES

With larger needles and MC, cast on 49 (49, 51) sts.

Begin Charts

Next row (RS) K2 (selvage sts), k0 (0, 1), p1, k1, pm, work 6-st rep of chart 2 to last 3 (3, 4) sts, pm, p1, k0 (0, 1), k2 (selvage sts).
Cont in pat as established, AT THE SAME TIME, inc 1 st each side (working inc sts into chart 2, inside 2 St st selvage sts each side) every 4th row 13 (10, 13) times, then every 6th row 3 (6, 4) times—81 (81, 85) sts.
Work even until piece measures 15 (16, 16)"/38 (40.5, 40.5)cm from beg, end with a WS row.

Cap Shaping

Bind off 3 sts at beg of next 2 rows, then 2 sts at beg of next 2 rows. Dec 1 st each side on next row, then every other row 6 (6, 7) times more. Work 1 row even. Bind off 2 sts at beg of next 4 rows, 3 sts at beg of next 4 rows, then 4 sts at beg of next 2 rows. Bind off rem 29 (29, 31) sts.

FINISHING
Block pieces lightly to measurements.

Sleeve Cuffs
With RS facing, using larger needles and CC, pick up and k 62 (62, 66) sts evenly across lower edge of sleeve. Work in k2, p2 rib for 6 (6, 6¾)"/15 (15, 16.5)cm. Bind off.

Sew shoulder seams. Sew side and sleeve seams. Set in sleeves.

Left Front Button Band
With RS facing, using smaller needles and MC, pick up and k 126 (138, 142) sts evenly along left front edge. Work in k2, p2 rib, with first and last 2 sts in garter st (k every row), for 1¼"/3cm. Bind off.
Place markers for 6 buttons along band, with the first 6 (7, 7)"/15 (18, 18)cm from lower edge, the last 1"/2.5cm below first neck dec, and 4 others spaced evenly between.

Right Front Buttonhole Band
Work to correspond to button band, working buttonholes opposite markers when band measures ½"/1.5cm by binding off 2 sts for each buttonhole, then casting on 2 sts over each pair of bound-off sts on foll row.

Collar
With RS facing, larger needles and CC, pick up and k 98 (98, 102) sts evenly around neck edge (not including front bands).
Next row (WS) K2, *k2, p2; rep from * to last 4 sts, k4.
Next row *K2, p2; rep from * to last 2 sts, k2.
Cont in rib pat as established, with first and last 2 sts in garter st, until collar measures 6 (6, 6¾)"/15 (15, 16.5)cm from beg. Bind off.

Sew on buttons. ●

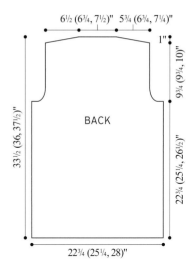

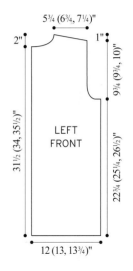

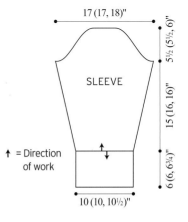

CHART 1

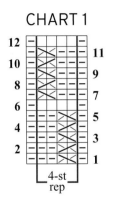

4-st rep

CHART 2

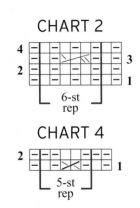

6-st rep

CHART 4

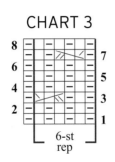

5-st rep

CHART 3

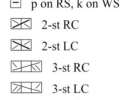

6-st rep

Stitch Key
☐ k on RS, p on WS

⊟ p on RS, k on WS

⊠ 2-st RC

⊠ 2-st LC

⊠ 3-st RC

⊠ 3-st LC

DRAGONFLY PULLOVER

Keen to prove that it's possible to "draw" with cables, I pulled out all the stops with this dragonfly knit with lace and cable stitches. Worked in summery cotton with breezy lace vents used as the wings of the dragonfly, it was the perfect summer sweater for this shoot in Los Angeles, California.

▄▄▄▄

SIZES
Small (Medium, Large, X-Large).
Shown in size Large.

KNITTED MEASUREMENTS
Bust 41 (43, 45, 47)"/104(109, 114, 119)cm
Length 28"/71cm
Upper Arm 15"/38cm

MATERIALS
• Original Yarn
12 (13, 13, 14) 1¾oz/50g balls (each approx 120yd/110m) of **Missoni/ Stacy Charles** Caprera (cotton) in #146 Green ❷
• Substitute Yarn
11 (12, 12, 13) 1¾oz/50g balls (each approx 136yd/125m) of **Tahki Yarns/ Tahki•Stacy Charles** BioLino (organic cotton/linen) in 1708 Lime ❷
• One pair each sizes 1 and 3 (2.25 and 3.25mm) needles, OR SIZE TO OBTAIN GAUGE
• One each sizes 1 and 3 (2 and 3.25mm) circular needles, 29"/74cm long
• Cable needle (cn)
• Stitch markers

GAUGE
24 sts and 33 rows to 4"/10cm over St st using larger needle.
TAKE TIME TO CHECK GAUGE.

STITCH GLOSSARY
1/1 LT (1/1 left twist) With RH needle behind LH needle, skip first st and k 2nd st tbl, insert RH needle into backs of both sts and k2tog tbl.

2/1 RC (2/1 right cross) Sl 1 st to cn and hold to back, k2, k1 from cn.

2/1 LC (2/1 left cross) Sl 2 sts to cn and hold to front, k1, k2 from cn.

2/1 RPC (2/1 right purl cross) Sl 1 st to cn and hold to back, k2, p1 from cn.

2/1 RYIC (2/1 right yarnover inc cross) Sl 1 st to cn and hold to back, k2, yo, k1 from cn—1 st inc'd.

2/1 LYIC (2/1 left yarnover inc cross) Sl 2 sts to cn and hold to front, k1, yo, k2 from cn—1 st inc'd.

2/2 RC (2/2 right cable) Sl 2 sts to cn and hold to back, k2, k2 from cn.

2/2 LC (2/2 left cable) Sl 2 sts to cn and hold to front, k2, k2 from cn.

2/2 LPC (2/2 left purl cable) Sl 2 sts to cn and hold to front, p2, k2 from cn.

2/2 RYC (2/2 right yarnover cable) Sl 2 sts to cn and hold to back, k2, yo, p2tog from cn.

2/2 LYC (2/2 left yarnover cable) Sl 2 sts to cn and hold to front, yo, p2tog, k2 from cn.

2/2 RDC (2/2 right dec cable) Sl 2 sts to cn and hold to back, k2, p2tog from cn—1 st dec'd.

2/2 RYIC (2/2 right yarnover inc cable) Sl 2 sts to cn and hold to back, k2, then from cn: yo, k1, knit yo of previous row tbl—1 st inc'd. **Note** On next row, k yo tbl.

2/2 LYIC (2/2 left yarnover inc cable) Sl 2 sts to cn and hold to front, yo, k1, knit yo of previous row tbl, k2 from cn—1 st inc'd. **Note** On next row, knit yo tbl.

2/3 RC (2/3 right cable) Sl 3 sts to cn and hold to back, k2, k3 from cn.

2/3 LC (2/3 left cable) Sl 2 sts to cn and hold to front, k3, k2 from cn.

2/3 LPC (2/3 left purl cable) Sl 2 sts to cn and hold to front, p3, k2 from cn.

2/3 RDC (2/3 right dec cable) Sl 3 sts to cn and hold to back, k2tog, k3tog from cn—3 sts dec'd.

2/3 LDC (2/3 left dec cable) Sl 2 sts to cn and hold to front, k3tog, ssk from cn—3 sts dec'd.

2/3 RYDC (2/3 right yarnover dec cable) Sl 3 sts to cn and hold to back, k2, yo, p3tog from cn—1 st dec'd.
2/3 LYDC (2/3 left yarnover dec cable) Sl 2 sts to cn and hold to front, yo, p3tog, k2 from cn—1 st dec'd.
3/3 LC (3/3 left cable) Sl 3 sts to cn and hold to front, k3, k3 from cn.
3/3 LPC (3/3 left purl cable) Sl 3 sts to cn and hold to front, p3, k3 from cn.

NOTE
Body of sweater is worked circularly to underarms, then divided for front and back and worked at the same time with separate balls.

BODY
With smaller circular needle, cast on 300 (312, 324, 336) sts. Join, taking care not to twist sts, and pm for beg of rnd.
Rnd 1 *K2, p2; rep from * around.
Rep rnd 1 for k2, p2 rib for 1½"/4cm.
Change to larger circular needle and work in rnds of St st (k every rnd), dec 43 sts evenly around on first rnd—257 (269, 281, 293) sts.
Knit 3 rnds.

Begin Chart
Next rnd K to 14 sts before end of rnd, pm, work row 1 of chart over 154 sts, pm, k to end.
Cont to work in rnds of St st and chart through chart row 140—247 (259, 271, 283) sts rem.
Knit 1 rnd, dec 1 st—246 (258, 270, 282) sts.
Work even in St st until piece measures 18½"/47cm from beg, end 4 sts before beg of rnd marker.

Armhole Shaping
Next rnd Bind off 8 sts (underarm), k until there are 115 (121, 127, 133) sts for front, join 2nd ball and bind off next 8 sts (underarm), k until there are 115 (121, 127, 133) sts for back. Working front and back at same time with separate balls, now working back and forth in rows of St st (k on RS, p on WS), bind off from each armhole edge 3 sts once, then 2 sts once. Dec 2 sts every RS row 3 times as foll: k2, k2tog, k to last 4 sts, ssk, k2—99 (105, 111, 117) sts.
Work even until armhole measures 4½"/11.5cm, end with a WS row.

Front Neck Shaping
Cont to work even on back sts, shape front neck as foll:
Next row (RS) K41 (44, 47, 50) sts, join 2nd ball and bind off center 17 sts, work to end.
Working both sides at same time, bind off from each neck edge 4 sts once, 3 sts once, 2 sts twice, then 1 st 4 times.
Work even until armhole measures 8½"/21.5cm, end with a WS row.

Shoulder and Back Neck Shaping
Bind off at each shoulder edge of front and back 6 (7, 8, 8) sts 2 (3, 4, 1) times, then 7 (8, 0, 9) sts 2 (1, 0, 3) times, AT THE SAME TIME, bind off center 23 sts of back for neck and, working both sides at same time, bind off from each neck edge 4 sts 3 times.

SLEEVES
With smaller straight needles, cast on 90 sts. Work in k2, p2 rib for 3½"/9cm, end with a WS row. Change to larger straight needles. Work in St st until piece measures 16"/40.5cm from beg, end with a WS row.

Cap Shaping
Bind off 4 sts at beg of next 2 rows, then 2 sts at beg of next 4 rows.
Next row (RS) K2, k2tog, k to last 4 sts, ssk, k2.
Rep last row every other row 3 times more, every 4th row twice, then every other row 4 times.
Work 1 row even. Bind off 2 sts at beg of next 4 rows, 3 sts at beg of next 2 rows, then 4 sts at beg of next 2 rows. Bind off rem 32 sts.

FINISHING
Block pieces to measurements (stretching dragonfly motif flat). Sew shoulder and side seams. Sew sleeve seams. Set in sleeves.

Neckband
With smaller straight needles, cast on 12 sts.
Row 1 (RS) K3, p2, k2, p2, k3.
Row 2 P3, k2, p2, k2, sl 3 wyif.
Rep rows 1 and 2 until short side measures 21"/53.5cm from beg. Bind off.
Sew ends tog. Sew neckband around neck edge, placing seam at center back neck. ●

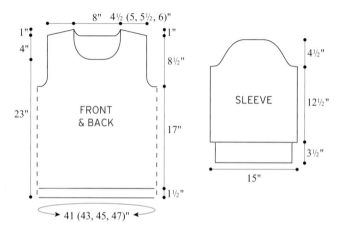

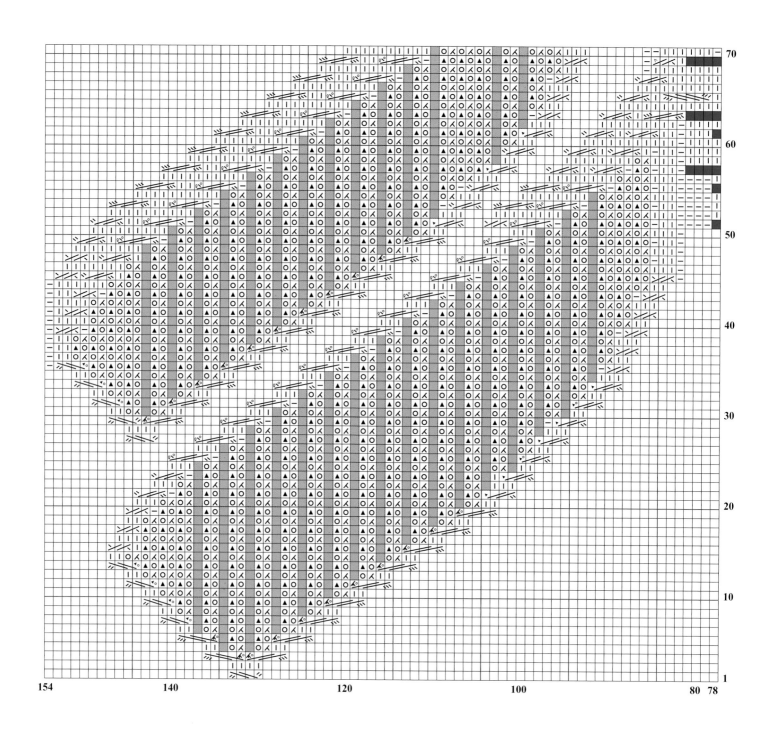

Stitch Key

I and ☐ Knit	▲ P2tog	2/1 RYIC	2/2 RYC
— Purl	1/1 LT	2/1 LYIC	2/2 LYC
▨ No stitch	2/1 LC	2/2 RC	2/2 RDC
O Yarn over	2/1 RC	2/2 LC	2/2 RYIC
⋋ K2tog	2/1 RPC	2/2 LPC	2/2 LYIC

2/3 RC	2/3 RYDC
2/3 LC	2/3 LYDC
2/3 LPC	3/3 LC
2/3 RDC	3/3 LPC
2/3 LDC	■ Cable continuation

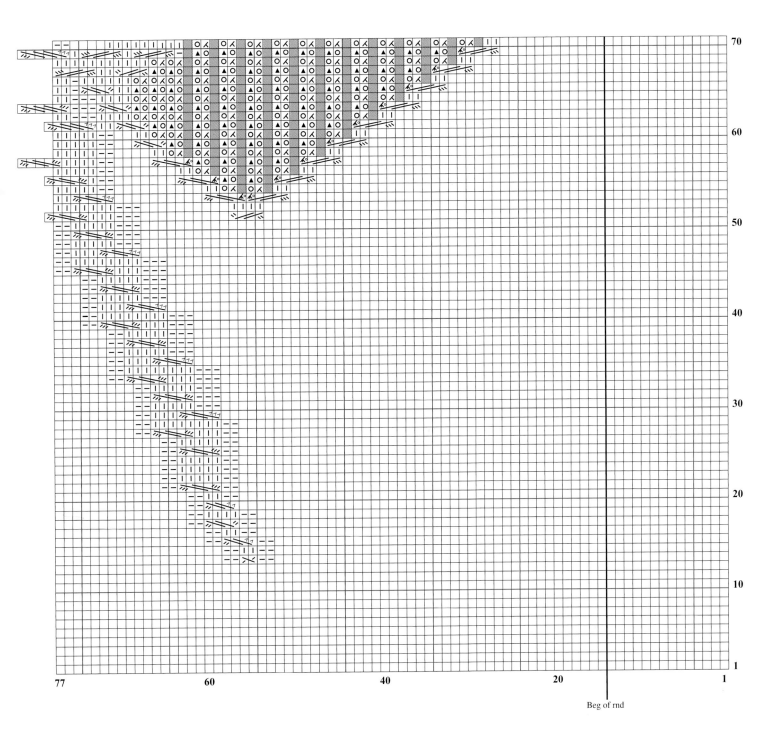

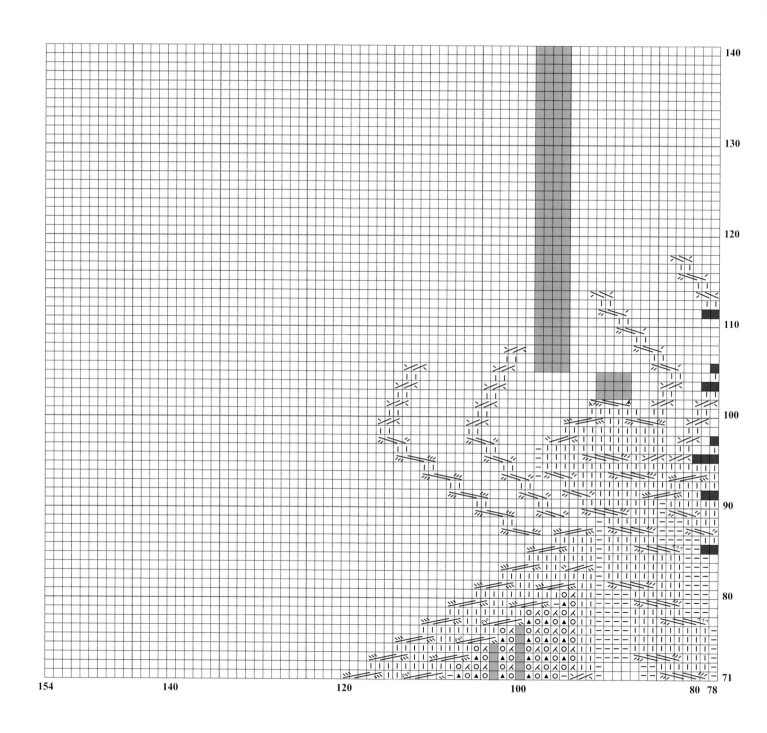

Stitch Key

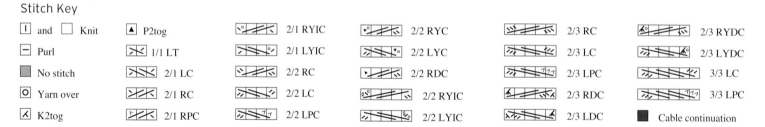

⊡ and ☐ Knit	▲ P2tog	2/1 RYIC	2/2 RYC	2/3 RC	2/3 RYDC
⊟ Purl	1/1 LT	2/1 LYIC	2/2 LYC	2/3 LC	2/3 LYDC
No stitch	2/1 LC	2/2 RC	2/2 RDC	2/3 LPC	2/3 LYDC
⊙ Yarn over	2/1 RC	2/2 LC	2/2 RYIC	2/3 RDC	3/3 LC
⊠ K2tog	2/1 RPC	2/2 LPC	2/2 LYIC	2/3 LDC	3/3 LPC
					Cable continuation

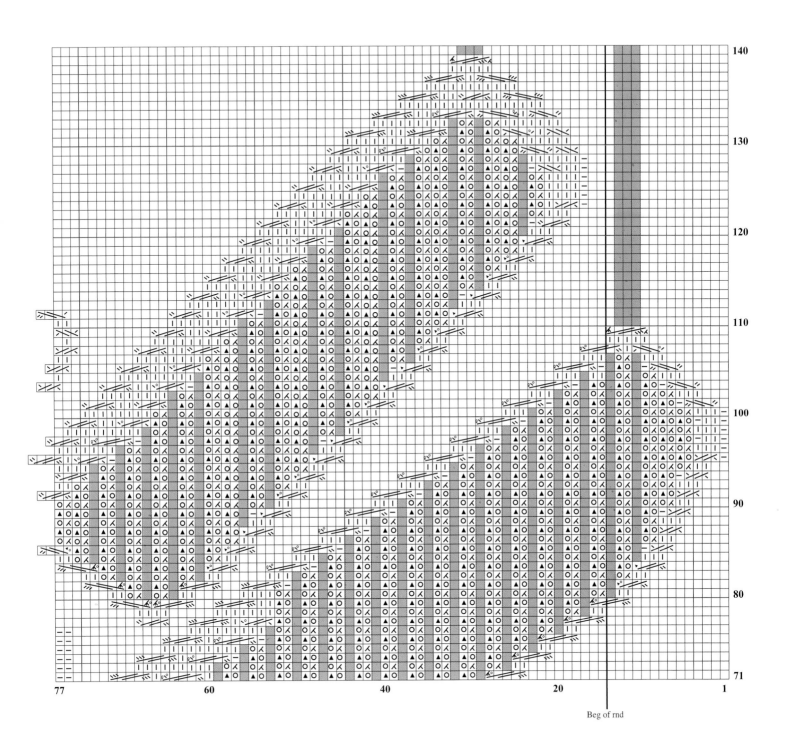

Beg of rnd

77　　　60　　　40　　　20　　　1

140
130
120
110
100
90
80
71

73

TRAVELING CABLES TURTLENECK

Reminiscent of the winding tendrils that traverse a vineyard, organically inspired cables flow with a life of their own. A variety of ribs pop up along the yoke, bottom edge, and sleeves of this graceful turtleneck, with twisting, turning cables sprouting from unexpected places.

SIZES
Small (Medium, Large, X-Large).
Shown in size Medium.

KNITTED MEASUREMENTS
Bust 37½ (40½, 44, 49)"/95 (103, 111.5, 124.5)cm
Length 23½ (24, 24½, 25)"/59.5 (61, 62, 63.5)cm
Upper Arm 16 (17, 18, 19)"/40.5 (43, 45.5, 48)cm

MATERIALS
• Original Yarn
8 (8, 9, 9) 3½oz/100g hanks (each approx 245yd/220m) of **Colinette** DK (wool) in #14 Pale Olive 🔳
• Substitute Yarn
16 (16, 18, 18) 1¾oz/50g balls (each approx 124yd/113m) of **Valley Yarn** Northfield (merino wool/baby alpaca/silk) in 24 Stone Blue 🔳
• One pair each sizes 5 and 7 (3.75 and 4.5mm) needles, OR SIZE TO OBTAIN GAUGES
• One size 5 (3.75mm) circular needle, 16"/40.5cm long
• Cable needle (cn)

GAUGES
• 28 sts and 29 rows to 4"/10cm over chart 2 using larger needles.
• 24 sts and 28 rows to 4"/10cm over rib pat using larger needles.
TAKE TIME TO CHECK GAUGES.

STITCH GLOSSARY
MB (make bobble) K into front, back, front, and back of st, turn, p4, turn, k4, sl first, 2nd, and 3rd sts over 4th st.
6-st BC (6-st Back Cable) Sl 3 sts to cn and hold to back, k3, k3 from cn.
6-st FC (6-st Front Cable) Sl 3 sts to cn and hold to front, k3, k3 from cn.
6-st BPC (6-st Back Purl Cross) Sl 3 sts to cn and hold to back, k3, p3 from cn.
6-st FPC (6-st Front Purl Cross) Sl 3 sts to cn and hold to front, p3, k3 from cn.
6-st BLC (6-st Back Loop Cross) Sl 3 sts to cn and hold to back, k3, then k1 tbl, p1, k1 tbl from cn.
6-st FLC (6-st Front Loop Cross) Sl 3 sts to cn and hold to front, k1 tbl, p1, k1 tbl, then k3 from cn.
6-st BPLC (6-st Back Purl Loop Cross) Sl 3 sts to cn and hold to back, k3 then p1, k1 tbl, p1 from cn.
6-st FPLC (6-st Front Purl Loop Cross) Sl 3 sts to cn and hold to front, p1, k1 tbl, p1, then k3 from cn.
9-st FLC (9-st Front Loop Cross) Sl 6 sts to cn and hold to front, k3, place last 3 sts from cn onto LH needle and k1 tbl, p1, k1 tbl, then k3 from cn.
9-st FPC (9-st Front Purl Cross) Sl 6 sts to cn and hold to front, k3, place last 3 sts from cn onto LH needle and p3, then k3 from cn.

RIB PATTERN
(multiple of 6 sts plus 3)
Row 1 (RS) *K3, p3; rep from * to last 3 sts, k3.
Row 2 *P3, k3; rep from * to last 3 sts, p3.
Rep rows 1 and 2 for rib pat.

BACK
With smaller needles, cast on 131 (143, 155, 173) sts.

For Sizes Small (Medium) Only
Row 1 (RS) K4, p3, k0 (3), p0 (3), work 9 sts of chart 1, work 99 sts of chart 2, work 9 sts of chart 3, p0 (3), k0 (3), p3, k4.

For Size Large Only
Row 1 (RS) K4, p3, [k3, p3] twice, work 9 sts of chart 1, work 99 sts of chart 2, work 9 sts of chart 3, [p3, k3] twice, p3, k4.

For Size X-Large Only
Row 1 (RS) K1, work 9 sts of chart 1, p3, [k3, p3] twice, work 9 sts of chart 1, work 99 sts of chart 2, work 9 sts of chart 3, [p3, k3] twice, p3, work 9 sts of chart 3, p3, k1.

For All Sizes
Cont to foll charts and work in established ribs through row 7 of chart 2. Change to larger needles and cont in pats until row 132 is completed. Then rep rows 131 and 132 until piece measures 22½ (23, 23½, 24)"/57 (58.5, 59.5, 61)cm from beg.

Shoulder and Neck Shaping
Cont in pat, bind off 10 (13, 14, 15) sts at beg of next 2 rows, then 11 (12, 13, 15) sts at beg of next 6 rows, AT THE SAME TIME, bind off center 27 (27, 31, 35) sts for neck and working both sides at once, bind off 3 sts from each neck edge 3 times.

FRONT
Work as for back until piece measures 21 (21½, 22, 22½)"/53 (54.5, 56, 57)cm from beg.

Neck and Shoulder Shaping
Work 55 (61, 65, 72) sts, place center 21 (21, 25, 29) sts on a holder for neck, join 2nd ball of yarn and work to end. Working both sides at once, bind off 4 sts from each neck edge once, 3 sts once, 2 sts twice, then 1 st once, AT THE SAME TIME, when same length as back to shoulders, shape shoulders as for back.

SLEEVES
With smaller needles, cast on 63 (63, 69, 69) sts. Work in rib pat for 2"/5cm. Change to larger needles.
Inc row (RS) K2, inc 1 by working 2 sts in next st, rib to last 4 sts, inc 1 st, k3.
Working inc sts into rib pat, rep inc row every 4th row 0 (0, 4, 7) times, then every 6th row 16 (18, 15, 14) times—97 (101, 109, 113) sts.
Work even until piece measures 19"/48cm from beg.
Bind off.

FINISHING
Block pieces to measurements. Sew shoulder seams.

Turtleneck
With circular needle, beg at left shoulder seam, pick up and k 20 sts to center front neck, work rib as established across 21 (21, 25, 29) sts from holder, pick up and k 20 sts from other side of neck, then pick up and k 45 (45, 49, 53) sts from back neck. Join and pm for beg of rnd.
Rnd 1 [K1 tbl, p1] 10 (10, 12, 14) times, work k3, p3 rib across center 21 sts, then *p1, k1 tbl; rep from * to last st, p1.
Rnd 2 *K1, p1; rep from * to center rib sts, work center rib sts then p1, k1 rib to end.
Rep rnds 1 and 2 until turtleneck measures 3"/7.5cm, then work p sts in twisted rib (instead of k sts) every other rnd by p1 tbl until turtleneck measures 7"/18cm. Bind off in rib.

Place markers 8 (8½, 9, 9½)"/20.5 (21.5, 23, 24)cm down from shoulders. Sew sleeves to armholes between markers.
Sew side and sleeve seams. ●

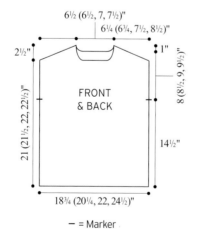

6½ (6½, 7, 7½)"
6¼ (6¾, 7½, 8½)"
2½"
1"
8 (8½, 9, 9½)"
21 (21½, 22, 22½)"

FRONT & BACK

14½"

18¾ (20¼, 22, 24½)"

━ = Marker

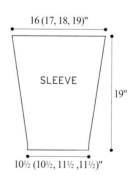

16 (17, 18, 19)"

SLEEVE

19"

10½ (10½, 11½ ,11½)"

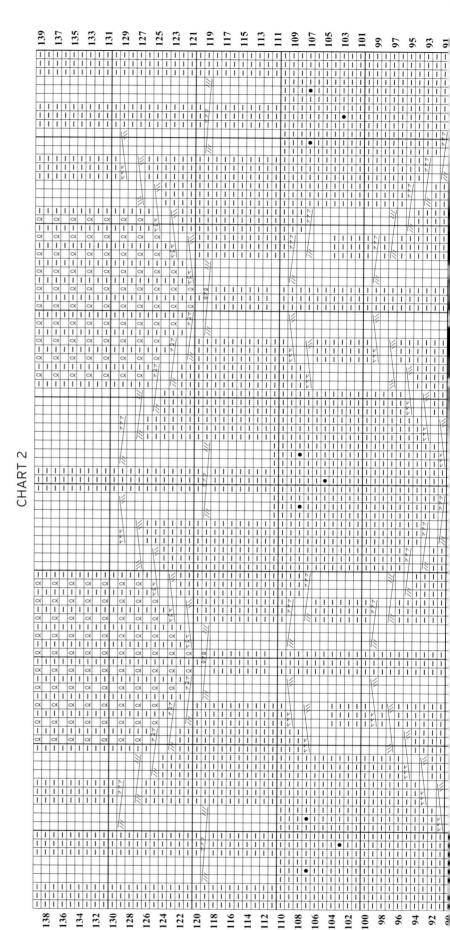

CHART 2

CHART 1

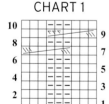

9 sts

CHART 3

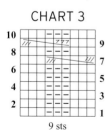

9 sts

Stitch Key

▢   k on RS, p on WS

▬   p on RS, k on WS

Ⓠ   k1 tbl

●   MB

   6-st BC

   6-st FC

   6-st BPC

   6-st FPC

   6-st BLC

   6-st FLC

   6-st BPLC

   6-st FPLC

   9-st FLC

   9-st FPC

99 sts

TRELLIS CARDIGAN

An interlaced pattern forms an allover woven trellis, intertwining with delicate twists of traveling cables across the chest and upper back. The cabled cuffs and collar provide a simple yet sturdy framework, putting the spotlight on the inventive, distinctive design of this button-down cardigan. Both this and the previous turtleneck were shot near the Montauk, New York lighthouse.

◼◼◼◼

SIZES
Small/Medium (Large/X-Large).
Shown in size Small/Medium.

KNITTED MEASUREMENTS
Bust 38 (50)"/96.5 (127)cm
Length 24¼ (27¼)"/61.5 (69)cm
Upper Arm 13½ (15¾)"/34.5 (40)cm

MATERIALS
• Original Yarn
17 (23) 1¾oz/50g balls (each approx 139yd/127m) of **Ilse Wolle/Skacel** Setana (wool/silk/microfiber) in #217 Plum ❸
• Substitute Yarn
20 (26) 1¾oz/50g balls (each approx 124yd/113m) of **Valley Yarns** Northfield (merino/baby alpaca/silk) in 08 Summer Plum ❸
• One pair each sizes 3 and 5 (3.25 and 3.75mm) needles, OR SIZE TO OBTAIN GAUGE
• Cable needle (cn)
• Seven ½"/3mm buttons

GAUGE
32 sts and 32 rows to 4"/10cm over cable pat foll chart or one 24-st rep to 3"/7.5cm using larger needles.
TAKE TIME TO CHECK GAUGE.

NOTE
When working left or right front, do not work cable if beg or end in middle of cable.

STITCH GLOSSARY
4-st RC Sl 2 sts to cn and hold to back, k2, k2 from cn.
4-st LC Sl 2 sts to cn and hold to front, k2, k2 from cn.
4-st RPC Sl 2 sts to cn and hold to back, k2, p2 from cn.
4-st LPC Sl 2 sts to cn and hold to front, p2, k2 from cn.

BACK
Note Read all instructions carefully before beginning.
With smaller needles, cast on 138 (178) sts.
Work in k2, p2 rib for 1"/2.5cm, end with a RS row.
Next row (WS) Purl, inc 16 (24) sts evenly across—154 (202) sts.
Change to larger needles. Beg with row 13 (1) of chart 1 as indicated, work to rep line, work 24-st rep 5 (7) times, end as indicated. Work rows 1–12 of chart 1 for 0 (1) times, then rep rows 13–36 a total of 4 times, piece measures approx 13 (14½)"/33 (37)cm from beg.
Work rows 37–66 once, AT THE SAME TIME, when piece measures 15½ (17)"/39.5 (43)cm from beg and row 58 of chart 1 is complete, beg armhole shaping.

Armhole Shaping
Note Cont foll chart 1 through row 66 during armhole shaping, then rep rows 67–90 to end of piece.
Bind off 4 sts at beg of next 2 rows, 3 sts at beg of next 4 (8) rows, 2 sts at beg next 4 (8) rows, then dec 1 st each side every other row 2 (4) times—122 (146) sts.
Working first and last st in rev St st (p on RS, k on WS), cont in pat until armhole measures 8 (9½)"/20.5 (24)cm.

Shoulder and Neck Shaping
Bind off 13 sts at beg of next 2 (0) rows, 12 (16) sts at beg of next 4 (6) rows, AT THE SAME TIME, bind off center 28 (30) sts and working both sides at once, bind off 5 sts from each neck edge twice.

LEFT FRONT
With smaller needles, cast on 71 (87) sts.
Row 1 (RS) *K2, p2; rep from * to last 3 sts, k3.
Cont in rib for 1"/2.5 cm, end with a RS row.
Next row (WS) Purl, inc 7 (15) sts evenly across—78 (102) sts.

Change to larger needles.
Beg with row 13 (1) of chart 1 as indicated, work to rep line, work 24-st rep 2 (3) times, end as indicated. Work rows 1–12 of chart 1 for 0 (1) times, then rep rows 13–36 a total of 4 times. Work rows 37–66 once, AT THE SAME TIME, when piece measures 15½ (17)"/39.5 (43)cm from beg and row 58 of chart 1 is complete, beg armhole shaping.

Armhole Shaping
Note As on back, cont foll chart 1 through row 66 during armhole shaping, then rep rows 67–90 to end of piece.
Bind off at beg of next RS row (armhole edge) 4 sts once, 3 sts 2 (4) times, 2 sts 2 (4) times, then dec 1 st every other row 2 (4) times—62 (74) sts.
Work even until armhole measures 7 (8½)"/17.5 (21.5)cm, end with a RS row.

Neck and Shoulder Shaping
Bind off 6 (7) sts at beg of next row (neck edge), then bind off 4 sts twice from neck edge, 3 sts twice, 2 sts twice, then 1 st once, AT THE SAME TIME, when same length as back to shoulders, shape shoulders by binding off 13 sts 1 (0) times, then 12 (16) sts 2 (3) times.

RIGHT FRONT
Work to correspond to left front, reversing shaping and beg and end chart 1 where indicated.

SLEEVES
With smaller needles, cast on 70 (86) sts. Work in k2, p2 rib for 1"/2.5cm, end with a RS row.
Next row (WS) Purl, inc 6 (14) sts evenly across—76 (100) sts. Change to larger needles.
Next row (RS) K2, work 24-st rep of chart 2 for 3 (4) times, k2. Cont foll chart 2, working incs into pat foll chart 2 by working 2 sts into 2nd st (beg inc) and 2 sts into 3rd st from end (end inc) as foll:
Inc 1 st each side every 6th row 5 times, [every 4th row once, every 8th row once] twice, every 6th row 3 times, then every 10th row 4 (1) times, AT THE SAME TIME, after row 84 of chart 2, rep rows 61–84 with added inc sts worked in rev St st—108 (126) sts after all inc. Work even until piece measures 17"/43cm from beg.

Cap Shaping
Bind off 4 sts at beg of next 2 rows, 3 sts at beg of next 2 (4) rows, then 2 sts at beg of next 2 (4) rows.
Dec 1 st each side every other row 4 (15) times, every 4th row 4 (0) times, then every other row 3 (0) times.
Bind off 2 sts at beg of next 4 rows, 3 sts at beg of next 2 rows, 4 sts at beg of next 2 rows, then 5 sts at beg of next 2 rows.
Bind off rem 36 sts.

FINISHING
Block pieces to measurements.

Front Bands
With smaller needles and RS facing, pick up and k 138 (154) sts from center left front edge.
Row 1 (WS) K1 (selvage st), *p2, k2; rep from * to last st, k1 (selvage st).
Work in rib for 6 rows more. Bind off.
Place markers on left front band for 7 buttons with first and last ½"/1.5cm from edges and 5 evenly spaced between.
Work right front band in same way, working buttonholes in 2nd row opposite markers as foll: yo, work 2 sts tog.
Sew on buttons to left front band.

Sew shoulder, side, and sleeve seams. Set sleeves in armholes.

Collar
With smaller needles and RS facing, beg after right front band and end before left front band, pick up and k 112 (118) sts evenly around neck.
Row 1 (RS) K4, [p2, k4] 17 (18) times, p2, k4.
Row 2 K2, M1, p1, [k1, M1, k1, p4] 17 (18) times, k1, M1, k1, p2, M1, k2.
Row 3 K2, p1, k2, *p2, sl 2 sts to cn and hold to back, k2, k2 from cn; rep from * to last 7 sts, p2, k2, p1, k2.
Work 3 rows even.
Rep last 4 rows until collar measures 5"/12.5cm. Bind off in pat. ●

CHART 1

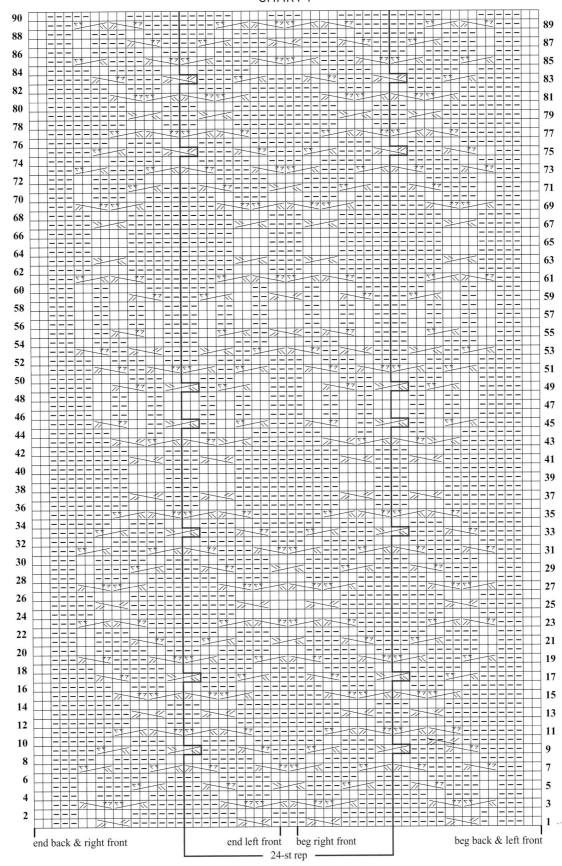

Stitch Key

- ☐ k on RS, p on WS
- ⊟ p on RS, k on WS
- 4-st RC
- 4-st LC
- 4-st RPC
- 4-st LPC

end back & right front   end left front   beg right front   beg back & left front

⊢——— 24-st rep ———⊣

CHART 2

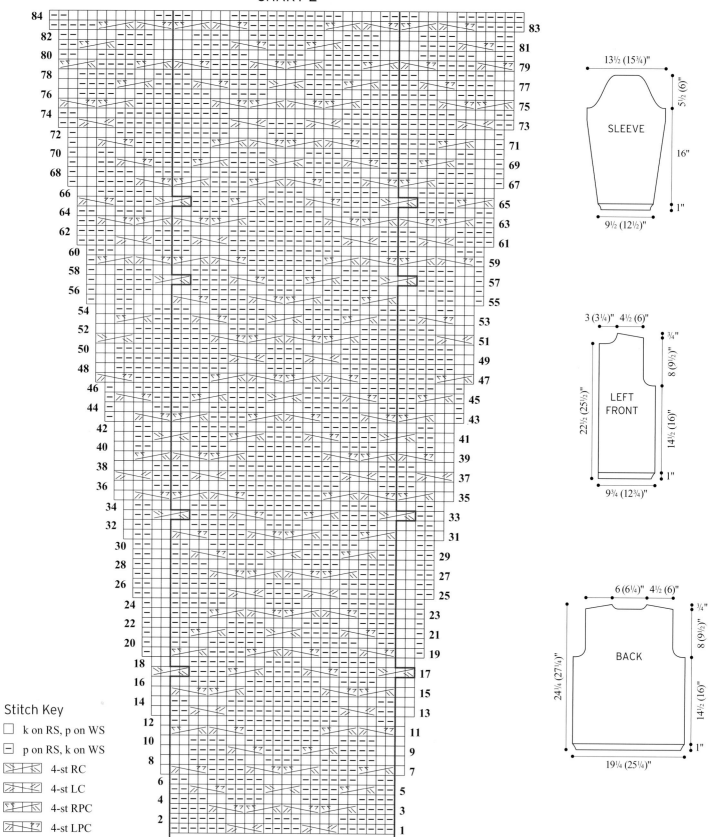

Stitch Key

☐ k on RS, p on WS

─ p on RS, k on WS

4-st RC

4-st LC

4-st RPC

4-st LPC

24-st rep

SLEEVE

13½ (15¾)"
5½ (6)"
16"
1"
9½ (12½)"

LEFT FRONT

3 (3¼)" 4½ (6)"
¾"
8 (9½)"
22½ (25½)"
14½ (16)"
1"
9¾ (12¾)"

BACK

6 (6¼)" 4½ (6)"
¾"
8 (9½)"
24¼ (27¼)"
14½ (16)"
1"
19¼ (25¼)"

CABLED-COLLAR PULLOVER

Textural, lace-filled cables give this V-neck a gently undulating scalloped edge. Strips of finely laddered lace and seeded rib run parallel to the cables, becoming the focal point of this otherwise understated pullover. We suggest its suitability for a crisp morning on a Miami beach, as seen here on a relaxed photo shoot.

SIZES
X-Small (Small, Medium, Large, X-Large). Shown in size Small.

KNITTED MEASUREMENTS
Bust 35½ (38, 40½, 43, 45½)"/89 (95, 101, 108, 114)cm
Length 20 (20, 20½, 21½, 22)"/51 (51, 52, 56)cm
Upper Arm 14 (14, 15, 16, 17)"/35.5 (35.5, 38, 40, 42.5)cm

MATERIALS
• Original Yarn
10 (10, 11, 12, 13) 1¾oz/50g balls (each approx 77yd/71m) of **Unger Escape** (rayon) in #107 Teal ⬤❹
• Substitute Yarn
5 (5, 6, 6, 7) 3½oz/100g balls (each approx 164yd/150m) of **Wool and the Gang** Tina Tape (Lyocell) in Dusty Blue ❹
• One pair each sizes 7 and 8 (4.5 and 5mm) needles, OR SIZE TO OBTAIN GAUGE
• One size G-6 (4.5mm) crochet hook
• Cable needle (cn)
• Stitch markers

GAUGE
19 sts and 27 rows to 4"/10cm over St st using larger needles.
TAKE TIME TO CHECK GAUGE.

STITCH GLOSSARY
10-st RC Sl 5 sts to cn and hold to back, p1, k1, yo, ssk, p1, work 5 sts from cn as foll: p1, k1, yo, ssk, p1.
10-st LC Sl 5 sts to cn and hold to front, p1, k1, yo, ssk, p1, work 5 sts from cn as foll: p1, k1, yo, ssk, p1.

BACK
With smaller needles, cast on 84 (90, 96, 102, 108) sts. Work in St st (k on RS, p on WS) for 2"/5cm. Change to larger needles. Cont in St st until piece measures 12"/30.5cm from beg, end with a WS row.

Armhole Shaping

Bind off 3 sts at beg of next 2 rows, then 2 sts at beg of next 2 (2, 2, 2, 4) rows.

Next dec row (RS) K1, k2tog, work to last 3 sts, ssk, k1.

Work 1 row even.

Rep last 2 rows 4 (4, 5, 5, 4) times more—64 (70, 74, 80, 84) sts. Work even until armhole measures 7 (7, 7½, 8½, 9)"/18 (18, 19, 23)cm, end with a WS row.

Shoulder and Neck Shaping

Bind off 6 (7, 8, 9, 9) sts at beg of next 4 rows, 7 (8, 8, 8, 10) sts at beg of next 2 rows, AT THE SAME TIME, bind off center 16 (16, 16, 18, 18) sts for neck and working both sides at once, bind off from each neck edge 3 sts once, then 2 sts once.

FRONT

Work as for back until armhole measures 1 (1, 1, 1½, 2)"/2.5 (2.5, 2.5, 4, 5)cm, end with a WS row.

Neck and Shoulder Shaping

Place markers to mark center 30 sts for neck.

Next row (RS) Work to marker, sm, work prep row 1 foll first half of chart (left front neck), join new yarn after first M1, work 2nd half of chart (right front neck), sm, work to end.

Next row (WS) Cont working both sides at once and work prep row 2 over center marked sts—there are now 36 sts between markers.

Keeping 18 sts each side of neck in chart pat, work dec as foll:

*__Next dec row (RS)__ Work to 3 sts before first marker, k2tog, k1, sm, work chart to marker, sm, k1, ssk, work to end.

Work 1 row even. Work dec row. Work 3 rows even.

Rep from * 3 (3, 4, 5, 5) times more, then work dec row every other row 8 (8, 6, 5, 5) times—19 (22, 24, 26, 28) sts each side.

Work even until same length as back to shoulders. Shape shoulders as for back.

SLEEVES

With smaller needles, cast on 39 sts.

Row 1 (WS) P2, *k2, p4, yo, p2tog, p3; rep from * to last 4 sts, k2, p2.

Row 2 (RS) *K2, p2, k2, p1, k1, yo, ssk, p1; rep from * to last 6 sts, k2, p2, k2.

Rep rows 1 and 2 for 2"/5cm, inc 0 (0, 1, 1, 2) sts on last WS row—39 (39, 40, 40, 41) sts.

Change to larger needles and work in St st as foll:

Work 4 rows even.

Inc row (RS) K2, M1, k to last 2 sts, M1, k2.

Rep inc row every 6th row 13 (13, 12, 10, 8) times, then every 4th row 0 (0, 3, 7, 11) times—67 (67, 72, 76, 81) sts.

Work even until piece measures 15½ (16, 16½, 17, 17½)"/39.5 (40.5, 42, 43, 44.5)cm from beg, end with a WS row.

Cap Shaping

Bind off 3 sts at beg of next 2 rows, then 2 sts at beg of next 4 rows.

Dec row (RS) K1, k2tog, k to last 3 sts, ssk, k1.

Rep dec row every other row 8 (8, 10, 11, 11) times, then every 4th row 0 (0, 0, 1, 2) times.

Bind off 2 sts at beg of next 4 rows, then 3 sts at beg of next 2 rows. Bind off rem 21 (21, 22, 22, 25) sts.

FINISHING

Block pieces to measurements. Sew shoulder seams. Set in sleeves. Sew side and sleeve seams.

With RS facing and crochet hook, work 1 row sl st, then 1 row backwards sc (from left to right) along back neck. ●

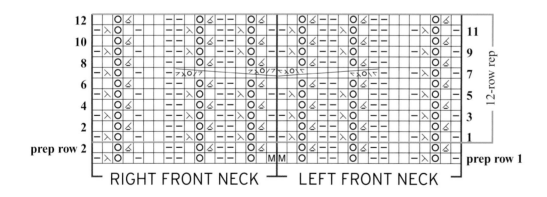

RIGHT FRONT NECK — LEFT FRONT NECK

Stitch Key

☐	k on RS, p on WS	⊠	ssk
⊟	p on RS, k on WS	◹	p2tog on WS
⊙	yo		10-st RC
Ⓜ	M1		10-st LC

CHAIN LINK CABLE PULLOVER

Deep ribbing at the lower hem grows upward into an allover lattice of braided knots, mimicking the classic chain link fence in fiber. It's framed on either side by tight braids, and, farther out, a syncopated rib. Slim, ribbed sleeves and a high V-neck add to this long, lean look.

■■■■

SIZES
X-Small (Small, Medium, Large).
Shown in size Small.

KNITTED MEASUREMENTS
Bust 36 (40, 44, 48)"/91.5 (101.5, 111.5, 122)cm
Length 26½ (27, 27½, 28)"/67.5 (68.5, 69.5, 71)cm
Upper Arm 12½ (12½, 13, 13½)"/32 (32, 33, 33.5)cm

MATERIALS
• Original Yarn
17 (18, 20, 22) 1¾oz/50g balls (each approx 96yd/88m) of **Adrienne Vittadini/JCA** Daniella (wool/cashmere) in #3 Grey (④)
• Substitute Yarn
15 (16, 18, 20) 1¾oz/50g hanks (each approx 110yd/101m) of **Shibui** Drift (extra fine merino/cashmere) in 11 Tar (④)
• One pair each sizes 6 and 7 (4 and 4.5mm) needles, OR SIZE TO OBTAIN GAUGES
• Cable needle (cn)
• Stitch holders

GAUGES
• 24 sts and 28 rows to 4"/10cm over body rib pat using larger needles.
• 80 sts in center cable panel foll chart = 12"/30.5cm wide.
TAKE TIME TO CHECK GAUGES.

STITCH GLOSSARY
4-st LC Sl 2 sts to cn and hold to front, k2, k2 from cn.
4-st RC Sl 2 sts to cn and hold to back, k2, k2 from cn.
4-st LPC Sl 2 sts to cn and hold to front, p2, k2 from cn.
4-st RPC Sl 2 sts to cn and hold to back, k2, p2 from cn.

BACK
With smaller needles, cast on 104 (116, 128, 140) sts.

Begin Chart
Row 1 (WS) [P4, k2] 3 (4, 5, 6) times, work row 1 of chart over next 68 sts as foll: work first 21 sts, then work 13-st rep twice, work rem 21 sts; [k2, p4] 3 (4, 5, 6) times. Cont to work in rib pat each side and center 68 sts rep chart rows 1–4 until piece measures 3½"/9cm from beg, end with chart row 4. Change to larger needles.
Inc row 5 (WS) P16 (22, 28, 34), k2, work chart row 5 over next 68 sts, k2, p16 (22, 28, 34)—116 (128, 140, 152) sts.
Row 6 (RS) For Small and Large Sizes Only: P1, k2, p3; then For All Sizes, [k4, p3, k2, p3] 1 (1, 2, 2) times, k4, p2; work 80 sts of chart row 6; p2, [k4, p3, k2, p3] 1 (1,2, 2) times, k4, then for Small and Large Sizes Only: p3, k2, p1. Cont in pats, rep chart rows 6–29, until piece measures 17½ (18, 18, 18)"/44.5 (45.5, 45.5, 45.5)cm from beg.

Armhole Shaping
Bind off 3 sts at beg of next 2 rows, bind off 2 sts at beg of next 4 (4, 6, 8) rows, then dec 1 st each side every other row 2 (3, 3, 4) times—98 (108, 116, 122) sts. Work even until armhole measures 8 (8, 8½, 9)"/20.5 (20.5, 21.5, 23)cm.

Shoulder and Neck Shaping
Bind off 8 (11, 12, 12) sts at beg of next 2 rows, then 9 (10, 11, 12) sts at beg of next 4 rows, AT THE SAME TIME, bind off center 26 (26, 28, 30) sts for neck and working both sides at once, bind off 5 sts from each neck edge twice.

FRONT
Work as for back until armhole measures 3"/7.5cm, end with a WS row.

V-neck Shaping

Mark center of row and cont armhole shaping.

Set-up row (RS) Work to 4 sts before marker, [M1, p1] 3 times, k1; join a 2nd ball of yarn, k1, [p1, M1] 3 times, work to end.

Next row (WS) Work to last 7 sts of V-neck, [p1, k1] 3 times, p1; on 2nd side, p1 [k1, p1] 3 times, work to end.

Dec row (RS) Work to last 8 sts of first side, k2tog, rib to end; on 2nd side, rib 6, ssk, work to end.

Rep dec row every other row 18 (18, 19, 20) times more, AT THE SAME TIME, when same length as back to shoulder, shape shoulder as for back.

Sl rem 7 sts each side to holders to be worked later for back neckband.

SLEEVES

With smaller needles, cast on 52 sts.

Row 1 (RS) *K4, p2; rep from * to last 4 sts, k4.

Work in k4, p2 rib as established for 3½"/9cm. Change to larger needles. Purl 1 row on WS.

Next row (RS) *K4, p3, k2, p3; rep from * to last 4 sts, k4.

Cont in rib as established for 1 row.

Inc row (RS) K2, M1, work to last 2 sts, M1, k2.

Working inc into rib pat, rep inc row every 8th (8th, 6th, 6th) row 10 (10, 12, 14) times more—74 (74, 78, 82) sts.

Work even until piece measures 17½"/44.5cm from beg.

Cap Shaping

Bind off 3 sts at beg of next 2 rows, then 2 sts at beg of next 4 rows.

Dec 1 st each side every other row 6 (6, 8, 10) times.

Bind off 2 sts at beg of next 4 rows, 3 sts at beg of next 2 rows, then 4 sts at beg of next 2 rows.

Bind off rem 26 sts.

FINISHING

Block pieces to measurements. Sew shoulder seams.

With smaller needles, work across 7 sts from one side of V-neck and cont in rib until band fits to center back neck, stretching slightly. Work other side in same way, then weave tog at center back neck. Sew neckband to back neck.

Set sleeves into armholes. Sew side and sleeve seams. ●

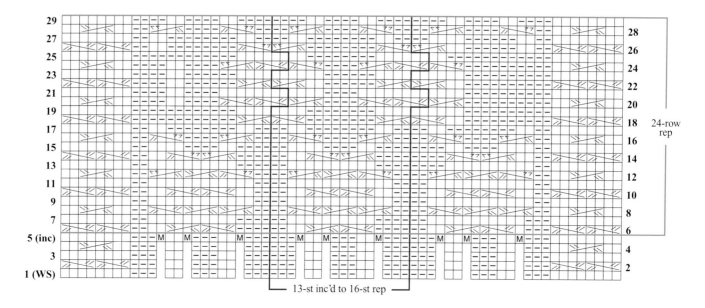

— 13-st inc'd to 16-st rep —

Stitch Key

☐ k on RS, p on WS

⊟ p on RS, k on WS

Ⓜ M1

4-st RC

4-st LC

4-st RPC

4-st LPC

7 (7, 7½, 7¾)" 4 (4¾, 5¼, 5½)"

1"

8 (8, 8½, 9)"

14 (14½, 14½, 14½)"

26½ (27, 27½, 28)"

FRONT & BACK

3½"

18 (20, 22, 24)"

12½ (12½, 13, 13½)"

3½ (3½, 4, 4½)"

SLEEVE

14"

3½"

8½"

GRIDDED PULLOVER

An orderly, rugged, no-nonsense network of alternating boxes and cables comprise the fabric of this undeniably masculine pullover with a roomy fit. It's anything but basic, given a more relaxed air with details like the easy ribbed cuffs and a mini V-neckline that smartly integrates with the ribbed collar.

SIZES
Men's X-Small (Small/Medium, Large, X-Large). Shown in size Large.

KNITTED MEASUREMENTS
Chest 42 (47, 52, 57)"/106.5 (119.5, 132, 144.5)cm
Length 26 (26½, 27, 27½)"/66 (67.5, 68.5, 69.5)cm
Upper Arm 19 (20, 21, 22)"/48 (50.5, 53.5, 56)cm

MATERIALS
• Original Yarn
14 (15, 15, 16) 1¾oz/50g balls (each approx 124yd/114m) of **Adrienne Vittadini/JCA** Sabrina (silk) in #2 Taupe ③
• Substitute Yarn
12 (13, 13, 14) 1¾oz/50g balls (each approx 153yd/140m) of **Katia** Silk Tweed (silk/mohair/polyamide/wool) in 53 Brown-Off-White-Light Brown ③
• One pair each sizes 5 and 7 (3.75 and 4.5mm) needles, OR SIZE TO OBTAIN GAUGE
• One size 5 (3.75mm) circular needle, 20"/50cm long
• Cable needle (cn)
• Removable stitch markers

GAUGE
22 sts and 30 rows to 4"/10cm over chart using larger needles.
TAKE TIME TO CHECK GAUGE.

K3, P3 RIB
(multiple of 6 sts plus 3)
Row 1 (WS) *P3, k3; rep from * to last 3 sts, p3.
Row 2 *K3, p3; rep from * to last 3 sts, k3.
Rep rows 1 and 2 for k3, p3 rib.

STITCH GLOSSARY
4-st RC Sl 2 sts to cn and hold to back, k2, k2 from cn.
4-st LC Sl 2 sts to cn and hold to front, k2, k2 from cn.

M1 Insert LH needle from front to back under strand between last st worked and next st on LH needle, knit strand through back loop.

M1 p-st Insert LH needle from front to back under strand between last st worked and next st on LH needle, purl strand through back loop.

BACK

With smaller needles cast on 117 (129, 141, 159) sts. Work in k3, p3 rib for 2"/5cm, end with a WS row. Change to larger needles. Work chart, beg with first st of chart and dec 2 (0, inc 2, dec 2) sts across first row—115 (129, 143, 157) sts. Work even until piece measures 25 (25½, 26, 26½)"/63.5 (65, 66, 67)cm from beg.

Shoulder and Neck Shaping

Bind off 9 (10, 11, 13) sts at beg of next 2 (8, 2, 4) rows, then 8 (0, 12, 14) sts at beg of next 6 (0, 6, 4) rows, AT THE SAME TIME, bind off center 31 sts for neck and working both sides at once, bind off from each neck edge 3 sts 3 times.

FRONT

Work as for back until piece measures 20½ (21, 21½, 22)"/58.5 (60, 61, 62)cm from beg, end with a WS row.

Divide for Split

Work 57 (64, 71, 78) sts, join 2nd ball of yarn and bind off center st, work to end. Working both sides at once, work 1 row even.
Dec row (RS) First Side: Work to last 3 sts of first side, ssk, k1; 2nd Side: K1, k2tog, work to end.
Rep dec row every RS row 5 times more. Work even for 3 rows.

Neck Shaping

Bind off from each neck edge 4 sts once, 3 sts twice, 2 sts 3 times, then 1 st twice, AT THE SAME TIME, when same length as back to shoulders, shape shoulders as for back.

SLEEVES

With smaller needles, cast on 57 sts. Work in k3, p3 rib for 2"/5cm, end with a WS row.
Change to larger needles and work chart, beg with first st of chart and inc 2 sts across first row—59 sts.
Cont in pat, inc 1 st each side every 4th row 9 (18, 24, 31) times, then every 6th row 14 (8, 4, 0) times—105 (111, 115, 121) sts. Work even until piece measures 19"/48.5cm from beg. Bind off.

FINISHING

Block pieces to measurements. Sew shoulder seams.

Neckband

With RS facing and circular needle, beg at right front neck edge, pick up and k 105 sts evenly around neck. Do not join. Work back and forth in k3, p3 rib, dec 1 st each side every RS row, for 1¼"/3cm. Bind off.

Neck Insert

With smaller needles, cast on 4 sts. Knit 1 row, purl 1 row.
Next row (RS) K1, M1 p-st, k2, M1 p-st, k1.
Next row and every WS row K the knit sts and p the purl sts.
Inc row (RS) Mark center 2 sts. Work as established to center sts, M1, k2, M1, work to end.
Cont to work inc row every RS row 3 times more, keeping new sts in k1, p1 rib.
Next row (RS) Work 7 sts, join new ball and work rem 7 sts.
Work even until piece measures 4"/10cm from beg, bind off. Sew into V of neckline.

Sew side and sleeve seams. ●

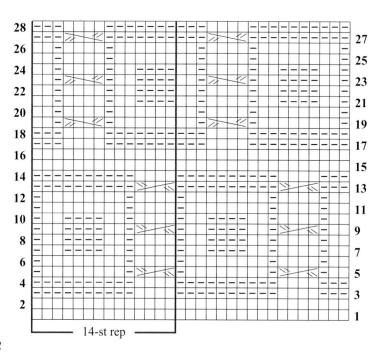

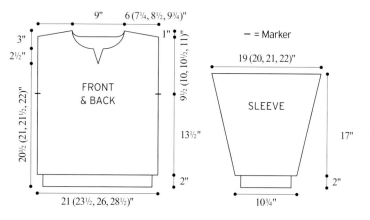

= Marker

Stitch Key

☐ k on RS, p on WS

⊟ p on RS, k on WS

▨ 4-st RC

▨ 4-st LC

14-st rep

PEAKED TWEED CARDIGAN

Wide diagonal cables vie with delicate twisted-stitch lines, resulting in a field of chevrons criss-crossing an overlapping V-necked cardigan. Wide ribs are nestled in the chevrons on the bottom edge and a more delicate fanning rib accent peeks from the front band, culminating in button loops.

SIZE
Medium/X-Large.

KNITTED MEASUREMENTS
Bust (buttoned) 55½"/147cm
Length 26½"/67cm
Upper Arm 19½"/50cm

MATERIALS
• Original Yarn
8 3½oz/100g hanks (each approx 220yd/203m) of **Reynolds/JCA** Turnberry Tweed (wool) in #81 Oat (4)
• Substitute Yarn
15 1¾oz/50g balls (each approx 122yd/113m) of **Tahki Yarns/ Tahki•Stacy Charles** Tara Tweed (wool/nylon) in #021 Mushroom Tweed (4)
• One pair each sizes 5 and 6 (3.75 and 4mm) needles, OR SIZE TO OBTAIN GAUGE
• Three 1½"/38mm toggle buttons
• Six ½"/13mm buttons (for inside as a backing button)
• Cable needle (cn)
• Removable stitch markers

GAUGE
20 sts and 26 rows to 4"/10cm over chart using larger needles.
TAKE TIME TO CHECK GAUGE.

STITCH GLOSSARY
LT (left twist) With RH needle behind LH needle, skip first st and k 2nd st tbl, insert RH needle into backs of both sts and k2tog tbl.
M1 Insert LH needle from front to back under strand between last st worked and next st on LH needle, knit strand through back loop.
M1 p-st Insert LH needle from front to back under strand between last st worked and next st on LH needle, purl strand through back loop.
4-st Right Slant Sl 1 st to cn and hold to back, k3, k1 from cn.

BACK
With larger needles, cast on 138 sts.
Row 1 (RS) K1, work 34-st rep of chart 4 times, k1.
Keeping 1 st each side as k1 for selvage sts, work chart through row 32, then rep rows 33–46 (14 rows) for body chevron pat until piece measures 25"/63.5cm from beg.

Shoulder and Neck Shaping
Next row (RS) Bind off 10 sts, work until there are 49 sts on needle, join another ball of yarn and bind off center 20 sts for neck, work to end.
Working both sides at once, bind off 10 sts at beg of next row (for left shoulder) then cont to shape neck binding off 3 sts from each neck edge 4 times, AT THE SAME TIME, bind off 10 sts at beg of next 2 rows, then 9 sts at beg of next 6 rows.

LEFT FRONT
With larger needles, cast on 70 sts.
Row 1 (RS) K1, work 34-st rep of chart twice, k1.
Keeping 1 st each side as k1 for selvage sts, work chart until piece measures 18"/45.5cm from beg, end with row 36.

Neck and Shoulder Shaping
Dec row (RS) K to last 5 sts, k2tog, k3.
Rep dec row every other row 20 times more, then every 4th row twice more, AT THE SAME TIME, when same length as back to shoulders, bind off 10 sts from shoulder edge twice, then 9 sts 3 times.

RIGHT FRONT

Work as for left front, reversing neck shaping by working dec at beg of RS rows as foll: K3, ssk, work to end. Work shoulder shaping at beg of WS rows.

SLEEVES

With larger needles, cast on 70 sts.
Keeping 1 st each side as k1 for selvage sts, work chart until piece measures 2"/5cm from beg.
Inc 1 st each side of next row (by M1 inside of selvage sts and working inc'd sts into pat), every 6th row 9 times, then every 8th row 5 times—100 sts.
Work even until piece measures 17"/43cm from beg. Bind off.

FINISHING

Block pieces to measurements. Sew shoulder seams.
Place markers at 9¾"/25cm down from shoulders. Sew sleeves to armholes between markers. Sew side and sleeve seams.

Left Front Band

With smaller needles and RS facing, beg at center back neck, pick up and k 60 sts to end of front neck shaping, then 96 sts along center straight front—156 sts.
Row 1 (WS) *K2, p2; rep from * to end.
Work even in k2, p2 rib for 9 rows more.
Buttonhole row (WS) Work 24 sts, bind off 2 sts, [work until there are 34 sts on needle, bind off 2 sts] twice, work to end.
Next row Work in rib as established, casting on 2 sts over each set of bound-off sts.
Work in rib for 2 more rows. Bind off in rib.

Right Front Band

With smaller needles and RS facing, pick up and k 97 sts along straight front band to neck shaping, then 61 sts to center back neck—158 sts.
Set-up row (WS) [P2, k2] 15 times, p6, *[k2, p2] 5 times, k5, k6, k5, p2; rep from * once more, [k2, p2] 4 times.
Work first 16 sts in established rib, work band wedge A over next 20 sts (see below), work 18 sts in established rib, work band wedge A over 20 sts, work 20 sts in established rib, work band wedge B over 2 sts (becomes 16 sts, see below), work in rib to end.
Cont as established through row 15 of band wedges.

Band Wedge A
(20 sts)
Row 1 (RS) K2, p4, k2tog, k1, M1 p-st, k2, M1 p-st, k1, ssk, p4, k2.
Row 2 P2, k4, p2, k1, p2, k1, p2, k4, p2.
Row 3 K2, p3, k2tog, k1, p1, M1, k2, M1, p1, k1, ssk, p3, k2.
Row 4 P2, k3, p2, k1, p4, k1, p2, k3, p2.
Row 5 K2, p2, k2tog, k1, p1, k1, M1 p-st, k2, M1 p-st, k1, p1, k1, ssk, p2, k2.
Row 6 P2, k2, p2, k1, p1, k1, p2, k1, p1, k1, p2, k2, p2.
Row 7 K2, p1, k2tog, [k1, p1] twice, M1, k2, M1, [p1, k1] twice, ssk, p1, k2.
Row 8 P2, k1, p2, k1, p1, k1, p4, k1, p1, k1, p2, k1, p2.
Row 9 K2, k2tog, [k1, p1] twice, k1, M1 p-st, k2, M1 p-st, [k1, p1] twice, k1, ssk, k2.
Row 10 P4, [k1, p1] twice, k1, p2, [k1, p1] twice, k1, p4.
Row 11 K1, k2tog, [k1, p1] 3 times, M1, k2, M1, p1, [k1, p1] twice, k1, ssk, k1.
Row 12 P3, [k1, p1] twice, k1, p4, [k1, p1] twice, k1, p3.
Row 13 K2tog, [k1, p1] 3 times, k1, M1 p-st, k2, M1 p-st, [k1, p1] 3 times, k1, ssk.
Row 14 P2, [k1, p1] 3 times, k1, p2, [k1, p1] 3 times, k1, p2.
Row 15 Bind off in pat to center 2 sts of peak, work 2 st I-cord on these sts for 2"/5cm, break yarn and tie off.

Band Wedge B
(2 sts inc'd to 16 sts)
Row 1 (RS) M1 p-st, k2, M1 p-st.
Row 2 K1, p2, k1.
Row 3 P1, M1, k2, M1, p1.
Row 4 K1, p4, k1.
Row 5 P1, k1, M1 p-st, k2, M1 p-st, k1, p1.

Row 6 K1, p1, k1, p2, k1, p1, k1.
Row 7 P1, k1, p1, M1, k2, M1, p1, k1, p1.
Row 8 K1, p1, k1, p4, k1, p1, k1.
Row 9 P1, k1, p1, k1, M1 p-st, k2, M1 p-st, k1, p1, k1, p1.
Row 10 [K1, p1] twice, k1, p2, [k 1, p1] twice, k1.
Row 11 P1, [k1, p1] twice, M1, k2, M1, p1, [k1, p1] twice.
Row 12 [K1, p1] twice, k1, p4, [k1, p1] twice, k1.
Row 13 P1, [k1, p1] twice, k1, M1 p-st, k2, M1 p-st, [k1, p1] 3 times.

Row 14 [K1, p1] 3 times, k1, p2, [k1, p1] 3 times, k1.
Row 15 Bind off in pat to center 2 sts of peak, work 2 st I-cord on these sts for 2"/5cm, break yarn and tie off.

Sew ends of I-cord down for button loops. Sew center back neck seam. Sew larger buttons on left front at level of button loops ½"/1.5cm from band into left front, using a backing button for strength. Sew rem small buttons on inside of right front band to correspond to inside buttonholes. ●

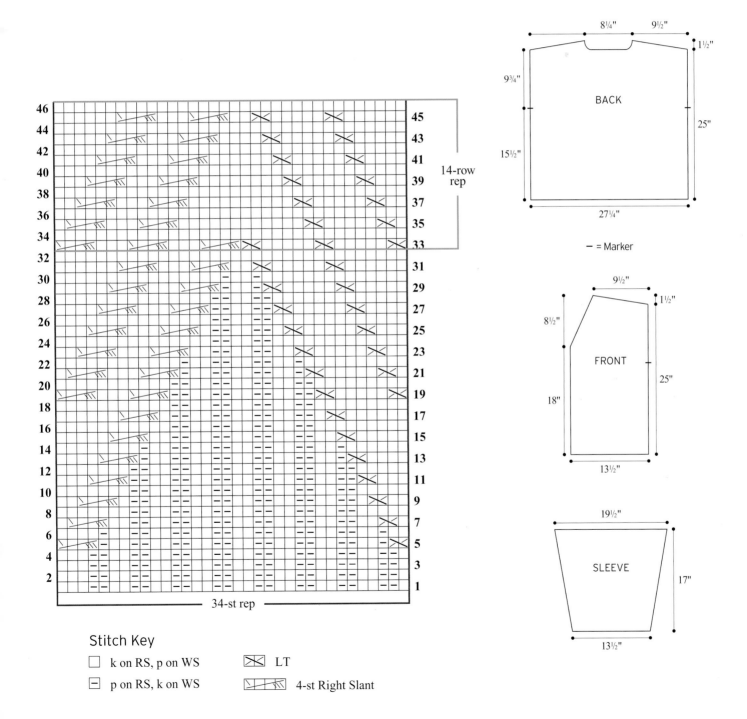

Stitch Key

- ☐ k on RS, p on WS
- ☒ LT
- ⊟ p on RS, k on WS
- 4-st Right Slant

14-row rep

34-st rep

— = Marker

BACK
8¼" 9½"
1½"
9¾"
25"
15½"
27¼"

FRONT
9½"
1½"
8½"
25"
18"
13½"

SLEEVE
19½"
17"
13½"

COUNTERPANE PULLOVER

When asked to design whatever I wanted I almost panicked. Like most creative people, I need parameters. Searching for focus, I landed on the idea of cables in a counterpane, a variation on a theme I had been working on. One simple motif repeated four times around adds up to so much more, and sometimes the simplest idea turns into something magnificent. We have recreated the original garment for the only new photo for this book. The original can be seen on page 103.

■■■■

SIZES
Small (Medium, Large). Shown in size Medium.

KNITTED MEASUREMENTS
Bust 40 (44, 48)"/101.5 (111.5, 122)cm
Waist 33 (36, 39)"/83.5 (91.5, 99)cm
Length 22 (24, 26)"/56 (61, 66)cm
Upper Arm 14¾ (16, 18)"/37.5 (40.5, 45.5)cm

MATERIALS
• Original Yarn
15 (17, 20) 1¾oz/50g balls (each approx 96yd/86m) of **Adrienne Vittadini/JCA** Eva (wool/alpaca) in #11 Green (3)
• Substitute Yarn
11 (12, 14) 1¾oz/50g hanks (each approx 145yd/132m) of **Brooklyn Tweed** Arbor (Targhee wool) in Gale (3)
• One pair each sizes 4 and 6 (3.5 and 4mm) needles, OR SIZE TO OBTAIN GAUGES
• One size 4 (3.5mm) circular needle, 16"/40cm long
• Cable needle (cn)
• Stitch holders
• Stitch markers

GAUGES
• 23 sts and 36 rows to 4"/10cm over charts using larger needles.
• 24 sts and 48 rows to 4"/10cm over garter st using smaller needles.
TAKE TIME TO CHECK GAUGES.

NOTE
Sweater is worked in 6 different sections then sewn together.

STITCH GLOSSARY
6-st RC Sl 2 sts to cn and hold to back, k4, k2 from cn.
6-st LC Sl 4 sts to cn and hold to front, k2, k4 from cn.
6-st RPC Sl 2 sts to cn and hold to back, k4, p2 from cn.
6-st LPC Sl 4 sts to cn and hold to front, p2, k4 from cn.
M1 Insert LH needle from front to back under strand between last st worked and next st on LH needle, knit strand through back loop.
M1 p-st Insert LH needle from front to back under strand between last st worked and next st on LH needle, purl strand through back loop.
RT (right twist) K2tog leaving sts on LH needle, k first st again, sl both sts from needle.

BOTTOM QUADRANTS (MAKE 2)
With larger needles, cast on 4 sts. Purl 1 row.
Next row (RS) K1, M1, k2, M1, k1.
Purl 1 row.
Next row [K2, M1] twice, k2—8 sts.
Purl 1 row.
Beg with row 1, work charts through row 90 (100, 108) —118 (128, 136) sts and piece measures approx 10 (11, 12)"/25.5 (28, 30.5)cm from beg (measured in center).*
Change to smaller needles and k next row, dec 5 sts over each 14-st cable section as foll: [k2tog, k1] 4 times, k2tog—98 (108, 116) sts.
Work in garter st (k every row) for 2"/5cm, end with a RS row. Bind off knitwise on WS.

BACK NECK QUADRANT
Work as for bottom quadrant to *—118 (128, 136) sts.

Shoulder and Neck Shaping
Bind off 8 (10, 11) sts at beg of next 2 rows, then 9 (10, 11) sts at beg of next 6 rows, AT THE SAME TIME, bind off center 24 sts for neck, and working both sides at once, bind off from each neck edge 4 sts 3 times.

FRONT NECK QUADRANT
Work as for bottom quadrant through row 80 (90, 98)—108 (118, 126) sts.

CHART 1–SECOND HALF

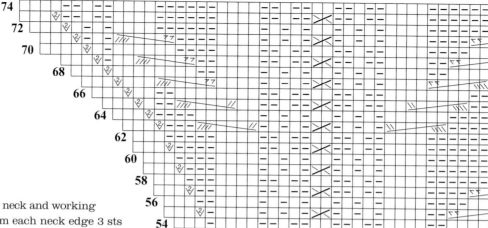

Neck and Shoulder Shaping
Place center 32 sts on holder for neck and working both sides at once, bind off from each neck edge 3 sts once, bind off 2 sts once, then dec 1 st every other row 3 times, AT THE SAME TIME, when same length as back to shoulder, shape shoulder as for back neck quadrant.

LEFT FRONT AND RIGHT BACK QUADRANT
Work same as bottom quadrant through row 90 (100, 108)—118 (128, 136) sts.
Next row (RS) Bind off 71 (77, 79) sts for side seam, place rem 47 (51, 57) sts on a holder for sleeve.

RIGHT FRONT AND LEFT BACK QUADRANT
Work same as bottom quadrant to 1 row before *.
Next row (WS) Bind off 71 (77, 79) sts for side seam, place rem 47 (51, 57) sts on a holder for sleeve.

CONSTRUCT BACK AND FRONT
Block all pieces to shape. Sew diagonal seams to form front and back. Sew shoulder seams.

SLEEVES
With larger needles, cont cable pat as established, and working from RS, work across sts from left front holder to last 2 sts, ssk, pm, with same yarn cont across sts from right back holder, knitting the first 2 sts tog—92 (100, 112) sts.
Work 3 rows even.
Dec row (RS) Work to 3 sts before marker, k2tog, k2, ssk, work to end.
Rep dec row every 4th row 14 (17, 21) times more—62 (64, 68) sts.
Work even until sleeve measures 10½ (10½, 11)"/26.5 (26.5, 28)cm, end with a WS row. Change to smaller needles and knit 1 row, dec 5 sts over each cable section as before—52 (54, 58) sts. Bind off knitwise on WS.

FINISHING
Sew side and sleeve seams.

Neckband
With RS facing and circular needle, beg at center back neck, pick up and k 39 sts to front holder, work 32 sts from holder, pick up 39 sts to centerback—110 sts. Join and work as foll:
Rnd 1 K1, work in k2, p2 rib to center 32 sts, work center 32 sts in cable pat as established, work p2, k2 rib over next 38 sts, RT, pm for end of rnd. Cont in this way, working RT every other rnd at center back, until neckband measures 2¼"/5.5cm. Knit 1 rnd, dec 5 sts over each center front cable section as before. Bind off rem 100 sts purlwise.

If necessary, wet block entire piece to measurements. ●

CHART 1–FIRST HALF

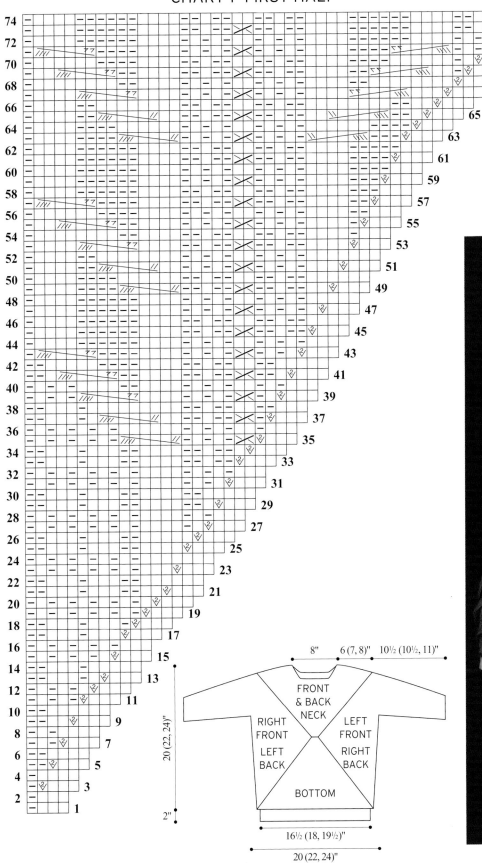

8"   6 (7, 8)"   10½ (10½, 11)"

FRONT & BACK NECK

RIGHT FRONT

LEFT FRONT

LEFT BACK

RIGHT BACK

BOTTOM

20 (22, 24)"

2"

16½ (18, 19½)"

20 (22, 24)"

CHART 2-SECOND HALF

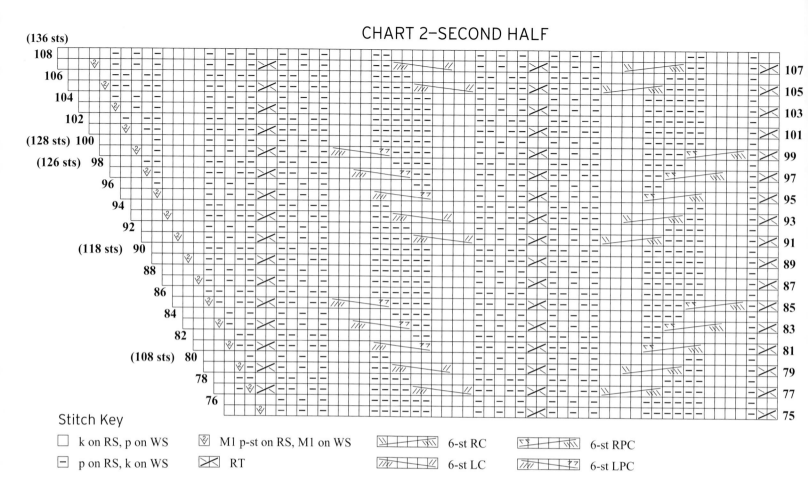

(136 sts)

(128 sts)

(126 sts)

(118 sts)

(108 sts)

Stitch Key

☐ k on RS, p on WS

– p on RS, k on WS

Ⓜ M1 p-st on RS, M1 on WS

⋈ RT

6-st RC

6-st LC

6-st RPC

6-st LPC

CHART 2-FIRST HALF

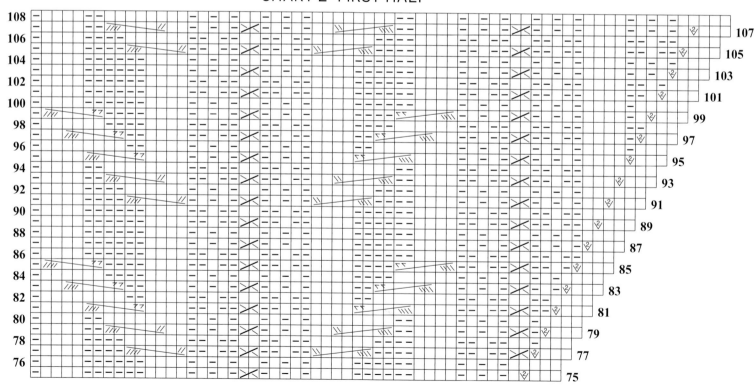

THE CABLE QUEEN

During a very sultry summer, 14-year-old Norah Gaughan took up knitting to beat the heat. "A friend taught me," she recalls. "It was a great way to justify sitting inside with the AC blasting." Later, she discovered Elizabeth Zimmermann's knitting book collection and became enamored of the craft.

As a student at Brown University in Providence, Rhode Island, Norah had dreams of becoming a scientist—a career in knitting was the furthest thing from her mind. "I had a few designs published while I was in school," she explains. "It never occurred to me I could do this for a living." Today, Norah is the design director for JCA, the company that distributes Reynolds, Unger, and Adrienne Vittadini yarns. She has been known to produce over 60 sweater designs a year, a number even she admits is staggering. Norah's first design for **VK**—a sleeveless bronze pullover in a cable-and-ladder pattern—appeared in the Spring/Summer 1987 issue.

"I love the challenge of inventing a complicated cable and enjoy knitting 'show-off' pieces—sweaters that make people come up to you and say 'Oh that's incredible, how did you do it?' " says the designer who is often referred to as the Cable Queen. "I came up with the idea for this sweater after teaching a class on counterpane cables. I was working on a more complex variation of this cable and decided to challenge myself by reworking it into a counterpane. I chose the yarn, a wool-alpaca blend, for its unique hand. It has a crisp surface that holds design detail well, but at the same time, it's incredibly soft and light—important for a cabled sweater because they can get bulky. Beyond the cable design, the basic sweater shape is clean and uncomplicated. I like to wear simple garments, but I like knitting difficult things—this sweater manages to combine both!"

FAIR ISLE YOKE SWEATER

Inspired by antique ornamental paisleys made in India for wealthy Victorian ladies, this sweater features the round yoke of a traditional Lopi pullover, but with wider sleeves, a loose high neck, and clean, ribless cast-on edges. This was designed for the 20th anniversary issue of **Vogue Knitting**, in a feature celebrating yarns that have stood the test of time, as Lopi certainly has.

■■■▢

SIZES
X-Small (Small, Medium, Large, X-Large). Shown in size Medium.

KNITTED MEASUREMENTS
Bust 38 (41, 44, 46, 48)"/96.5 (104, 111.5, 117, 122)cm
Length 22½ (23½, 24, 25, 25½)"/57 (59.5, 61, 63.5, 64.5)cm
Upper Arm 16 (16½, 17¼, 18, 19)"/40.5 (42, 44, 45.5, 48)cm

MATERIALS
• Original Yarn and Colors
5 (6, 6, 7, 7) 3½oz/100g skeins (each approx 110yd/100m) of **Ístex** Álafosslopi (wool) in #389 Burnt Red (MC) **⑤**
2 skeins in #452 Dk Grey Tweed (B)
1 skein each in #166 Jade (A), #719 Field (C), and #392 Rust (D)
• Substitute Colors
1238 Dusk Red (MC), 9967 Teal Heather (A), 0053 Acorn Heather (B), 9964 Golden Heather (C), 9971 Amber Heather (D)
• One size 10 (6mm) circular needle, 24"/60cm long, OR SIZE TO OBTAIN GAUGE
• One each sizes 8 and 10 (5 and 6mm) circular needles, 16"/40cm long
• Stitch markers
• Stitch holders

GAUGE
13 sts and 18 rows to 4"/10cm over St st using larger needle.
TAKE TIME TO CHECK GAUGE.

NOTE
Body and sleeves are each worked in one piece to the underarms.

BODY
With longer, larger needle and MC, cast on 124 (134, 144, 150, 156) sts. Join, taking care not to twist sts, and pm for beg of rnd. Work in rnds of St st (k every rnd) until piece measures 13 (13½, 14, 14½, 15)"/33 (34, 35.5, 37, 38)cm from beg.
Next rnd K58 (63, 67, 70, 73) sts, sl next 8 (9, 10, 10, 11) sts onto holder for underarm, k to last 4 (4, 5, 5, 5) sts, sl rem sts in rnd and first 4 (5, 5, 5, 6) sts at beg of rnd onto holder for underarm, dropping marker. Do not cut yarn.

SLEEVES
With shorter, larger needle and MC, cast on 44 (44, 46, 46, 48) sts. Join, taking care not to twist sts, and pm for beg of rnd. Work in rnds of St st until piece measures 9 (9, 9, 8, 6)"/23 (23, 23, 20, 15)cm from beg.
Inc rnd K1, M1, k to last st, M1, k1.
Rep inc rnd every 8th rnd 3 (4, 4, 5, 6) times more—52 (54, 56, 58, 62) sts.
Work even until piece measures 17½"/44.5cm from beg.
Sl last 4 (4, 5, 5, 5) sts and first 4 (5, 5, 5, 6) sts onto holder for underarm—44 (45, 46, 48, 51) sts.
Sl sts of first sleeve onto a spare needle.

YOKE
With longer, larger needle and MC, k44 (45, 46, 48, 51) sts of first sleeve, k54 (58, 62, 65, 67) front sts, k44 (45, 46, 48, 51) sts of 2nd sleeve, then k54 (58, 62, 65, 67) back sts—196 (206, 216, 226, 236) sts. Place marker for beg of rnd.
Next rnd Knit, inc 4 sts evenly around—200 (210, 220, 230, 240) sts.
Work even for 0 (2, 2, 4, 4) rnds.

Begin Chart
Work rnds 1–36 of chart, changing to shorter needle as needed—120 (126, 132, 138, 144) sts.
With MC only, work even for 1 rnd.

Dec rnd *K4, k2tog; rep from * around—100 (105, 110, 115, 120) sts.

Work even for 1 (1, 1, 2, 2) rnds.

Next dec rnd *K1, k2tog; rep from * around, end k4 (0, 2, 4, 0)—68 (70, 74, 78, 80) sts.

Change to smaller needle.

Knit 1 rnd. Work in k1, p1 rib for 2½"/6.5cm.

Change to B and cont in rib for 1 rnd.

Bind off loosely in rib.

FINISHING

Block pieces to measurements.

Using Kitchener st (see page 174), graft underarms. ●

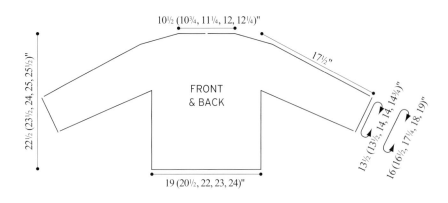

10½ (10¾, 11¼, 12, 12¼)"

17½"

22½ (23½, 24, 25, 25½)"

FRONT & BACK

13½ (13½, 14, 14, 14¾)"

16 (16½, 17¼, 18, 19)"

19 (20½, 22, 23, 24)"

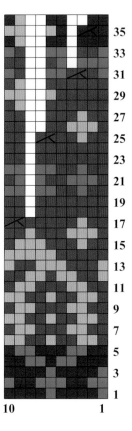

35
33
31
29
27
25
23
21
19
17
15
13
11
9
7
5
3
1

10   1

Stitch and Color Key

■ MC
■ A
■ B
■ C
■ D
□ no stitch
☒ k2tog

HIS AND HERS

What better place to shoot a hip men's turtleneck with a coordinating woman's cardigan in a cool Tribeca loft than in the only special men's issue of **Vogue Knitting**? Sharing design elements without becoming too matchy-matchy, both pieces feature a stockinette stitch body contrasted with a deeply etched zigzag texture.

HIS PULLOVER

SIZES
Men's Small (Medium, Large, X-Large). Shown in size Medium.

KNITTED MEASUREMENTS
Chest 42 (44½, 46½, 48½)"/106.5 (113, 118, 123)cm
Length 25 (25, 26, 27)"/63.5 (63.5, 66, 68.5)cm
Upper Arm 21 (21, 22, 23)"/53 (53, 56, 58.5)cm

MATERIALS
• Original Yarn
24 (25, 27, 29) 1¾oz/50g balls (each approx 52yd/48m) of **Adrienne Vittadini Yarns/JCA** Emma (cotton/viscose/silk) in #11 Taupe (5)
• Substitute Yarn
15 (15, 17, 18) 1¾oz/50g balls (each approx 87yd/80m) of **Katia** Big Alabama (cotton/acrylic) in 6 Beige (5)
• One pair each sizes 8 and 9 (5 and 5.5mm) needles, OR SIZE TO OBTAIN GAUGES
• One size 8 (5mm) circular needle, 16"/40cm long

GAUGES
• 14 sts and 19 rows to 4"/10cm over St st using larger needles.
• 20 sts and 20 rows to 4"/10cm over twisted ridge pat using smaller needles.
TAKE TIME TO CHECK GAUGES.

TWISTED RIDGE PATTERN
(multiple of 5 sts plus 1)
Row 1 (RS) *K1, p1, k 2nd st on LH needle tbl, k first st on LH needle, then sl both sts from needle tog, p1; rep from * to last st, k1.
Row 2 *P1, k1, wyif p 2nd st on LH needle, p first st on LH needle, then sl both sts from needle tog, k1; rep from * to last st, p1.
Rep rows 1 and 2 for twisted ridge pat.

BACK
With smaller needles, cast on 74 (78, 82, 86) sts.
Work in k2, p2 rib for 2½"/6.5cm. Change to larger needles.

Cont in St st (k on RS, p on WS) until piece measures 14½ (14½, 15, 15½)"/37 (37, 38, 39.5)cm from beg, end with a RS row. Change to smaller needles. Purl 1 row, inc 32 (33, 34, 35) sts evenly across—106 (111, 116, 121) sts.
Cont in twisted rib pat for 10½ (10½, 11, 11½)"/26.5 (26.5, 28, 29)cm. Bind off.

FRONT

Work as for back until piece measures 22 (22, 23, 24)"/56 (56, 58.5, 61)cm from beg.

Neck Shaping

Next row (RS) Work 46 (48, 50, 52) sts, join a 2nd ball of yarn and bind off center 14 (15, 16, 17) sts, work to end.
Working both sides at once, bind off from each neck edge 4 sts once, 3 sts once, 2 sts twice, then 1 st once.
Work even until same length as back.
Bind off rem 34 (36, 38, 40) sts each side for shoulders.

SLEEVES

With smaller needles, cast on 46 (46, 50, 50) sts. Work in k2, p2 rib for 2½"/6.5cm. Change to larger needles.
Cont in St st, inc 1 st each side every 4th row 17 (17, 16, 18) times—80 (80, 82, 86) sts.
Work even until piece measures 17"/43cm from beg, end with a RS row. Change to smaller needles.
Purl 1 row, inc 31 (31, 34, 35) sts evenly across—111 (111, 116, 121) sts.
Work even until piece measures 21"/53cm from beg. Bind off.

FINISHING

Block pieces to measurements. Sew shoulder seams.

Turtleneck

With circular needle, pick up and k 84 (84, 88, 88) sts evenly around neck edge. join and pm for beg of rnd.
Work in rnds of k2, p2 rib for 7"/18cm. Bind off in rib.

Sew sleeves along ridge patterned yoke. Sew side and sleeve seams. ●

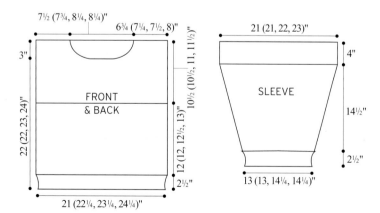

HER CARDIGAN

■■■◻

SIZES
Small (Medium, Large, X-Large).
Shown in size Medium.

KNITTED MEASUREMENTS
Bust (buttoned) 39½ (41½, 43½, 45½)"/100 (105, 110.5, 115.5)cm
Length 20½ (21, 21½, 22)"/52 (53, 54.5, 56)cm
Upper Arm 18½ (19½, 20½, 21½)"/47 (49, 52, 55)cm

MATERIALS
• Original Yarn
17 (18, 20, 21) 1¾oz/50g balls (each approx 52yd/48m) of **Adrienne Vittadini Yarns/JCA** Emma (cotton/viscose/silk) in #19 Lt Green (**5**)
• Substitute Yarn
11 (11, 13, 13) 1¾oz/50g balls (each approx 87yd/80m) of **Katia** Big Alabama (cotton/acrylic) in 19 Lemon Yellow (**5**)
• One pair each sizes 8 and 9 (5 and 5.5mm) needles, OR SIZE TO OBTAIN GAUGES
• Six 1"/25mm buttons
• Removable stitch markers

GAUGES
• 14 sts and 19 rows to 4"/10cm over St st using larger needles.
• 20 sts and 20 rows to 4"/10cm over twisted ridge pat using smaller needles.
TAKE TIME TO CHECK GAUGES.

TWISTED RIDGE PATTERN

(multiple of 5 sts plus 1)

Row 1 (RS) *K1, p1, k 2nd st on LH needle tbl, k first st on LH needle, then sl both sts from needle tog, p1; rep from * to last st, k1.

Row 2 *P1, k1, wyif, p 2nd st on LH needle, p first st on LH needle, then sl both sts from needle tog, k1; rep from * to last st, p1.

Rep rows 1 and 2 for twisted ridge pat.

BACK

With larger needles, cast on 68 (72, 76, 79) sts. Purl 2 rows. Beg with a knit row, cont in St st (k on RS, p on WS) until piece measures 10½"/26.5cm from beg, end with a RS row. Change to smaller needles.

Purl 1 row, inc 28 (29, 30, 32) sts evenly across—96 (101, 106, 111) sts.

Cont in twisted rib pat for 10 (10½, 11, 11½)"/25.5 (26.5, 28, 29)cm. Bind off.

LEFT FRONT

With larger needles, cast on 35 (37, 39, 41) sts. Purl 2 rows. Beg with a knit row, cont in St st (k on RS, p on WS) until piece measures 10½"/26.5cm from beg, end with a RS row. Change to smaller needles.

Purl 1 row, inc 13 (14, 14, 15) sts evenly across— 48 (51, 53, **56) sts.**

Next row (RS) P1 (0, 1, 0), rep from * of row 1 of twisted ridge pat, end k1, p1 (0, 1, 0).

Cont to work as established until piece measures 17½ (18, 18½, 19)"/44.5 (45.5, 47, 48)cm from beg, end with a RS row.

Neck Shaping

Next row (WS) Bind off 6 (6, 7, 7) sts, work pat to end. Cont to shape neck binding off from neck edge 6 sts once, 3 sts twice, then 2 sts once—28 (31, 32, 35) sts. Work even until same length as back. Bind off.

RIGHT FRONT

Work to correspond to left front, reversing neck shaping (beg of RS rows).

SLEEVES

With larger needles, cast on 37 (38, 40, 41) sts. Purl 2 rows. Beg with a RS row, cont in St st, inc 1 st each side every 6th row 8 (9, 10, 11) times —53 (56, 60, 63) sts.

Work even until piece measures 15 (15, 15½, 15½)"/38 (38, 39.5, 39.5)cm from beg.

Next row (RS) K1, M1, k to last st, M1, k1.

Purl 1 row.

Rep last 2 rows 6 times more— 67 (70, 74, 77) sts. Bind off.

FINISHING

Block pieces to measurements. Sew shoulder seams.

Neckband

With smaller needles, pick up and k 86 (86, 90, 90) sts evenly around neck edge. Work in k2, p2 rib for 1¼"/3cm. Bind off in rib.

Place markers 9¼ (9¾, 10¼, 10¾)"/23.5 (24.5, 26, 27.5)cm down from shoulders on back and front pieces. Sew sleeves to armholes between markers.

Sew side and sleeve seams.

Front Bands

With smaller needles and RS facing, pick up and k 78 (80, 82, 84) sts evenly along left front edge. Work in k2, p2 rib for 1¼"/3cm. Bind off in rib. Place markers for buttons ¾"/2cm from top and bottom edges and 4 others evenly spaced between. Work right front band in same way, working buttonholes opposite each marker at center of band by yo, k2tog (or p2tog in rib, as necessary).

Sew on buttons. ●

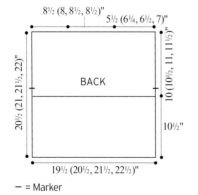

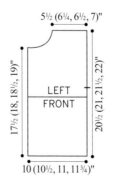

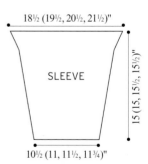

─ = Marker

MITERED CARDIGAN

It's a fact: garter stitch is mathematically perfect for mitered knitting. The structure of each mitered module is accentuated by the light striping of a multi-colored plied yarn, and the sharpness of the design contrasts nicely with the closure-less edges, minimal shaping, and a neck-hugging collar.

SIZES
X-Small (Small, Medium, Large, X-Large). Shown in size Small.

KNITTED MEASUREMENTS
Bust (closed) 40 (44, 48, 52, 56)"/101.5 (111.5, 122, 132, 142)cm
Length 23 (24, 25½, 27, 27¾)"/58.5 (61, 65, 68.5, 70.5)cm
Upper Arm 17 (18, 19, 20, 21)"/43 (46, 48, 51, 53)cm

MATERIALS
• Original Yarn
14 (16, 17, 19, 20) 1¾oz/50g balls (each approx 104yd/96m) of **Reynolds/JCA** Odyssey (wool) in #502 Dk Green (4)
• Substitute Yarn
7 (8, 9, 10, 10) 3½oz/100g hanks (each approx 210yd/192m) of **Malabrigo** Hojas (superwash merino wool) in RIO880 Hojas (4)
• One pair size 7 (4.5mm) needles, OR SIZE TO OBTAIN GAUGE
• One size 7 (4.5mm) circular needle, 29"/74cm long
• Removable stitch markers

GAUGE
19 sts and 36 rows to 4"/10cm over garter st using size 7 (4.5mm) needles.
TAKE TIME TO CHECK GAUGE.

STITCH GLOSSARY
Dec row *K to 2 sts before marker, ssk, sm, k2tog; rep from * to end.

NOTES
1) 3-needle bind-offs are indicated on schematics with red lines.
2) Always pick up sts with the RS facing.
3) Always use 3-needle bind-off with RS held together.

BACK
Section 1
With circular needle, using knit cast-on, cast on 144 (156, 174, 186, 198) sts. Do not join, work back and forth in rows.
***Row 1** K48 (52, 58, 62, 66), pm, k48 (52, 58, 62, 66), pm, k48 (52, 58, 62, 66).

Row 2 (RS) Work dec row (see Stitch Glossary).
Row 3 Knit.
Rep last 2 rows 22 (24, 27, 29, 31) times more, there are 2 sts between markers. Remove markers.
Sl first 26 (28, 31, 33, 35) sts to a straight needle. With points of 2 needles at center of section, bind off using 3-needle bind-off.

Section 2
With circular needle, cast on 48 (52, 58, 62, 66) sts (for lower edge), pick up and k 48 (52, 58, 62, 66) sts along side edge of section 1 (for center back), cast on 48 (52, 58, 62, 66) sts (for top edge). Beg at *, complete as for section 1.

Section 3
With circular needle, cast on 62 (62, 65, 67, 66) sts, pm, pick up and k 48 (52, 58, 62, 66) sts along top edge of section 2, pm, cast on 62 (62, 65, 67, 66) sts—172 (176, 188, 196, 198) sts.
**Row 1 Knit.
Row 2 (RS) Work dec row.
Rep last 2 rows 22 (24, 27, 29, 31) times more. There are 2 sts between markers. Sl first 40 (38, 38, 38, 35) st to a straight needle. With points of 2 needles at center of section, bind off using 3-needle bind-off.

Section 4
With circular needle, cast on 62 (62, 65, 67, 66) sts, pm, pick up and k48 (52, 58, 62, 66) sts along top edge of section 1, pm, pick up and k 62 (62, 65, 67, 66) sts along side edge of section 3—172 (176, 188, 196, 198) sts.
Beg at **, complete as for section 3.

LEFT FRONT
Section 1
Work as for section 1 of back.

Section 2
With circular needle, cast on 62 (62, 65, 67, 66) sts, pm, pick up and k48 (52, 58, 62, 66) sts along top edge of section 1, pm, cast on 81 (81, 84, 86, 85) sts (for center front and collar) —191 (195, 207, 215, 217) sts.
***Row 1 Knit.
Row 2 (RS) Work dec row.

Rep last 2 rows for a total of 4"/10cm.

Collar Shaping
Beg at longest edge, bind off 19 sts (this forms one half of back neck of collar), then cont to work dec as before until there are 2 sts between markers. Sl first 40 (38, 38, 38, 35) sts to a straight needle and bind off using 3-needle bind-off.

RIGHT FRONT
Section 1
Work as for section 1 of back.

Section 2
With circular needle, cast on 81 (81, 84, 86, 85) sts (for collar and center front), pm, pick up and k 48 (52, 58, 62, 66) sts along top edge of section 1, pm, cast on 62 (62, 65, 67, 66) sts—191 (195, 207, 215, 217) sts.
Beg at ***, complete as for section 2 of left front.

SLEEVES
With straight needles, cast on 43 (48, 53, 58, 63) sts.
Work in garter st (k every row) for 2"/5cm.
Inc row (RS) K2, M1, k to last 2 sts, M1, k2.
Rep inc row every 14th row 8 times more—61 (66, 71, 76, 81) sts.
Work even until piece measures 16"/40.5cm from beg.
Work inc row on next RS row, then every 4th row 9 times more—81 (86, 91, 96, 101) sts. Bind off.

FINISHING
Sew shoulder seams. Place markers at 8½ (9, 9½, 10, 10½)"/21.5 (23, 24, 25.5, 26.5)cm down from shoulders.
Sew sleeves to armholes between markers.
Sew side and sleeve seams.
Sew collar to back neck edge. Sew collar seam at center back neck.

Front Edge Trim
With circular needle, pick up and k 1 st in each st along center fronts and around back neck collar edge. Knit 2 rows. Bind off knitwise on WS. ●

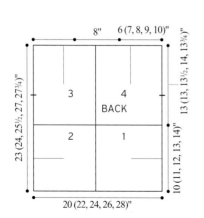

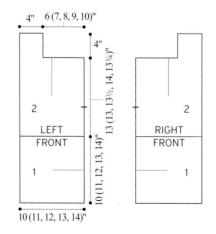

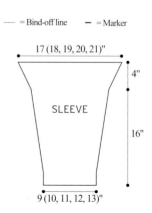

— = Bind-off line   — = Marker

MOBIUS HOODED PULLOVER

I tweaked the traditional Frost Flowers motif, making it reversible to accommodate the Mobius-loop front and hood border. The cropped length and generous sleeves are an invitation to layer, while the stockinette body and simple ribbed cuffs put the spotlight on the stunning, face-framing Mobius.

■■■■

SIZES
Small (Medium, Large, X-Large). Shown in size Medium.

KNITTED MEASUREMENTS
Bust 36 (40½, 45, 49)"/91.5 (103, 114, 124.5)cm
Length 17½ (18, 18½, 19)"/44.5 (45.5, 47, 48)cm
Upper Arm 15 (16, 17, 18)"/38 (41, 43, 46)cm

MATERIALS
• Original Yarn
13 (14, 16, 18) 1¾oz/50g balls (each approx 110yd/90m) of **Trendsetter Yarns** Spiral (acrylic/polyamide) in #96 Aqua (4)
• Substitute Yarn
11 (12, 13, 15) 1¾oz/50g hanks (each approx 137yd/125m) of **Berroco** Maya (pima cotton/baby alapaca) in 5630 Lagoon (4)
• One pair each sizes 6 and 7 (4 and 4.5mm) needles, OR SIZE TO OBTAIN GAUGE
• Removable stitch markers

GAUGE
19 sts and 24 rows to 4"/10cm over St st using larger needles.
TAKE TIME TO CHECK GAUGE.

TWO-SIDED FROST FLOWERS
(over 34 sts)
Row 1 Sl 2 (purlwise wyib on all odd rows), p3, p2tog tbl, k4, yo, k2, yo, ssk, p2, yo, p2tog, k2, yo, ssk, yo, k4, p2tog, p3, k2.
Row 2 Sl 2 (purlwise wyif on all even rows), k2, k2tog, p4, yo, k1, p2, yo, p2tog, k2, yo, ssk, p2, yo, p2tog, k1, yo, p4, ssk, k2, p2.
Row 3 Sl 2, p1, p2tog tbl, k4, yo, p2, k2, yo, ssk, p2, yo, p2tog, k2, yo, ssk, p2, yo, k4, p2tog, p1, k2.
Row 4 Sl 2, k2tog, p4, yo, k3, p2, yo, p2tog, k2, yo, ssk, p2, yo, p2tog, k3, yo, p4, ssk, p2.
Row 5 Sl 2, k3, k2tog, p4, yo, k2, yo, ssk, p2, yo, p2tog, k2, yo, ssk, yo, p4, ssk, k5.
Row 6 Sl 2, p2, k2tog tbl, k4, yo, p3, yo, p2tog, k2, yo, ssk, p2, yo, p2tog, p1, yo, k4, p2tog, p4.
Row 7 Sl 2, k1, k2tog, p4, yo, k4, yo, ssk, p2, yo, p2tog, k2, yo, ssk, k2, yo, p4, ssk, k3.
Row 8 Sl 2, k2tog tbl, k4, yo, p5, yo, p2tog, k2, yo, ssk, p2, yo, p2tog, p3, yo, k4, p2tog, p2.
Rows 9–16 Rep rows 1–8.
Row 17 Sl 2, yo, ssk, p2, yo, p2tog, yo, k4, p2tog, p6, p2tog tbl, k4, yo, p2, yo, p2tog, yo, ssk, k2.
Row 18 Sl 2, p2, k2, yo, ssk, k1, yo, p4, ssk, k4, k2tog, p4, yo, k3, yo, ssk, p4.
Row 19 Sl 2, yo, ssk, p2, yo, p2tog, p2, yo, k4, p2tog, p2, p2tog tbl, k4, yo, p4, yo, p2tog, yo, ssk, k2.
Row 20 Sl 2, p2, k2, yo, ssk, k3, yo, p4, ssk, k2tog, p4, yo, k5, yo, ssk, p4.
Row 21 Sl 2, yo, ssk, p2, yo, p2tog, yo, p4, ssk, k6, k2tog, p4, yo, p2, yo, p2tog, yo, ssk, k2.
Row 22 Sl 2, p2, k2, yo, ssk, p1, yo, k4, p2tog, p4, p2tog tbl, k4, yo, p1, k2, yo, ssk, p4.
Row 23 Sl 2, yo, ssk, p2, yo, p2tog, k2, yo, p4, ssk, k2, k2tog, p4, yo, k2, p2, yo, p2tog, yo, ssk, k2.
Row 24 Sl 2, p2, k2, yo, ssk, p3, yo, k4, p2tog, p2tog tbl, k4, yo, p3, k2, yo, ssk, p4.
Rows 25–32 Rep rows 17–24.
Rep rows 1–32 for two-sided frost flowers.

BACK
With smaller needles, cast on 102 (114, 126, 138) sts.

Row 1 (RS) K2, *p2, k2; rep from * to end.
Cont in k2, p2 rib for 3"/7.5cm, dec 16 (18, 20, 22) sts evenly across last WS row—86 (96, 106, 116) sts.
Change to larger needles. Cont in St st (k on RS, p on WS) until piece measures 17½ (18, 18½, 19)"/44.5 (45.5, 47, 48)cm from beg. Bind off.

FRONT

Note The front begins at right center top of hood, then is worked down right side of front to lower ribbed edge, is turned at hem and worked up to center top of hood on opposite side of front.
Beg at center top of hood, with larger needles, cast on 58 sts.
Row 1 (RS) K24, work 34 sts in two-sided frost flowers pat.
Work even with first 24 sts in St st and last 34 sts in two-sided frost flowers pat until piece measures 12"/30.5cm from beg (end of hood). On next RS row, bind off 23 sts, work to end.
Next row Work even on 35 sts.

Begin Right Front

Next row (RS) Cast on 19 (23, 28, 33) sts to LH needle and knit these sts for shoulder, cont in frost flowers to end—54 (58, 63, 68) sts.
Next row (WS) Work 34-st frost flowers band and rem st in St st. Work even for 10 (12, 14, 16) rows.
Inc row (RS) Work to 2 sts before 34-st frost flowers band, M1, k2, complete 34-st frost flower band.
Rep inc row every 8th row 9 times more—64 (68, 73, 78) sts. Place marker on both sides of last inc row. Work even until piece measures 14½ (15, 15½, 16)"/37 (38, 39.5, 40.4)cm from shoulder cast-on, end with a RS row.
Next inc row (WS) Work 34-st frost flowers band, then inc 6 (6, 9, 8) sts evenly across rem St sts—70 (74, 82, 86) sts. Change to smaller needles.
Next row (RS) [K2, p2] 9 (10, 12, 13) times, work 34-st frost flowers band.
Work even in frost flowers and k2, p2 rib for 3"/7.5cm, end with WS row.
Next row (RS) Bind off 36 (40, 48, 52) rib sts, work to end. Work even on rem 34 sts in frost flowers pat for 1½"/38cm, end with a RS row.

Begin Left Front

Next row (WS) Cast on 36 (40, 48, 52) sts to LH needle and knit these sts for left front, work rem 34 sts in frost flowers—70 (74, 82, 86) sts.
At this point, the RS and WS are reversed.
Next row (WS) Work 34 sts in frost flowers, [k2, p2] 9 (10, 11, 12) times to end of row.
Cont in k2, p2 rib and frost flowers until 3"/7.5cm from cast-on row, end with a WS row. Change to larger needles.
Next row (RS) K and dec 6 (6, 9, 8) sts evenly across rib sts, work rem 34 sts in frost flowers—64 (68, 73, 78) sts.
Work even until same length as right front to marker, end with a WS row.
Next dec row (RS) Work to last 4 sts in St st, ssk, k2, work frost flowers to end.
Rep dec row every 8th row 9 times more—54 (58, 63, 68) sts. Work even for 10 (12, 14, 16) rows.
Next row (RS) Bind off 19 (23, 28, 33) sts (for shoulder), work to end.
Work 1 row even.
Next row (RS) Cast on 23 sts to LH needle and knit these sts, work frost flowers to end.
Work even on all 58 sts for 2nd half of hood for 12"/30.5cm. Bind off.

SLEEVES

With smaller needles, cast on 86 (90, 98, 102) sts. Work in k2, p2 rib as for back for 3"/7.5cm, dec 15 (14, 17, 16) sts evenly spaced across last WS row—71 (76, 81, 86) sts.
Change to larger needles. Cont in St st until piece measures 19"/48cm from beg. Bind off.

FINISHING

Block pieces lightly to measurements.
Fold up front at lower hem so both sides are in St st. Sew top of hood seam along cast-on and bind-off edges of front. Sew shoulder seams.
Place markers at 7½ (8, 8½, 9)"/19 (20.5, 21.5, 23)cm from shoulders. Sew sleeves to armholes between markers. Sew side and sleeve seams. ●

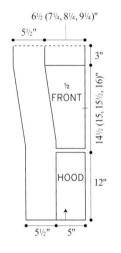

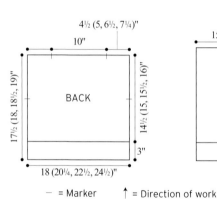

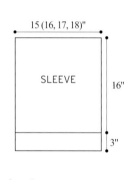

— = Marker   ↑ = Direction of work

SCARF-COLLAR CARDIGAN

Transform a simple cardigan into a unique, eye-catching garment by adding a tapered cable-and-rib collar that drapes beautifully from the cropped length. It's an exercise in asymmetry that you'll want to flaunt. The deep ribbing around the waistline and clean stockinette stitch maintain a sleek, chic fit to balance the striking collar.

■■■▢

SIZES
X-Small (Small, Medium, Large, 1X, 2X). Shown in size Small.

KNITTED MEASUREMENTS
Bust (closed) 34 (36, 38, 40, 45, 49)"/86 (91.5, 96.5, 101.5, 114, 124.5)cm
Length 18½ (19, 19½, 20½, 21½, 22)"/47 (48, 49.5, 52, 54.5, 56)cm
Upper Arm 10½ (11¼, 12, 12½, 13¼, 14)"/26.5 (28.5, 30.5, 32, 33.5, 35.5)cm

MATERIALS
• 5 (6, 6, 7, 7, 8) 3½oz/100g hanks (each approx 215yd/198m) of **Berroco** Ultra Alpaca (super fine alpaca/Peruvian wool) in #6207 Salt & Pepper (▣)
• One pair each sizes 5 and 7 (3.75 and 4.5mm) needles, OR SIZE TO OBTAIN GAUGE
• Cable needle (cn)

GAUGE
20 sts and 26 rows to 4"/10cm over St st using larger needles.
TAKE TIME TO CHECK GAUGE.

STITCH GLOSSARY
4-st RC Sl 2 sts to cn and hold to back, k2, k2 from cn.
12-st LC Sl 8 sts to cn and hold to front, k4, k8 from cn.

BACK
With smaller needles, cast on 129 (135, 141, 147, 159, 165) sts.
Row 1 (RS) K3, *p3, k3; rep from * to end.
Work in k3, p3 rib for 4"/10cm, dec 34 (35, 36, 37, 37, 33) sts evenly across last WS row—95 (100, 105, 110, 122, 132) sts. Change to larger needles.
Cont in St st (k on RS, p on WS), dec 1 st each side every 6th row 5

times—85 (90, 95, 100, 112, 122) sts.
Work even until piece measures 10 (10, 10, 10½, 11, 11)"/25.5
(25.5, 25.5, 26.5, 28, 28)cm from beg.

Armhole Shaping
Bind off 4 sts at beg of next 2 rows, 3 sts at beg of next 2 rows,
2 sts at beg of next 4 (4, 4, 4, 6, 8) rows, then 1 st at beg of
next 0 (2, 4, 6, 8, 10) rows—63 (66, 69, 72, 78, 82) sts.
Work even until armhole measures 7½ (8, 8½, 9, 9½, 10)"/19
(20.5, 21.5, 23, 24, 25.5)cm.

Shoulder Shaping
Bind off 6 (7, 7, 7, 8, 9) sts at beg of next 4 rows, then 7 (6, 7, 8,
8, 8) sts at beg of next 2 rows. Bind off rem 25 (26, 27, 28, 30,
30) sts for back neck.

LEFT FRONT
With smaller needles, cast on 51 (57, 63, 63, 69, 75) sts. Work
in k3, p3 rib for 4"/10cm, dec 17 (20, 23, 21, 21, 22) sts evenly
across last WS row—34 (37, 40, 42, 48, 53) sts.
Change to larger needles.
Cont in St st, dec 1 st at beg of RS rows every 6th row 5
times—29 (32, 35, 37, 43, 48) sts.
Work even until piece measures 10 (10, 10, 10½, 11, 11)"/25.5
(25.5, 25.5, 26.5, 28, 28)cm from beg, end with a WS row.

Armhole Shaping
Next row (RS) Bind off 4 sts, work to end.
Cont to shape armhole, binding off 3 sts from armhole edge
once, 2 sts 1 (2, 2, 2, 3, 4) times, 1 st 1 (1, 3, 4, 6, 7) times—19 (20,
21, 22, 24, 26) sts.
Work even until armhole measures same as back to shoulder.

Shoulder Shaping
Bind off 6 (7, 7, 7, 8, 9) sts from armhole edge twice, then 7 (6, 7,
8, 8, 8) sts once.

RIGHT FRONT
Work as for left front, reversing all shaping.

SLEEVES
With smaller needles, cast on 57 (63, 63, 69, 75, 75) sts.
Work in k3, p3 rib as for back for 4"/10cm, dec 4 (7, 4, 7, 9, 5)
sts evenly across last WS row—53 (56, 59, 62, 66, 70) sts.
Change to larger needles. Work even until piece measures
18"/45.5cm from beg.

Cap Shaping
Bind off 3 sts at beg of next 2 rows, then 2 sts at beg of next 2 rows.
Dec row (RS) K2, k2tog, k to last 4 sts, ssk, k2.
Rep dec row every other row 1 (2, 3, 4, 4, 5) times more, every

4th row 6 (6, 6, 6, 7, 7) times, then every other row 3 times.
Bind off 2 sts at beg of next 2 rows, then 3 sts at beg of next 2
rows. Bind off rem 11 (12, 13, 14, 16, 18) sts.

CABLED SCARF FRONT
With larger needles, cast on 61 sts.
Row 1(RS) Work row 1 of chart 1 over 16 sts, [work 10-st rep
of chart 2] 4 times, work sts 11–15 of chart 2.
Cont in charts as established for a total of 8 rows from beg.
Dec row (RS) Work 19 sts, ssk, work to end.
Rep dec row every 8th row 35 times more—25 sts.
Work even until piece measures 53 (54, 55½, 58, 60, 61)"/134.5
(137, 141, 147, 152, 155)cm from beg. Bind off.

FINISHING
Block lightly to measurements, omitting ribbing.
Sew shoulder seams. Set in sleeves. Sew side and sleeves
seams.
Pin or baste chart 2 edge of cabled scarf front in place along
inside edge of cardigan allowing 11"/15cm to hang free at
center right front and 10"/25.5cm at center left front.
Sew in place, leaving edge along ribbed hem free. ●

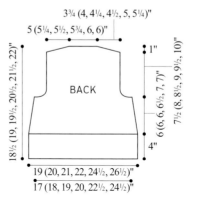

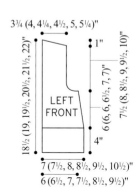

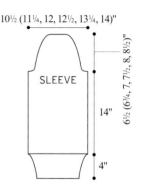

CHART 1

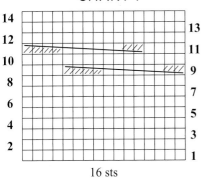

16 sts

CHART 2

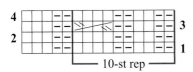

— 10-st rep —

Stitch Key

☐ K on RS, p on WS

⊟ P on RS, k on WS

〰〰〰 12-st LC

〰〰 4-st RC

CABLED BOLERO

One of my most-knit designs ever, this loose-fitting bolero is comprised of cabled pentagons, one knit onto another with no seaming. Even the sleeve begins as a pentagon before being worked into the ribbing. Leave off the button for a less structured look. Take special care, especially when working with superwash wool, to wash and block your swatch as you will your finished piece.

■■■▭

SIZES
X-Small (Small, Medium, Large, X-Large). Shown in size Small.

KNITTED MEASUREMENTS
*Bust (closed) 33 (36, 39, 42, 45)"/84 (91.5, 99, 106.5, 114.5)cm
Length (from center back neck) 11 (12, 13, 14, 15)"/28 (30.5, 33, 35.5, 38)cm
*Finished bolero is loose fitting. For a tighter fit, work a smaller size or use smaller needles for a tighter gauge.

MATERIALS
• Original Yarn
11 (13, 15, 17, 19) 1¾oz/50g balls (each approx 92yd/85m) of **Berroco** Pure Merino (extra fine merino) in #8528 Cocoon (4)
• Substitute Yarn
11 (13, 15, 17, 19) 1¾oz/50g hanks (each approx 95yd/87m) of **Trendsetter Yarns** Merino 8-Ply (superfine merino wool) in 7800 Ecru (4)
• One pair size 9 (5.5mm) needles, OR SIZE TO OBTAIN GAUGE
• Cable needle (cn)
• Tapestry needle
• One 1¼"/32cm button
• Stitch markers (optional)

GAUGE
18 sts and 24 rows to 4"/10cm over St st using size 9 (5.5mm) needles.
TAKE TIME TO CHECK GAUGE.

STITCH GLOSSARY
8-st RC Sl 4 sts to cn and hold to back, k4, k4 from cn.

NOTE
Always pick up stitches with the RS facing.

BODY
Pentagon 1
Cast on 132 (142, 152, 162, 172) sts. *Purl 1 row on WS.
Set-up row (RS) K1 (selvage st), beg with chart row 9 (7, 5, 3, 1), work 26 (28, 30, 32, 34) sts of chart 5 times, k1 (selvage st).
Cont as established through row 30 of chart—12 sts.
Cut yarn.
With tapestry needle, thread yarn through remaining sts, pull tightly to cinch, secure, and sew seam (one full st in from the edge).

Pentagons 2–7
Cast on 105 (113, 121, 129, 137) sts, pick up and k 27 (29, 31, 33, 35) sts along edge of previous pentagon (see diagram)—132 (142, 152, 162, 172) sts.
Beg at *, complete as for pentagon 1.

Pentagons 8–10
Cast on 79 (85, 91, 97, 103) sts, pick up and k 26 (28, 30, 32, 34) sts along edge of an existing pentagon, then 27 (29, 31, 33, 35) sts along side of next pentagon (see diagram)—132 (142, 152, 162, 172) sts.
Beg at *, complete as for pentagon 1.

Pentagon 11
Cast on 53 (57, 61, 65, 69) sts, pick up and k 26 (28, 30, 32, 34) sts along edge of pentagon 5, 26 (28, 30, 32, 34) sts along edge of pentagon 4, 27 (29, 31, 33, 35) sts along side of pentagon 10 (see diagram)—132 (142, 152, 162, 172) sts.
Beg at *, complete as for pentagon 1.

LEFT SLEEVE
Cast on 27 (29, 31, 33, 35) sts, pick up and k 26 (28, 30, 32, 34) sts along edge of pentagon 8, 26 (28, 30, 32, 34) sts

along edge of pentagon 6, 26 (28, 30, 32, 34) sts along edge of pentagon 5, 27 (29, 31, 33, 35) sts along edge of Pentagon #11 (see diagram)—132 (142, 152, 162, 172) sts.

Beg at *, work as for pentagon 1 through row 20 (20, 16, 16, 12) of chart—72 (72, 92, 92, 112) sts.

Work 16 rows even, working cable every 10th row as established. Work dec row as foll:

Sizes X-Small and Small K1, *k1, p2, k1, ssk, p2, k2tog, k1, p2, k1; rep from * 4 times more, k1—62 sts.

Sizes Medium and Large K1, *p1, k2, p2, k1, ssk, p2, k2tog, k1, p2, k2, p1; rep from * 4 times more, k1—82 sts.

Size X-Large K1, *k1, p2, k2, p2, k1, ssk, p2, k2tog, k1, p2, k2, p2, k1; rep from * 4 times more, k1—102 sts.

Work even in k2, p2 rib as established for 4½"/11.5cm. Bind off.

RIGHT SLEEVE

Work to correspond to left sleeve, foll diagram for picking up sts.

COLLAR

Cast on 34 sts. Purl 1 row. Work in cable and rib pat as foll:

Rows 1, 3, 7, and 9 (RS) Sl 3 wyib, [p2, k2] twice, p2, k8, [p2, k2] twice, p2, k3.

Row 2 and all WS rows P3, [k2, p2] twice, k2, p8, [k2, p2] twice, k2, p3.

Row 5 Sl 3 wyib, [p2, k2] twice, p2, 8-st RC, [p2, k2] twice, p2, k3.

Row 10 Rep row 2.

Rep rows 1–10 for cable and rib pat.

On next row 1 of cable and rib pat, work buttonhole as foll: Work 16 sts, yo, k2tog, work to end.

Cont in cable and rib pat until left edge of collar (end of RS rows) fits along first row of pentagons in body—1 st of body to 1 row of collar. Bind off.

Sew collar in place. Sew button to end of collar, opposite buttonhole. ●

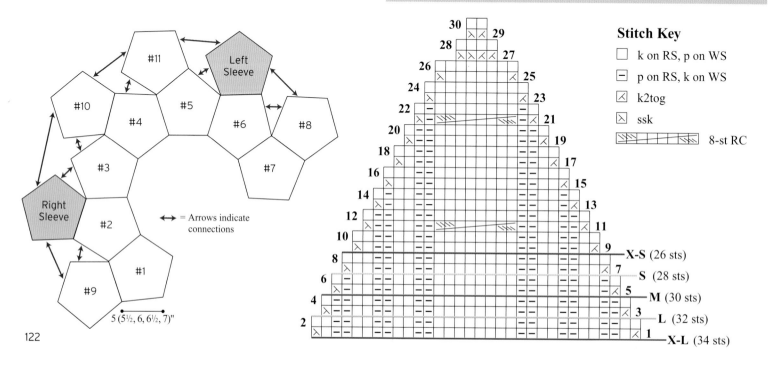

Stitch Key

☐ k on RS, p on WS

⊟ p on RS, k on WS

⊠ k2tog

⊠ ssk

8-st RC

= Arrows indicate connections

5 (5½, 6, 6½, 7)"

X-S (26 sts)
S (28 sts)
M (30 sts)
L (32 sts)
X-L (34 sts)

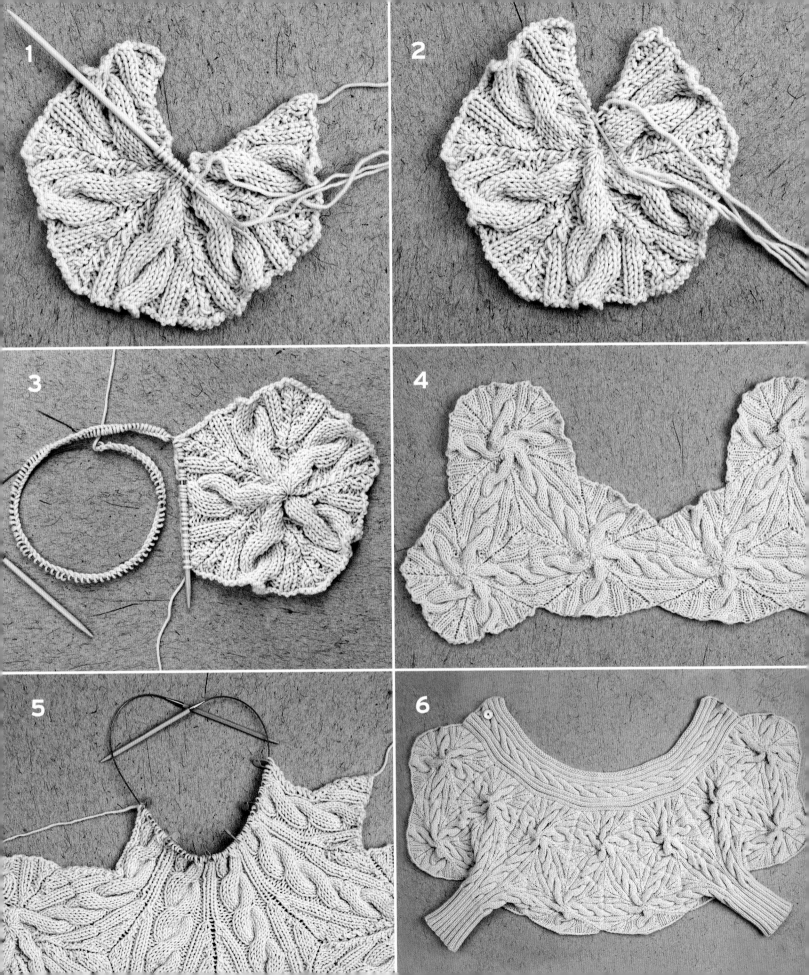

KALEIDOSCOPIC CABLES COAT

Repeating an element can make a pattern appear more complex than it really is, a concept illustrated here. The collar is a lattice of rib, twists, and cables; the same lattice is centered in three identical triangles making up each front of the coat, and repeated again as a godet insert on the back.

▬▬▬▬

SIZES
Small (Medium, Large, X-Large, 2X-Large). Shown in size Medium.

KNITTED MEASUREMENTS
Bust 34 (38, 42, 46, 50)"/86 (96.5, 106.5, 117, 127)cm
Length 29"/73.5cm
Upper Arm 12 (13, 14, 15, 16)"/30.5 (33, 35.5, 38, 40.5)cm

MATERIALS
• Original Yarn
25 (25, 26, 28, 29) 1¾oz/50g balls (each approx 92yd/85m) of **Berroco** Pure Merino in #8529 Cadet (④)
• Substitute Yarn
25 (25, 26, 28, 29) 1¾oz/50g hanks (each approx 95yd/87m) of **Trendsetter Yarns** Merino 8-Ply (superfine merino wool) in 269 Aquamarine (④)
• One pair each sizes 7 and 9 (4.5 and 5.5mm) needles, OR SIZE TO OBTAIN GAUGE
• Cable needle (cn)
• Stitch holders
• Removable stitch markers

GAUGE
18 sts and 24 rows to 4"/10cm over moss st using larger needles.
TAKE TIME TO CHECK GAUGE.

MOSS STITCH
(an even number of sts)
Row 1 (RS) *K1, p1; rep from * to end.
Row 2 K the knit sts and p the purl sts.
Row 3 *P1, k1; rep from * to end.
Row 4 K the knit sts and p the purl sts.
Rep rows 1–4 for moss st.

STITCH GLOSSARY
4-st RC Sl 2 sts to cn and hold to back, k2, k2 from cn.
4-st LC Sl 2 sts to cn and hold to front, k2, k2 from cn.
4-st RPC Sl 2 sts to cn and hold to back, k2, p2 from cn.
4-st LPC Sl 2 sts to cn and hold to front, p2, p2 from cn.
6-st RC Sl 4 sts to cn and hold to back, k2, k4 from cn.
6-st LC Sl 2 sts to cn and hold to front, k4, k2 from cn.
RT (right twist) K2tog leaving sts on LH needle, k first st again, sl both sts from needle.

BACK
Note Back is made in two pieces for the first 17"/43cm.

Right Back
With larger needles, cast on 52 (54, 58, 64, 68) sts.
Work in moss st for 1½"/4cm. Cont in moss st as foll:
Dec row (RS) K1, k2tog, work to end.
Work 3 rows even.
Rep last 4 rows 12 times more.
Rep dec row. Work 5 rows even.
Rep last 6 rows 6 times more—32 (34, 38, 44, 48) sts and piece measures 17"/43cm from beg. Place sts on a holder.

Left Back
With larger needles, cast on 52 (54, 58, 64, 68) sts.
Work in moss st for 1½"/4cm. Cont in moss st as foll:
Dec row (RS) Work to last 3 sts, ssk, k1.
Work 3 rows even
Rep last 4 rows 12 times more.
Rep dec row. Work 5 rows even.
Rep last 6 rows 6 times more—32 (34, 38, 44, 48) sts.
Place sts on a holder.

Top of Back

With RS facing and cont in pat, work across right back and then left back with one ball of yarn—64 (68, 76, 88, 96) sts. Work 3 (3, 1, 1, 1) rows even. Dec 1 st each side on next row, every other row 0 (0, 1, 7, 11) times, every 4th row 7 (13, 16, 13, 11) times, then every 6th row 6 (2, 0, 0, 0) times—36 (36, 40, 46, 50) sts.

Work even until piece measures 29"/73.5cm from beg. Bind off.

GODET

Note When working chart 1 for godet, work rows 1 and 2 ten times, rows 1–10 once, then rows 11–26 twice. When working chart 2 for godet, work rows 1–40 once.

With larger needles cast on 88 sts. Purl 1 row.

Row 1 (RS) K1, work 20 sts in moss st, p2, work row 1 of chart 1 over 42 sts, p2, work 20 sts in moss st, k1.

Work 1 row even.

Dec row (RS) K2tog, work to last 2 sts, ssk.

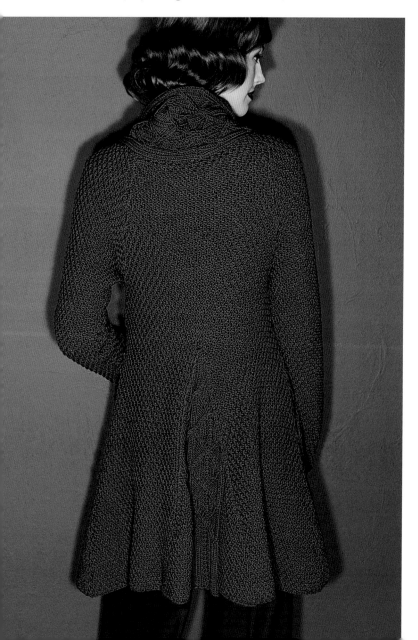

Rep dec row every other row 14 times, then every 4th row 8 times—42 sts and end with row 26 of chart 1.

Work rows 1–40 of chart 2.

Cut yarn, thread yarn through rem 2 sts, pull up and secure.

FRONTS (MAKE 2)

Note When working chart 1 for fronts, work rows 1 and 2 five times, rows 1–10 once, then rows 11–26 twice. When working chart 2 for fronts, work rows 1–40 once.

With larger needles, cast on 260 sts.

Set-up row (WS) P1, pm, [p86, pm] 3 times, p1.

Begin Chart 1

Row 1 (RS) K1, *sm, work 20 sts in moss, p2, work row 1 of chart 1, p2, work 20 sts in moss; rep from * twice more, sm, k1.

Row 2 P1, *sm, work 20 sts in moss, k2, work row 2 of chart 1, k2, work 20 sts in moss, sm; rep from * twice more, sm, p1.

Dec row (RS) K1, *sm, k2tog, work to 2 sts before next marker, ssk; rep from * twice more, sm, k1.

Rep dec row every other row 18 times more, then every 4th row 3 times—128 sts and end with row 26 of chart 1.

Begin Chart 2

Row 1 (RS) K1, *sm, work 42 sts of chart 2; rep from * twice more, sm, k1.

Cont in pat as established through row 40.

Cut yarn, thread through rem 8 sts, pull up, and secure.

SLEEVES

Cast on 36 (36, 38, 38, 40) sts. Work in moss st, inc 1 st each side (working inc sts into moss st) every 10th (8th, 6th, 6th, 6th) row 4 (5, 2, 10, 14) times, then every 12th (10th, 8th, 8th, 8th) row 5 (6, 11, 5, 2) times—54 (58, 64, 68, 72) sts.

Work even until piece measures 18"/45.5cm from beg. Place marker at each end for beg of armhole.

Raglan Cap Shaping

Dec row (RS) K1, k2tog, work to last 3 sts, ssk, k1.

Rep dec row every 4th row 11 (12, 11, 10, 10) times, then every 6th (2nd, 2nd, 2nd, 2nd) row 1 (2, 6, 9, 11) times.

Bind off rem 28 sts.

COLLAR (MAKE 2)

Cast on 52 sts.

Row 1 (RS) K3, p2, work row 1 of chart 1 to last 5 sts, p2, k3.

Row 2 P3, k2, work chart to last 5 sts, k2, p3.

Rep last 2 rows until piece measures 24½ (25, 25½, 26, 26½)"/62 (63.5, 64.5, 66, 67.5)cm from beg.

Bind off for center back collar seam.

FINISHING

Sew raglan sleeve caps to top 8½ (9, 9½, 10, 10½)" of back and to upper triangle on side edge of fronts (see assembly diagram). Sew side and sleeve seams. Sew collar to top edge (it should cover one wedge of each front, tops of sleeves, and across back neck). Sew godet into back slit. ●

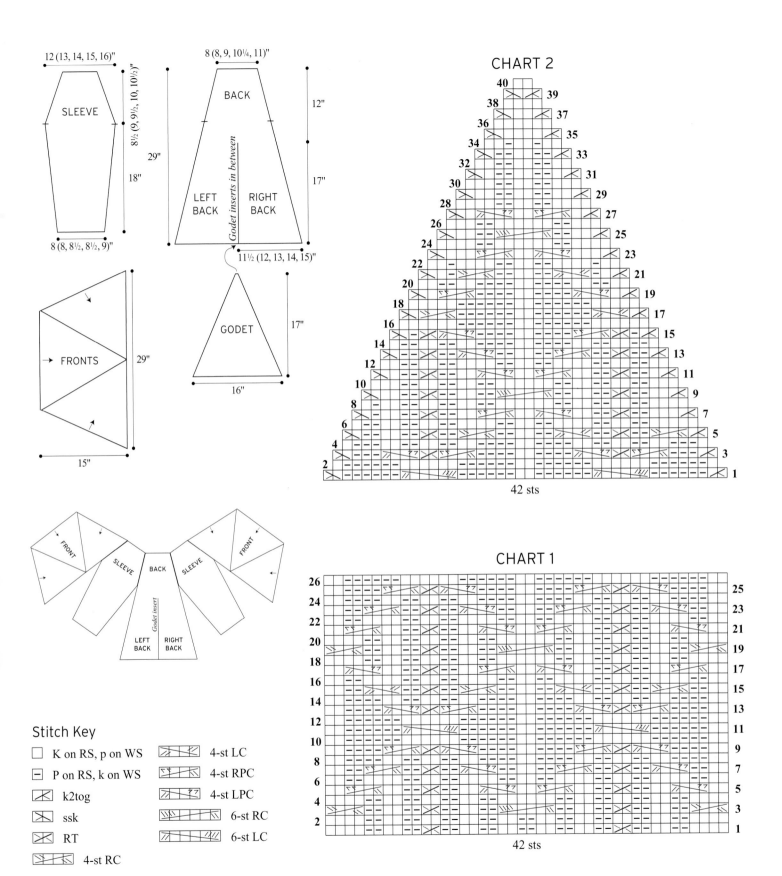

CHART 2

40
38 39
36 37
34 35
32 33
30 31
28 29
26 27
24 25
22 23
20 21
18 19
16 17
14 15
12 13
10 11
8 9
6 7
4 5
2 3
1

42 sts

CHART 1

26
24 25
22 23
20 21
18 19
16 17
14 15
12 13
10 11
8 9
6 7
4 5
2 3
1

42 sts

12 (13, 14, 15, 16)"

SLEEVE

8½ (9, 9½, 10, 10½)"

29"

18"

8 (8, 8½, 8½, 9)"

8 (8, 9, 10¼, 11)"

BACK

12"

17"

LEFT
BACK

RIGHT
BACK

Godet inserts in between

11½ (12, 13, 14, 15)"

GODET

17"

16"

FRONTS

29"

15"

FRONT

SLEEVE

BACK

SLEEVE

FRONT

Godet insert

LEFT
BACK

RIGHT
BACK

Stitch Key

☐ K on RS, p on WS

⊟ P on RS, k on WS

⧖ k2tog

⧗ ssk

⧓ RT

⧘ 4-st RC

⧗ 4-st LC

⧖ 4-st RPC

⧘ 4-st LPC

⧗ 6-st RC

⧘ 6-st LC

MEDALLION SHAWL

This airy, breezy wrap is a web-like crescent of hexagons. A simple double yarnover lace motif repeats six times per hexagon, creating a snowflake effect. The motifs are joined together with an innovative bit of easy crochet, and all that's left is for you to wrap it around your shoulders.

■■■□

KNITTED MEASUREMENTS
Hexagon (point to point) 8"/20.5cm
Shawl 34½" x 32"/87.5cm x 81.5cm

MATERIALS
• 4 1¾oz/50g skeins (each approx 144yd/133m) of **Berroco** Ultra Alpaca Light (super fine alpaca/Peruvian highland wool) in #4283 Lavender Mix ③
• One size 7 (4.5mm) circular needle, 16"/40cm long, OR SIZE TO OBTAIN GAUGE
• One set (5) size 7 (4.5mm) double-pointed needles (dpn)
• One size F-5 (3.75mm) crochet hook
• Stitch marker
• Tapestry needle

GAUGE
1 hexagon = 8"/20.5cm after blocking.
TAKE TIME TO CHECK GAUGE.

HEXAGONS (MAKE 15)
Cast on 96 sts. Join, taking care not to twist sts, and pm for beg of rnd.
Rep chart 6 times around working through row 20, changing to dpn when sts no longer fit comfortably on needle.
Cut yarn with a 12"/30.5cm tail. Thread through 36 rem sts and cinch tightly to close.

FINISHING
Block hexagons lightly. Arrange hexagons according to placement diagram and join with crochet hook, holding WS tog, as foll:
To join along one edge: Sc in first and 2nd sts, ch 7, skip 5, sc in next 2 sts, ch 7, skip 5, sc in last 2 sts.
To join along two or more edges: Sc in first and 2nd sts, ch 7, skip 5, *sc in next 2 sts, ch 8, skip 6, sc in last st of hexagon, sc in first st of next hexagon, ch 8, skip 6; rep from *, end ch 7, skip 5, sc in last 2 sts.
To work outside edging: Work same as joining two or more edges, and working at each outside point as foll: sc in last 2 sts, ch 4, sc in first 2 sts. ●

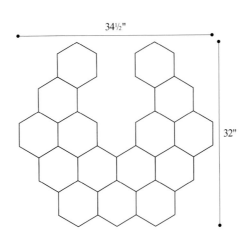

34½"

32"

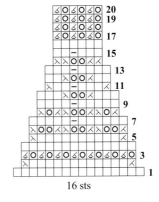

16 sts

Stitch Key
☐ K on RS, p on WS	☒ SKP
⊟ P on RS, k on WS	◿ P2tog
◹ K2tog	O Yo

BRAIDED CABLES VEST

I employed an illusory effect wherein multiple small side-by-side cables appear to be much larger ribbed braids. An optional cord belt sneaks through the back waist ribbing before showing itself across the fronts, brilliantly minimizing any bulk from a bulky yarn.

SIZES
Small (Medium, Large, 1X, 2X).
Shown in size Small.

KNITTED MEASUREMENTS
Bust (closed) 36 (40, 44, 48, 52)"/91.5 (101.5, 111.5, 122, 132)cm
Length 24 (24½, 25, 26½, 27)"/61 (62, 63.5, 67.5, 68.5)cm

MATERIALS
• Original Yarn
5 (6, 7, 8, 8) 3½oz/100g hanks (each approx 103yd/94m) of **Berroco** Peruvia Quick (wool) in #9100 Cream (5)
• Substitute Yarn
2 8⁴⁄₅oz/250g hanks (each approx 478yd/437m of **Cascade Yarns** Ecological Wool (natural Peruvian wool) in 8010 Ecru (5)
• One pair each sizes 9 and 11 (5.5 and 8mm) needles, OR SIZE TO OBTAIN GAUGE
• One extra size 11 (8mm) needle
• One size J-10 (6mm) crochet hook
• Cable needle (cn)
• Stitch holders
• Stitch markers

GAUGE
12 sts and 16 rows to 4"/10cm over St st using larger needles.
TAKE TIME TO CHECK GAUGE.

STITCH GLOSSARY
6-st RC Sl next 3 sts to cn and hold to back, p1, k1, p1, then p1, k1, p1 from cn.
6-st LC Sl next 3 sts to cn and hold to front, p1, k1, p1, then p1, k1, p1 from cn.
M1 Insert LH needle from front to back under strand between last st worked and next st on LH needle, knit strand through back loop.
M1 p-st Insert LH needle from front to back under strand between last st worked and next st on LH needle, purl strand through back loop.

BACK
With smaller needles, cast on 62 (70, 78, 82, 90) sts.
Row 1 (WS) P2, *k2, p2; rep from * to end.
Cont in k2, p2 rib for 10 rows. Change to larger needles.
Dec row (RS) Knit, dec 8 (10, 12, 10, 12) sts evenly across—54 (60, 66, 72, 78) sts.
Beg with a purl row, cont in St st (k on RS, p on WS) until piece measures 5 (5, 5, 5½, 5½)"/12.5 (12.5, 12.5, 14, 14)cm from beg, end with a WS row.

Side Shaping
Dec row (RS) K2, k2tog, k to last 4 sts, ssk, k2.
Work even for 11 rows.
Rep dec row once more—50 (56, 62, 68, 74) sts.
Work even until piece measures 9 (9, 9, 9½, 9½)"/23 (23, 23, 24, 24)cm from beg, inc 0 (2, 0, 2, 0) sts evenly across last row, end with a WS row—50 (58, 62, 70, 74) sts.
Change to smaller needles.
Work in k2, p2 rib for 10 rows, dec 0 (2, 0, 2, 0) sts evenly spaced across last row—50 (56, 62, 68, 74) sts.
Change to larger needles.
Cont in St st for 1"/2.5cm, end with a WS row.
Inc row (RS) K2, M1, k to last 2 sts, M1, k2.
Work even for 11 rows.
Rep inc row once more—54 (60, 66, 72, 78) sts.
Work even until piece measures 16 (16, 16, 17, 17)"/40.5 (40.5, 40.5, 43, 43)cm from beg, end with a WS row.

Armhole Shaping
Bind off 3 (4, 4, 5, 6) sts at beg of next 2 rows, then 2 (2, 2, 3, 3) sts at beg of next 2 rows.
Dec row (RS) K2, k2tog, k to last 4 sts, ssk, k2.
Purl 1 row.
Rep last 2 rows 2 (3, 4, 4, 4) times more—38 (40, 44, 46, 50) sts.
Work even until armhole measures 7 (7½, 8, 8½, 9)"/17.5 (19, 20.5, 21.5, 23)cm, end with a WS row.

Neck Shaping
Next row (RS) K12 (13, 15, 16, 18) sts, join a 2nd ball of yarn and bind off center 14 sts for neck, k to end.
Working both sides at once, bind off from each neck edge 5 sts twice, end with a WS row. Bind off rem 2 (3, 5, 6, 8) sts each side for shoulders.

LEFT FRONT
With smaller needles, cast on 46 (50, 54, 58, 62) sts.

Begin Chart
Row 1 (WS) P3, pm, work chart row 1 over next 29 sts, pm, p2, [k2, p2] 3 (4, 5, 6, 7) times.
Row 2 K2, [p2, k2] 3 (4, 5, 6, 7) times, sm, work chart row 2, sm, k3. Keeping 29 sts in chart, 3 sts at front edge in St st, and rem sts in k2, p2 rib, work even for 9 rows more.
Change to larger needles.
Dec row (RS) K2tog, [p2, k2tog] 3 (4, 5, 6, 7) times, sm, work chart row 12, sm, k3—42 (45, 48, 51, 54) sts.
Next row (WS) P3, sm, work chart row 13, p1, [k2, p1] 3 (4, 5, 6, 7) times.
Next row (RS) K1, [p2, k1] 3 (4, 5, 6, 7) times, sm, work chart row 14, sm, k3.
Cont in pats as established until piece measures 5 (5, 5, 5½, 5½)"/12.5 (12.5, 12.5, 14, 14)cm from beg, end with a WS row.

Side Shaping
Dec row 1 (RS) K1, p2tog, work to end.
Work even for 11 rows.
Dec row 2 (RS) K1, k2tog, work to end—40 (43, 46, 49, 52) sts.
Work even until piece measures 12½ (12½, 12½, 13, 13)"/31.5 (31.5, 31.5, 33, 33)cm from beg, end with a WS row.
Inc row (RS) K1, M1 p-st, work to end.
Work even for 11 rows.
Rep inc row once more—42 (45, 48, 51, 54) sts.
Work even until piece measures same length as back to underarm, end with a WS row.

Armhole Shaping
At armhole edge, bind off 3 (4, 4, 5, 6) sts once, then 2 (2, 2, 3, 3) sts once, end with a WS row. Dec 1 st from armhole edge on next row, then every other row 2 (3, 4, 4, 4) times more—34 (35, 37, 38, 40) sts.
Work even until piece measures same length as back to shoulder.

Shoulder Shaping and Neck Extension
Bind off 2 (3, 5, 6, 8) sts at beg of next RS row—32 sts.
Work even for 6"/15cm, end with a WS row. Place sts on holder.

RIGHT FRONT
With smaller needles, cast on 46 (50, 54, 58, 62) sts.

Begin Chart

Row 1 (WS) P2, [k2, p2] 3 (3, 4, 5, 6, 7) times, pm, work chart row 1 over next 29 sts, pm, p3.

Row 2 K3, sm, work chart row 2 over next 29 sts, sm, k2, [p2, k2] 3 (4, 5, 6, 7) times.

Keeping 29 sts in chart pat, 3 sts at front edge in St st, and rem sts in k2, p2 rib, work even for 9 rows more.

Change to larger needles.

Dec row (RS) K3, sm, work chart row 12, sm, k2tog, [p2, k2tog] 3 (4, 5, 6, 7) times—42 (45, 48, 51, 54) sts.

Next row (WS) P1, [k2, p1] 3 (4, 5, 6, 7) times, sm, work chart row 13, sm, p3.

Next row (RS) K3, sm, work chart row 14, sm, k1, [p2, k1] 3 (4, 5, 6, 7) times.

Cont in pats as established until piece measures 5 (5, 5, 5½, 5½)"/12.5 (12.5, 12.5, 14, 14)cm from beg, end with a WS row.

Side Shaping

Dec row 1 (RS) Work to last 3 sts, p2tog, k1.

Work even for 11 rows.

Dec row 2 (RS) Work to last 3 sts, ssk, k1— 40 (43, 46, 49, 52) sts.

Work even until piece measures 12½ (12½, 12½, 13, 13)"/31.5 (31.5, 31.5, 33, 33)cm from beg, end with a WS row.

Inc row (RS) Work to last st, M1 p-st, k1.

Work even for 11 rows.

Rep inc row once more—42 (45, 48, 51, 54) sts.

Cont to work same as for left front, reversing armhole and shoulder shaping, end with a RS row.

FINISHING

Lightly block pieces to measurements. Sew shoulder seams. To join neck extensions, place 32 sts from left front holder on larger needle ready for a WS row, then place 34 sts from right front holder on larger needle ready for a RS row. With RS held tog, work 3-needle bind-off. Sew neck extension along back neck edge.

Sew side seams.

Armhole Edging

With RS facing and crochet hook, join yarn with a sl st in underarm seam.

Rnd 1 (RS) Ch 1, working from left to right, sc evenly around armhole edge, making sure that work lies flat, join rnd with a sl st in first sc. Fasten off.

Tie

With smaller needles, cast on 3 sts. Work in St st for 48 (51, 54, 58, 62)"/122 (129.5, 133, 147.5, 157.5)cm. Bind off. From WS, insert one end of tie up to RS between first p2 (p2, k2, k2, p2) sts on left side of back waist ribbing, centering it from top to bottom. Inserting tie between each set of p2 (p2, k2, k2, p2) sts, weave tie over and under each set of k2 (k2, p2, p2, k2) sts. End by inserting tie end down to WS between last p2 (p2, k2, k2, p2) sts. Even up ends. From WS, insert right end of tie up between 2 purl sts at LH side of right front cable and left end between 2 purl sts at RH side of left front cable. ●

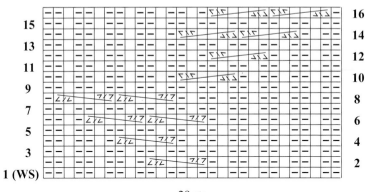

29 sts

Stitch Key

☐ k on RS, p on WS

⊟ p on RS, k on WS

6-st RC

6-st LC

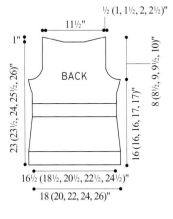

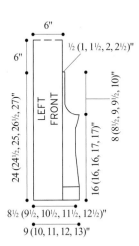

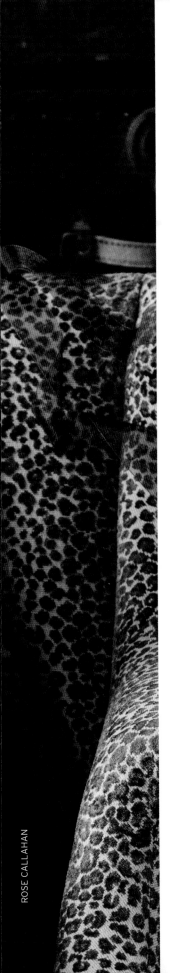

CRISS-CROSS CABLES PULLOVER

A cabled yoke reminiscent of braided holiday garlands is the focal point of a short-sleeve turtleneck that carries about it an air of winter and fireplaces. At the top of the yoke, the cabling segues naturally into the deep ribbing of the high and cozy turtleneck.

SIZES
X-Small (Small, Medium, Large, 1X, 2X). Shown in size Small.

KNITTED MEASUREMENTS
Bust 32 (34½, 37¼, 41, 45, 50)"/81.5 (87, 94.5, 104, 114, 127)cm
Length 23½ (24, 24½, 26, 26½, 27)"/59.5 (61, 62, 66, 67.5, 68.5)cm
Upper Arm 11 (12, 12½, 13, 14¼, 16)"/ 28 (30.5, 31.5, 33, 36, 40.5)cm

MATERIALS
• Original Yarn
7 (7, 8, 9, 11, 12) 1¾oz/50g balls (each approx 130yd/119m) of **Berroco** Blackstone Tweed (wool/superkid mohair/angora rabbit hair) in #2614 Cranberry Bog (4)
• Substitute Yarn
8 (8, 9, 10, 12, 13) 1¾oz/50g balls (each approx 122yd/112m) of **Tahki Yarns/Tahki•Stacy Charles** Tara Tweed (wool/nylon) in #016 Cherry Tweed (4)
• Two each sizes 5 and 7 (3.75 and 4.5mm) circular needle, 16"/40cm long and 29 (29, 32, 32, 40, 40)"/75 (75, 80, 80, 100, 100)cm long, OR SIZE TO OBTAIN GAUGE
• One set (5) each sizes 5 and 7 (3.75 and 4.5mm) double-pointed needles (dpn)
• Cable needle (cn)
• 4 stitch markers—one in a different color for beg of rnd

GAUGE
18 sts and 25 rnds to 4"/10cm over St st using larger needles.
TAKE TIME TO CHECK GAUGE.

STITCH GLOSSARY
4-st RC Sl 2 sts to cn and hold to back, k2, k2 from cn.
4-st LC Sl 2 sts to cn and hold to front, k2, k2 from cn.
4-st RPC Sl 2 sts to cn and hold to back, k2, p2 from cn.
4-st LPC Sl 2 sts to cn and hold to front, p2, k2 from cn.
4 to 2-st RC dec Sl 2 sts to cn and hold to back, k2tog, k2tog from cn.
6-st RPC Sl 4 sts to cn and hold to back, k2, sl last 2 sts from cn to LH needle and p them, then k2 from cn.
6-st LPC Sl 4 sts to cn and hold to front, k2, sl last 2 sts from cn to LH needle and p them, then k2 from cn.

NOTE
Body and sleeves are worked in the round separately, then joined at underarms. Yoke is then worked in the round.

BODY
With longer, smaller circular needle, cast on 154 (168, 180, 198, 218, 240) sts. Join, taking care not to twist sts, and place different colored marker for beg of rnd.
Work in k1, p1 rib for 3½"/9cm.
Change to longer, larger needle.
Knit 1 rnd, dec 10 (12, 12, 14, 16, 16) sts evenly around—144 (156, 168, 184, 202, 224) sts.
Cont in St st (k every rnd) for 6 (6, 6, 9, 9, 9) rnds.
Next rnd K72 (78, 84, 92, 101, 112), pm, k to end.
Dec rnd K2, k2tog, k to 4 sts before first marker, ssk, k2, sm, k2, k2tog, k to 4 sts before last marker, ssk, k2—2 sts dec'd.
Rep dec rnd every 8th rnd 3 times more—128 (140, 152, 168, 186, 208) sts.
Work even until piece measures 12½ (12½, 12½, 13, 13, 13)"/31.5 (31.5, 31.5, 33, 33, 33)cm from beg.
Inc rnd K2, M1, k to 2 sts before first marker, M1, k2, sm, k2, M1, k to 2 sts before last marker, M1, k2.
Rep inc rnd every 4th rnd 3 times more—144 (156, 168, 184, 202, 224) sts.
Work even until piece measures 16 (16, 16, 16½, 16½, 16½)"/40.5 (40.5, 40.5, 42, 42, 42)cm from beg.
Next rnd Work to 6 sts before first marker, bind off 12 sts, dropping marker, k to 6 sts before last marker, bind off 12 sts, dropping marker. Leave sts on needle for yoke.

SLEEVES

With smaller dpn, cast on 46 (50, 52, 54, 60, 68) sts. Divide sts over 4 dpn and join, taking care not to twist sts. Place marker for beg of rnd. Work in k1, p1 rib for 2"/5cm. Change to larger dpn and work in St st for 1"/2.5cm more.
Inc rnd K2, M1, k to last 2 sts, M1, k2.
Work 5 rnds even, then rep inc rnd—50 (54, 56, 58, 64, 72) sts. Work even until piece measures 5 (5, 5½, 5½, 6, 6)"/12.5 (12.5, 14, 14, 15, 15)cm from beg.
Next rnd K to last 6 sts, bind off 12 sts, dropping marker, k to end—38 (42, 44, 46, 52, 60) sts.

YOKE

Joining rnd Using longer, larger circular needle, k38 (42, 44, 46, 52, 60) sts of first sleeve (left sleeve), pm, k60 (66, 72, 80, 89, 100) sts of body (front), pm, k38 (42, 44, 46, 52, 60) sts of 2nd sleeve (right sleeve), pm, k60 (66, 72, 80, 89, 100) rem sts of body (back), place different colored marker for beg of rnd—196 (216, 232, 252, 282, 320) sts.

For Sizes Small (Medium) Only

Next rnd Knit, dec 2 (2) sts on left sleeve, 2 (2) sts on front, 2 (2) sts on right sleeve, and 0 (2) sts on back—210 (224) sts.

For All Sizes

Knit 6 (9, 12, 6, 4, 1) rnds.

For Sizes Large (1X, 2X) Only

Dec rnd Dec 2 sts evenly across each piece—8 sts dec'd. Work 1 rnd even.
Rep last 2 rnds 6 (8, 11) times more—196 (210, 224) sts.

For All Sizes

Inc rnd [K6, kfb, kfb, k6] 14 (15, 16, 14, 15, 16) times—224 (240, 256, 224, 240, 256) sts.

BEGIN CHART

Note Change to shorter, larger circular needle, when there are too few sts to fit comfortably on longer circular needle.
Rnd 1 Work 16-st rep 14 (15, 16, 14, 15, 16) times around. Cont chart through rnd 40—84 (90, 96, 84, 90, 96) sts. Change to shorter, smaller needle and rep rnd 40 of chart for 9"/23cm. Bind off loosely in pat.

FINISHING

Block to measurements. ●

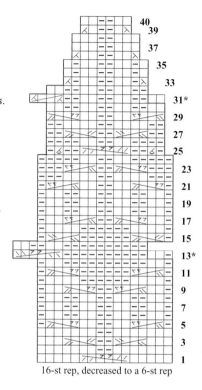

16-st rep, decreased to a 6-st rep

Stitch Key

☐ k on RS, p on WS
⊟ p on RS, k on WS
☒ k2tog
⊠ ssk
⬚ p2tog
▱ 4-st RC
▱ 4-st LC
▱ 4-st RPC
▱ 4-st LPC
▱ 4 to 2-st RC dec
▱ 6-st RPC
▱ 6-st LPC

*Rnd 13 Work to rep line, work rep around, working final cable at the end of the rnd.
Rnd 14 End rnd with k2, p1.
*Rnd 31 Work to rep line, work rep around, working the final dec cable at the end of the rnd.
Rnd 32 End rnd with k1.

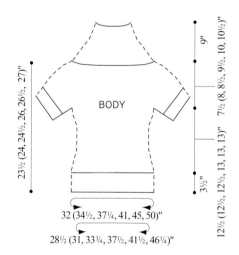

CABLED PONCHO

Full confession: This cabled piece actually began its life as a skirt, but in the end it wanted to be a poncho. Worked side to side in a rhythmic rib-and-cable pattern, increases and decreases slope the shoulders for a graceful fit, and open sides keep you warm without restricting motion.

■■□□

SIZES
Small/Large (Large/1X). Shown in size Small/Large.

KNITTED MEASUREMENTS
Width (at one lower edge) 40 (45)"/ 101.5 (114)cm
Length 27 (29½)"/68.5 (75)cm

MATERIALS
• Original Yarn
12 (15) 1¾oz/50g balls (each 127yd/117m) of **Berroco** Blackstone Tweed Metallic (wool/mohair/angora/ other fibers) in #4601 Clover Honey (4)
• Substitute Yarn
13 (16) 1¾oz/50g balls (each approx 122yd/113m) of **Tahki Yarns/ Tahki•Stacy Charles** Tara Tweed (wool/ nylon) in #021 Mushroom Tweed (4)
• One each sizes 5 and 7 (3.75 and 4.5mm) circular needle, 40"/100cm long, OR SIZE TO OBTAIN GAUGE
• One size 5 (3.75mm) circular needle, 24"/60cm long
• Cable needle (cn)
• Removable stitch markers

GAUGE
20 sts and 27 rows to 4"/10cm over cable chart pat using larger needle.
TAKE TIME TO CHECK GAUGE.

NOTES
1) Poncho is worked in one piece (see schematic for direction of knitting) with center line inc's, an opening for neck, then center line dec's.
2) Schematic shows a side view. The center line inc/dec form placement of poncho along shoulders (see photo).

STITCH GLOSSARY
6-st RC Sl 3 sts to cn and hold to back, k3, k3 from cn.
6-st LC Sl 3 sts to cn and hold to front, k3, k3 from cn.
M1 Insert LH needle from front to back under strand between last st worked and next st on LH needle, knit strand through back loop.
M1 p-st Insert LH needle from front to back under strand between last st worked and next st on LH needle, purl strand through back loop.

PONCHO
With longer, smaller needle, cast on 143 sts.
Row 1 (WS) P1, *k1, p1; rep from * to end.
Cont in k1, p1 rib for 3 rows more.
Change to larger needle.
Next row (WS) Cast on 3 sts, p to end.

Begin Charts
Cast on 3 sts—149 sts.
Row 1 (RS) Beg with row 1, st 1 on chart 1, work to end of rep line, work 13-st rep 4 times more, then work to end of chart 1, pm, k3, pm, beg with row 1, st 1 on chart 2, work to end of rep line, work 13-st rep 4 times more, work to end of chart 2—149 sts.
Row 2 Work even, foll row 2 of charts as established with center 3 sts worked as p3 on this and every WS row.
Cont to work 8-row reps of charts 1 and 2, AT THE SAME TIME, work inc rows as foll:
*Next inc row (RS)** Work chart 1 to marker, M1 or M1 p-st (foll chart pat), sm, k3, sm, M1 or M1 p-st (foll chart pat), work chart 2 to end—2 sts inc'd.
Next row Work even.
Next inc row Work chart 1 to marker, M1 or M1 p-st (foll chart pat), sm, k3, sm, M1 or M1 p-st (foll chart pat), work chart 2 to end—2 sts inc'd.
Next inc row Work chart 2 to marker, M1 or M1 p-st (foll chart pat), sm, p3, sm, M1 or M1 p-st (foll chart pat), work chart 1 to end—2 sts inc'd.
Rep from * 20 (25) times more, working inc'd sts into chart pats—275 (305) sts.

Size Small/Large Only

Next inc row (RS) Work chart 1 to marker, M1 or M1 p-st (foll chart pat), sm, k3, sm, M1 or M1 p-st (foll chart pat), work chart 2 to end—2 sts inc'd.
Next row (WS) Work even.
Next inc row (RS) Work chart 1 to marker, M1 or M1 p-st (foll chart pat), sm, k3, sm, M1 or M1 p-st (foll chart pat), work chart 2 to end—279 sts.

Size X-Large/1X Only

Next row (RS) Work even.

There are 138 (151) sts and 10 (11) cable reps on EACH side of center 3 sts—279 (305) sts.

Neck Opening

Next row (WS) Work even to marker, sm, p2, join a 2nd ball of yarn and M1 p-st, p1, sm, work to end.
Cont to work even on 140 (153) sts each side for a total of 14"/35.5cm from beg of opening, end with a WS row.

Rejoin Halves

Next row (RS) Work to first marker, k1, k last st of first side tog with first st of 2nd side, work to end—279 (305) sts.
Next row (WS) Work even on all sts.
Note Center dec is worked with first and last st of center 3 sts. Adjust marker placement as necessary to keep center 3 sts marked.

Dec row 1 (RS) Work chart 1 to 1 st before 3 marked sts, k2tog, k1, ssk, work chart 2 to end.
Row 2 Work even.
Row 3 Rep dec row 1.
Dec row 4 (WS) Work chart 2 to 1 st before 3 marked sts, p2tog tbl, p1, p2tog, work chart 1 pat to end.
Rep rows 1–4 for 20 (24) times more, then rep row 1 once (0 times) more. Work 1 row even. There are 70 sts and a total of 5 cable reps each side once again, end with a RS row on the 149 sts.
Change to longer, smaller needle.
Next row (WS) Bind off 3 sts, purl to end.
Next row (RS) Bind off 3 sts, work in k1, p1 rib to end.
Cont in k1, p1 rib for 3 rows more.
Bind off in rib.

FINISHING

Fold 3 sts along each side edge of poncho to WS and sew in place, forming a hem facing.

Collar

With RS facing and shorter needle, pick up and k 128 sts evenly around neck opening. Join and pm for beg of rnd. Work in k1, p1 rib for 1"/2.5cm. Knit 1 rnd. Work in k2, p2 rib for 1¾"/4.5cm. Knit 1 rnd. Work in k1, p1 rib for 1"/2.5cm more. Bind off loosely in rib. ●

CHART 1

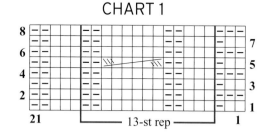

8
6
4
2
21
7
5
3
1
13-st rep

CHART 2

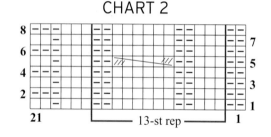

8
6
4
2
21
7
5
3
1
13-st rep

STITCH KEY

☐ k on RS, p on WS
⊟ p on RS, k on WS
6-st RC
6-st LC

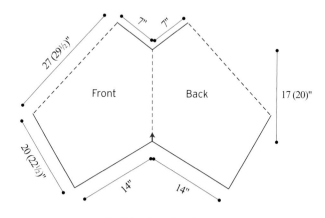

Front   Back

27 (29½)"
20 (22½)"
7"   7"
17 (20)"
14"   14"

↑ = Direction of work
⋮ = Center line inc's and dec's

140

FUNNEL-NECK PULLOVER

Serpentine traveling cables flare across the bodice of this funnel-neck pullover, pooling and separating into a sharp collection of ribs and twisted cables. Worked in the round from the top down, it's divided for the armholes and rejoined once the armholes are complete. Three-quarter-length sleeves are later picked up and worked down. You'll recognize the diagonal lines of cables I am so fond of here and as far back as 1997 (see the Traveling Cables Turtleneck on pages 74-79 and the Trellis Cardigan on pages 80-84).

■■■■

SIZES
Small (Medium, Large, X-Large).
Shown in size Small.

KNITTED MEASUREMENTS
Bust 39 (39, 41½, 43)"/99 (99, 105.5, 109)cm*
Length 25 (25¾, 26¼, 26¾)"/63.5 (65.5, 66.5, 68)cm
Upper Arm 13⅓ (14, 14½, 15¼)"/33.5 (35.5, 37, 38.5)cm
*As this garment is worked from the top down, the yoke is roomy; therefore, the first two sizes have the same bust measurement, with the other two sizes just a couple of inches wider. Determine your size from the length and upper arm measurements.

MATERIALS
• Original Yarn
10 (10, 11, 12) 1¾oz/50g balls (each approx 132yd/121m) of **Bergère de France** Pure Mérino Français (wool) in #295-391 Palmier (Aqua) (4)
• Substitute Yarn
11 (11, 12, 13) 1¾oz/50g balls (each approx 122yd/112m) of **Classic Elite Yarns** Liberty Wool (washable wool) in 7814 Mallard (4)
• Two size 7 (4.5mm) circular needles, each 16"/40 and 24"/60cm long, OR SIZE TO OBTAIN GAUGE
• One set (5) size 7 (4.5mm) double-pointed needles (dpn)
• Stitch markers
• Cable needle (cn)

GAUGE
20 sts and 28 rnds to 4"/10cm over St st using size 7 (4.5mm) needles.
TAKE TIME TO CHECK GAUGE.

STITCH GLOSSARY
M1 Insert LH needle from front to back under strand between last st worked and next st on LH needle, knit strand through back loop.
M1R Insert LH needle from back to front under strand between last st worked and next st on LH needle, knit strand through front loop.
M1 p-st Insert LH needle from front to back under strand between last st worked and next st on LH needle, purl strand through back loop.

M1R p-st Insert LH needle from back to front under strand between the last st worked and next st on LH needle, purl strand through back loop.

4-st RC Sl 2 sts to cn and hold to back, k2, k2 from cn.

4-st LC Sl 2 sts to cn and hold to front, k2, k2 from cn.

4-st RPC Sl 2 sts to cn, hold to back, k2, p2 from cn.

4-st LPC Sl 2 sts to cn, hold to front, p2, k2 from cn.

NECK CABLE

(over 12 sts)

Rnds 1, 2, 3, and 5 P4, k4, p4.

Rnd 4 P4, 4-st RC, p4.

Rnd 6 Rep rnd 1.

Rep rnds 1–6 for neck cable.

NOTES

1) Pullover is worked from the top down in the round to the top of the armhole, then worked back and forth in two pieces for the armhole opening, then joined and worked in the round once more to the lower edge.

2) Side and center pattern shaping in lower body are worked simultaneously, read carefully before beginning to knit.

NECK

With shorter circular needle, cast on 124 sts. Join, taking care not to twist sts, and pm for beg of rnd.

Rnd 1 K2, [p2, k2] 6 times, work neck cable over 12 sts, k2, [p2, k2] 12 times, work neck cable over 12 sts, [k2, p2] 6 times.

Cont in pats as established until rnds 1–6 of neck cable have been worked 3 times, then work rnd 1 once more. When last rnd is complete, remove marker, k1, pm for new beg of rnd.

Shoulder Shaping

Note Work inc'd sts into k2, p2 rib. Change to longer circular needle when sts no longer fit comfortably on shorter needle.

Inc rnd 1 *K1, p2, k2, M1, [p2, k2] 5 times, work 12 sts of neck cable as established, [k2, p2] 5 times, M1R, k2, p2, k1*, place side marker, rep between *s once more—128 sts.

Inc rnd 2 [K1, p2, k2, M1, work in pat to 5 sts before marker, M1R, k2, p2, k1] twice—4 sts inc'd.

Inc rnd 3 [K1, p2, k2, M1 p-st, work in pat to 5 sts before marker, M1R p-st, k2, p2, k1] twice— 4 sts inc'd.

Inc rnd 4 Rep inc rnd 3—140 sts.

Inc rnds 5 and 6 Rep inc rnd 2.

Inc rnd 7 and 8 Rep inc rnd 3.

Inc rnd 9 Rep inc rnd 2—160 sts.

Inc rnd 10 [K1, p2, k2, M1, k1, pm, work in pat to 5 sts before marker, M1R, pm, k2, p2, k1] twice —164 sts.

Begin Chart

Note Work inc'd sts into St st (k every rnd).

Rnd 1 [K1, p2, k2, M1, k to marker, sm, work chart over 68 sts, k to marker, M1R, sm, k2, p2, k1] twice —4 sts inc'd.

Cont in this way to inc 4 sts every rnd and work chart as

established through rnd 28 (28, 30, 32) of chart, end last rnd 3 sts before beg of rnd marker—276 (276, 284, 292) sts.

Divide for Armhole Openings

Note Front and back will be now worked back and forth, at the same time, using separate balls of yarn.

Next rnd (RS) Bind off last 3 sts of previous rnd and first 3 sts of rnd, work in pat (without increasing) to 3 sts before side marker (remove 2nd shaping marker 5 sts before side marker), join 2nd ball of yarn and bind off 6 sts (3 on each side of side marker), work in pat to end, turn—264 (264, 272, 280) sts, 132 (132, 136, 140) sts each for front and back.

Next row (WS) [P to marker, sm, work chart as established, p to marker] twice.

Armhole Shaping

Row 1 (RS) [K to marker, sm, work chart as established, k to marker] twice.

Rows 2 and 4 [P to marker, sm, work chart as established, p to marker] twice.

Dec rows 3 and 5 [K3, k2tog, k to marker, sm, work chart as established, k to last 5 sts, ssk, k3] twice—2 sts dec'd each piece.

Row 6 Rep row 2.

Rep rows 1–6, working chart as established, 5 times more —108 (108, 112, 116) each for front and back.

Rep rows 1 and 2 to work even 0 (3, 4, 5) times more.

Join to Work Body in the Round

Next rnd (RS) K to marker, sm, work chart as established, k to end of first side, place side marker, cont with working yarn, k to marker, sm, work chart as established, k to end of rnd, place new marker for beg of rnd.

Work 2 rnds even in pats as established over 216 (216, 224, 232) sts.

Next rnd [K16 (16, 18, 20), pm, k4, work chart as established over 68 sts, pm, k4, pm, k16 (16, 18, 20)] twice.

Side Shaping

Note Read before continuing to knit. Dec's at side and inc's for k4, p4 rib pat are worked simultaneously.

Next rnd [K3, k2tog (side shaping dec), work to marker, M1 p-st (rib shaping inc), sm, k4, sm, work chart as established, sm, k4, sm, M1 p-st (rib shaping inc), work to last 5 sts, ssk (side shaping dec), k3] twice.

Cont in pats as established, rep side shaping dec every 4th row 2 (2, 0, 0) times, then every 8th (8th, 10th, 12th) row 7 (7, 7, 5) times more, AT THE SAME TIME, rep rib shaping inc every 4th row 19 times more, working inc'd sts into a p4, k4 rib by working inc's as foll: 3 M1 p-st inc's, then [4 M1 inc's, 4 M1 p-st inc's] twice, AT THE SAME TIME, when rnd 104 of chart is complete, cont to work dec's as established and work center 64 sts in center cable pat as foll:

Rnd 1 *Work in pat to chart marker, p2, k2, p2, 4-st LC, [p2, k2] twice, p28, pm, [k2, p2] twice, 4-st RC, p2, k2, p2, sm, work in pat to side marker; rep from * once more.

Rnds 2, 3, and 4 *Work in pat to chart marker, p2, k2, p2, k4, [p2, k2] twice, p to marker, sm, [k2, p2] twice, k4, p2, k2, p2, sm, work in pat to side marker; rep from * once more.

Dec rnd 5 *Work in pat to chart marker, p2, k2, p2, k4, [p2, k2] twice, p2tog (center shaping dec), p to 2 sts before marker, p2tog (center shaping dec), sm, [k2, p2] twice, k4, p2, k2, p2, sm, work in pat to side marker; rep from * once more—4 sts dec'd.

Rnd 6 Rep rnd 2.

Rnd 7 *Work in pat to chart marker, p2, k2, p2, 4-st LC, [p2, k2] twice, p to marker, sm, [k2, p2] twice, 4-st RC, p2, k2, p2, sm, work in pat to side marker; rep from * once more. Rep rnds 2–7 for center cable pat, AT THE SAME TIME, rep center shaping dec's as in rnd 5 every 12th row 3 times more—232 (232, 248, 264) sts when all shaping is complete, 116 (116, 124, 132) for each front and back.

Work 3 rnds even in pats after final rib shaping inc.

Rib set-up rnd *P1, k2, p1, M1 p-st, k2, [p2, k2] 0 (1, 2) times, [p2, k2] 7 times, work 8 sts in cable pat as established, [k2, p2] 3 times, M1, k1, p2, k2, p1, M1 p-st, [k2, p2] 3 times, k2, work cable as established over 8 sts, [k2, p2] 7 times, [k2, p2] 0 (1, 2) times, k2, p1, M1 p-st, k2, p1; rep from * once more —240 (240, 256, 272) sts.

Cont in k2, p2 rib and cable pats as established for 2½"/6.5cm. Bind off purlwise.

SLEEVES

With RS facing and dpn, beg at underarm, pick up and k 66 (70, 72, 76) evenly around armhole opening. Join and pm for beg of rnd. Work 8 rnds in St st (k every rnd).

Dec rnd K2, k2tog, k to last 4 sts, ssk, k2—2 sts dec'd.

Rep dec rnd every 8th (6th, 8th, 6th) rnd 8 (10, 9, 11) times more—48 (48, 52, 52) sts.

Work even until sleeve measures 11 (11, 11½, 12)"/28 (28, 29, 30.5)cm.

Next rnd *K2, p2; rep from * around.

Rep last rnd for k2, p2 rib for 3"/7.5cm. Bind off in rib.

FINISHING

Block lightly to measurements. •

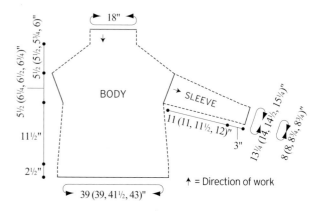

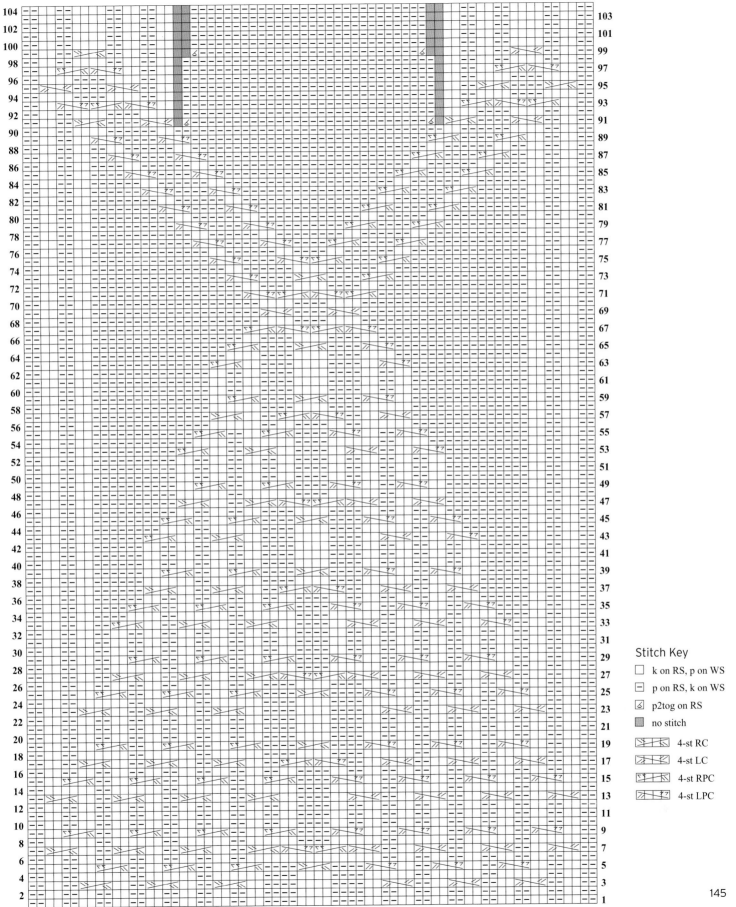

Stitch Key

☐ k on RS, p on WS

– p on RS, k on WS

◿ p2tog on RS

▨ no stitch

⧄⧅ 4-st RC

⧄⧅ 4-st LC

⧄⧅ 4-st RPC

⧄⧅ 4-st LPC

68 sts

145

CABLE AND CHEVRON TOP

Mirrored increases and decreases establish the bias-knit central chevron panel, which organically shapes the shoulder and fashions a gently curving hemline. Bold honeycomb and twist cables add flattering, strong vertical lines on this cap-sleeved top, which can be worn with or without a shirt underneath.

SIZES
Small (Medium, Large, X-Large, 2X-Large). Shown in size Medium.

KNITTED MEASUREMENTS
Bust 39 (43, 47, 51, 55)"/99 (109, 119, 129.5, 139.5)cm
Length (measured at side seam) 26"/66cm

MATERIALS
• Original Yarn
13 (15, 16, 17, 19) 1¾oz/50g hanks (each approx 87yd/80m) of **Dale Garn** Cotinga (wool/alpaca) in #4654 Purple (⬤)
• Substitute Yarn
6 (7, 7, 7, 8) 3½oz/100g skeins (each approx 218yd/199m) of **Plymouth Yarn Company** Worsted Merino (superwash merino) in 0048 Fuchsia (⬤)
• One pair each sizes 6 and 8 (4 and 5mm) needles, OR SIZE TO OBTAIN GAUGE
• One size 6 (4mm) circular needle, 16"/40cm long
• Removable stitch markers

GAUGE
18 sts and 24 rows to 4"/10cm over St st using larger needles.
TAKE TIME TO CHECK GAUGE.

NOTES
1) The chevron chart creates a biased fabric that exaggerates the shoulder shaping and creates a biased hemline. Measure length at side edges.
2) Front neck looks more like a V-neck in shaping, a more rounded neckline will be created when the neckband is worked.

STITCH GLOSSARY
M1 Insert LH needle from front to back under strand between last st worked and next st on LH needle, knit strand through back loop.
M1 p-st Insert LH needle from front to back under strand between last st worked and next st on LH needle, purl strand through back loop.
4-st RC Sl 2 sts to cn and hold to back, k2, k2 from cn.
4-st RC Sl 2 sts to cn and hold to front, k2, k2 from cn.
8-st RC Sl 4 sts to cn and hold to back, k4, k4 from cn.

BACK
With smaller needles, cast on 114 (122, 134, 146, 154) sts.
Row 1 (WS) P2, *k2, p2; rep from * to end.
Cont in k2, p2 rib as established for 3"/7.5cm, end with a WS row.
Next dec row (RS) [K7 (9, 7, 7, 7), k2tog] 12 (10, 14, 16, 16) times, k6 (12, 8, 2, 10)—102 (112, 120, 130, 138) sts.

Begin Chart
Note Row 1 of chart is a WS row.
Change to larger needles.
Row 1 (WS) P9 (14, 18, 23, 27), pm, work chart over 84 sts, pm, p to end.
Row 2 (RS) K to marker, sm, work chart over 84 sts, sm, k to end.
Cont to work chart in this way through row 24, working sts outside markers in St st (k on RS, p on WS), rep rows 1–24 three times more, then rep rows 1–23 once more.

Shoulder and Neck Shaping
Note Due to biasing in fabric, back neck is shaped but appears straight.
Bind off 4 (5, 6, 7, 8) sts at beg of next 4 rows. Mark center 12 sts on last row.
Next row (RS) Bind off 4 (5, 6, 7, 8) sts, work to marked sts (do not work the M1), join 2nd ball of yarn and bind off center 12 sts (do not work the M1), work to end.
Working both sides at once, bind off 4 (5, 6, 7, 8) at shoulder edge at beg of next 3 rows, then bind off 5 (5, 6, 7, 7) sts at beg of next 2 rows, AT THE SAME TIME, bind off 5 sts from each neck edge twice. Bind off rem sts each side.

Chart column numbers (top): 24 22 20 18 16 14 12 10 8 6 4 2

84 sts

Chart column numbers (bottom): 23 21 19 17 15 13 11 9 7 5 3 1 (WS)

FRONT

Work as for back until 24-row chart has been worked 4 times, then work rows 1–3 once more, working both inc in last row 2 as M1. Mark center 12 sts on last row.

Shoulder and Neck Shaping

Note Front neck is shaped by eliminating inc each side of center neck.
Next row (RS) Work to center marked sts, (do not work the M1), join 2nd ball of yarn and bind off center 12 sts (do not work the M1), work to end.
Working both sides at once, cont in pats as established for 19 rows more.
Bind off 4 (5, 6, 7, 8) sts at beg of next 4 rows.
Next row (RS) Bind off 4 (5, 6, 7, 8) sts, work to last st of first side, M1, k1; k1, M1 at beg of 2nd side, work to end.
Next row Bind off 4 (5, 6, 7, 8) sts, work to end.
Next row (RS) Bind off 4 (5, 6, 7, 8) sts, work to last st of first side, M1 p-st, k1; k1, M1 p-st at beg of 2nd side, work to end.
Next row Bind off 4 (5, 6, 7, 8) sts, work to end.
Next row (RS) Bind off 5 (6, 6, 7, 7) sts, work to last st of first side, M1 p-st, k1; k1, M1 p-st at beg of 2nd side, work to end.
Next row Bind off 5 (6, 6, 7, 7) sts, work to end.
Bind off rem sts each side.

FINISHING

Block pieces to measurements. Sew shoulder seams.

Neckband

With RS facing and circular needle, pick up and k 100 sts evenly around neck edge. Join and pm for beg of rnd.
Rnd 1 *K2, p2; rep from * to end.
Rep rnd 1 for k2, p2 rib for 1"/2.5cm. Bind off in rib.

Armhole Trim

Place markers at each side edge 10"/25.5cm from shoulder. With RS facing and smaller needle, pick up and k 45 sts from marker to shoulder, pm, then pick up and k 45 sts from shoulder to 2nd marker—90 sts.
Row 1 (WS) P2, *k2, p2; rep from * to end.
Dec row 2 (RS) K1, ssk, work in rib as established to 2 sts before shoulder marker, k2tog, sm, ssk, work to last 3 sts, k2tog, k1—4 sts dec'd.
Rep dec row every other row 3 times more. Bind off in pat on WS.
Rep for other armhole.

Sew side and underarm seams, leaving lower 3"/7.5cm of rib unseamed for side vent. ●

Stitch Key

☐	k on RS, p on WS	Ⓜ	M1
⊟	p on RS, k on WS	Ⓟ	M1 p-st
⊠	ssk		4-st RC
⊠	k2tog		4-st LC
⊠	p2tog		8-st RC
⊠	p2tog tbl		

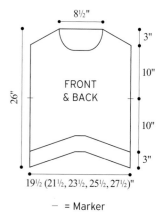

8½"
3"
10"
FRONT & BACK
26"
10"
3"
19½ (21½, 23½, 25½, 27½)"

− = Marker

PLAID PULLOVER

This casual, chic, oversized drop-shoulder pullover features textured stripes and intarsia color blocks with dotted vertical stripes of Swiss darning, or duplicate stitch, to complete the plaid illusion. The photographer took it for a stroll along the streets of SoHo in New York City, where it fit right in.

■■■◻

SIZES
Small (Small, Medium, Large, X-Large). Shown in size Medium.

KNITTED MEASUREMENTS
Bust 40 (44, 48, 52)"/101.5 (111.5,122, 132)cm
Length 24 (24½, 25, 25½)"/61 (62, 63.5, 64.5)cm
Upper Arm 14 (14, 16, 17)"/35.5 (35.5, 40.5, 43)cm

MATERIALS
• 3 (3, 4, 4) 1¾oz/50g hanks (each approx 159yd/145m) of **The Fibre Co.** Road to China Light (baby alpaca/silk/camel/cashmere) in Lapis (A) 🔳2🔳
• 2 (3, 3, 3) hanks in Apatite (B)
• 3 (3, 3, 4) hanks in Cobalt (C)
• 2 hanks each in Citrine (D) and Grey Pearl (E)
• One pair each sizes 2 and 4 (2.75 and 3.5mm) needles, OR SIZE TO OBTAIN GAUGE
• One size 2 (2.75mm) circular needle, 16"/40cm long
• Removable stitch markers

GAUGE
24 sts and 35 rows to 4"/10cm over St st using larger needles.
TAKE TIME TO CHECK GAUGE.

NOTES
1) When changing colors, twist yarns on WS to prevent holes in work.
2) Use a separate bobbin for each color section. Do not carry yarn across back of work.

BACK
With smaller needles and C, cast on 134 (146, 158, 170) sts.
Row 1 (WS) P2, *k2, p2; rep from * to end.
Row 2 (RS) K2, *p2, k2; rep from * to end.
Rep rows 1 and 2 for k2, p2 rib for 2"/5cm, end with a RS row. Change to larger needles.
Next row (WS) [P7 (8, 9, 10), p2tog] 14 times, p to end —120 (132, 144, 156) sts.

Begin Chart 1
For Size Small Only
Row 1 (RS) Beg with st 6, work chart to end of rep, work 52-st rep once, work next 21 sts of chart.

For Sizes Medium (Large, X-Large) Only
Note Work sts outside chart at each edge to correspond to chart throughout.
Row 1 (RS) With B, k1 (7, 13), work 52-st rep twice, work to end of chart; with B, k1 (7, 13).

For All Sizes
Cont to work chart as established until piece measures 22½ (23, 23½, 24)"/57 (58.5, 59.5, 61)cm from beg, end with a WS row.

Shoulder Shaping
Bind off 5 (6, 7, 8) sts at beg of next 6 (10, 12, 12) rows, then bind off 6 (7, 0, 0) sts at beg of next 6 (2, 0, 0) rows. Bind off rem 54 (58, 60, 60) sts for back neck.

FRONT
Work as for back until piece measures 20½ (21, 21½, 22)"/52 (53.5, 54.5, 56)cm, end with a WS row. Mark center 16 (20, 22, 22) sts on last row.

Neck and Shoulder Shaping
Next row (RS) Work to marker, join 2nd ball of yarn and bind off center 16 (20, 22, 22) sts, work to end.
Working both sides at once, bind off from each neck edge 4 sts once, 3 sts twice, 2 sts twice, then dec 1 st at each neck edge every other row 5 times, AT THE SAME TIME,

when piece measures same as back to shoulders, shape shoulders as for back.
Sew shoulder seams.

SLEEVES
Place markers 7 (7, 8, 8½)"/18 (18, 20.5, 21.5)cm down from shoulder seam on front and back. With RS facing, using larger needles and E, pick up and k 84 (84, 96, 102) sts between markers.

Begin Chart 2
Note Beg chart 2 with row 2. Chart alignment will begin in row 15. Work sts outside chart at right edge to correspond to chart.
Row 2 (WS) With E, work row 2 of chart over all sts.
Dec row 3 (RS) With B, work chart row 3, dec 1 st each side—2 sts dec'd.

Row 15 (RS) With B, k1, k2tog, k4 (4, 10, 13), work chart over 52 sts, work first 10 (10, 16, 19) sts of rep once more, k2tog, k1—2 sts dec'd.
Cont to work chart as established through row 104, then work rows 1–33 once more, AT THE SAME TIME, dec 1 st each side every 16th (16th, 10th, 8th) row 7 (7, 12, 13) times more—56 (56, 58, 62) sts.
Change to smaller needles.
Row 34 (WS) With D, purl, dec 2 (2, 0, 0) sts evenly across —54 (54, 58, 62) sts.
Work in k2, p2 rib for 1¾"/4.5cm. Bind off in rib.

FINISHING
Sew side and sleeve seams.

Neckband
With RS facing, using circular needle and C, pick up and k 54 (58, 60, 60) sts along back neck edge, then pick up and k 86 (90, 92, 92) sts along front neck edge—140 (148, 152, 152) sts. Join and pm for beg of rnd.
Rnd 1 *K2, p2; rep from * around.
Rep rnd 1 for k2, p2 rib for 3"/7.5cm. Bind off in rib. ●

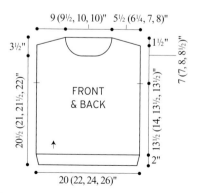

9 (9½, 10, 10)"   5½ (6¼, 7, 8)"

1½"

3½"

7 (7, 8, 8½)"

20½ (21, 21½, 22)"

13½ (14, 13½, 13½)"

FRONT & BACK

2"

20 (22, 24, 26)"

14 (14, 16, 17)"

SLEEVE

15¾"

1¾"

6½ (6½, 7, 7½)"

↑ = Direction of work   — = Marker

CHART 1

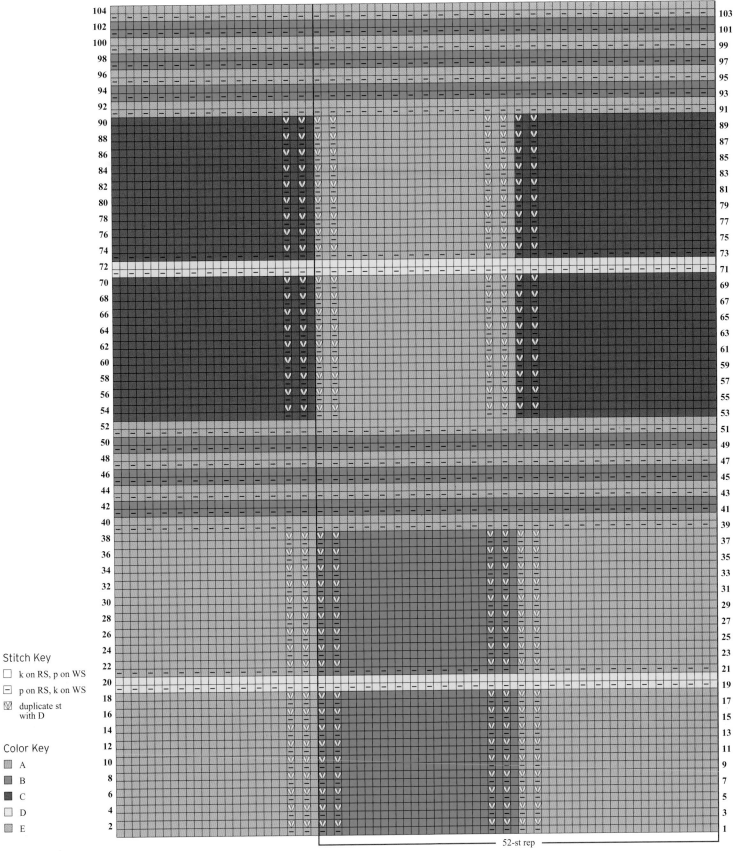

Stitch Key

☐ k on RS, p on WS

⊟ p on RS, k on WS

Ⓥ duplicate st with D

Color Key

▨ A

▨ B

▨ C

▨ D

▨ E

52-st rep

CHART 2

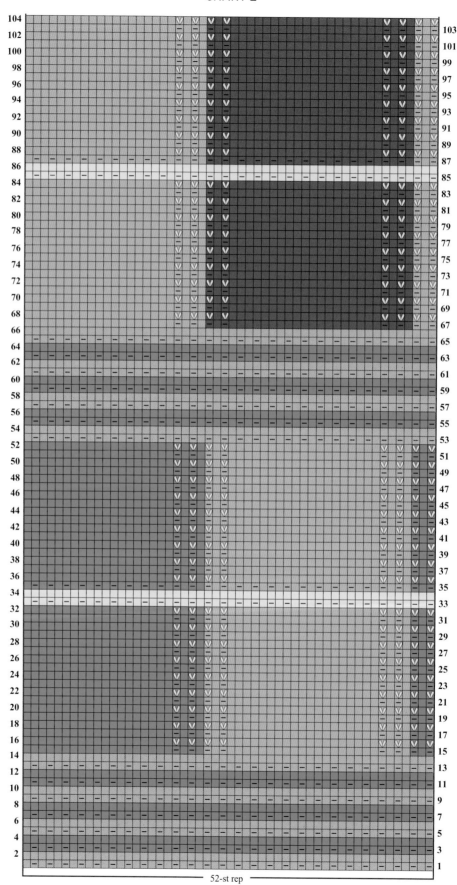

52-st rep

Stitch Key

☐ k on RS, p on WS

⊟ p on RS, k on WS

☒ duplicate st with D

Color Key

▨ A

▨ B

■ C

☐ D

▨ E

GUERNSEY PULLOVER

Traditional Guernsey textures and mitered knitting combine to form the front yoke of this relaxed pullover. The raglan slopes and wide V-neckline are automatically formed by the miter in the front. In the back, the same Guernsey stitches are worked straight across the top while full-fashioned decreases form the sloping raglan sleeves.

SIZES
Small/Medium (Large). Shown in size Small/Medium.

KNITTED MEASUREMENTS
Bust 42 (44)"/106.5 (111.5)cm
Length 26"/66cm
Upper Arm 12½ (13¾)"/32 (35)cm

Materials
• 8 (9) 1¾oz/50g balls (each approx 126yd/115m) of **Fibre Natura/ Universal Yarn** Dona (superwash wool) in #112 Smoky Peach (3)
Note This yarn amount reflects a bracelet length sleeve. For traditional full-length sleeve, add 1 more ball of yarn to the amount.
• One pair each sizes 5 and 6 (3.75 and 4mm) needles, OR SIZE TO OBTAIN GAUGE
• One size 5 (3.75mm) circular needle, 24"/60cm long
• Removable stitch markers

GAUGE
21 sts and 30 rows to 4"/10cm over St st using larger needles.
TAKE TIME TO CHECK GAUGE.

NOTE
To ensure that the back length to the armhole matches the front to the armhole, make the front first.

FRONT
With larger needles, cast on 110 (118) sts.
Purl 1 row, knit 3 rows.
Next row (WS) P2, *k2, p2; rep from * to end.
Next row (RS) K2, *p2, k2; rep from * to end.
Rep last 2 rows once more. For large size only, dec 2 sts evenly across last row—116 sts.
Beg with a (WS) purl row, work in St st (k on RS, p on WS), until piece measures 9"/23cm from beg. On last WS row, pm after 55 (58) sts to mark center front.

V-Opening Shaping
Dec row 1 (RS) K to 3 sts before center marker, ssk, k1, remove marker; join 2nd ball of yarn, on 2nd side, k1, k2tog, k to end.

Work both sides at once with separate balls of yarn as foll:
Dec row 2 (WS) First Side: P to last 3 sts, p2tog, p1; Second Side: P1, p2tog tbl, p to end.
Rep last 2 rows 24 times more—5 (8) sts rem each side.
Next row (RS) Bind off 5 (8) sts from first side, leave last st on needle and pick up and k 54 sts evenly along front edge to center front, pick up and k 1 st in center of v-opening, pick up and k 55 sts along other side of neck, then k 5 (8) sts from second side. Place markers to mark center 3 sts at center of v-opening.
Next row (WS) Bind off 5 (8) sts, p next st, k to marker, sm, p1, k1, p1, sm, k to last 2 sts, p2.
Next row (RS) K to 1 st before marker, p1, sm, k3, sm, p1, k to end.
Next row (WS) P2, k to marker, sm, p1, k1, p1, sm, k to last 2 sts, p2.
Next row (RS) K to 1 st before marker, p1, sm, k3, sm, p1, k to end.
Dec row (WS) P to 2 sts before marker, k2tog, sm, p1, k1, p1, sm, ssk, p to end—109 sts.

Begin Front Chart
Row 1 (RS) Work first 9 sts of chart, work 12-st rep twice, work center 43 sts of chart, work 12-st rep twice, work last 9 sts of chart.
Cont to work front chart in this way through row 59—71 sts. Bind off on next WS row.

BACK
With larger needles, cast on 110 (118) sts.
Purl 1 row, knit 3 rows.
Next row (WS) P2, *k2, p2; rep from * to end.
Next row (RS) K2, *p2, k2; rep from * to end.
Rep last 2 rows once more. For large size only, dec 2 sts evenly across last row—116 sts.
Beg with a (WS) purl row, work in St st until piece measures 17"/43cm from beg, or until piece measures same length as front to end of V-opening shaping.

Raglan Armhole Shaping
Next row (RS) Bind off 4 (7) sts, k to end.
Next row (WS) Bind off 4 (7) sts, k to end—102 sts.
Knit 2 rows.
Dec row (RS) K1, ssk, k to last 3 sts, k2tog, k1—100 sts.
Purl 1 row.

Begin Back Chart
Row 1 (RS) Work first 26 sts of chart, work 12-st rep 4 times, work last 26 sts of chart.
Cont to work back chart in this way through row 71—52 sts. Bind off purlwise on next WS row.

RIGHT SLEEVE
With smaller needles, cast on 50 (54) sts.
Row 1 (WS) P2, *k2, p2; rep from * to end.

Row 2 (RS) K2, *p2, k2; rep from * to end.
Rep rows 1 and 2 for k2, p2 rib for 2½"/6.5cm.
Next row (RS) Knit, dec 4 (2) sts evenly across—46 (52) sts.
Change to larger needles. Beg with a purl row, work in St st for 3 rows.
Inc row (RS) K2, kfb, k to last 4 sts, kfb, k3.
Rep inc row every 8th row 9 times more—66 (72) sts.
Work even until piece measures approx 14"/35.5cm from beg. If a traditional length is desired, work even for 3"/7.5cm more.

Raglan Cap Shaping
Bind off 4 (7) sts at beg of next 2 rows—58 sts.
Dec row (RS) K2, k2tog, k to last 4 sts, ssk, k2.
Work even for 3 rows. Rep dec row. Work even for 1 row.
Rep the last 6 rows 10 times more—14 sts.

Top of Cap Shaping
Row 1 (RS) Bind off 5 sts, k to end—9 sts.
Rows 2, 4, 6, and 8 Purl.
Row 3 Bind off 2 sts, k to last 4 sts, ssk, k2.
Row 5 K2, ssk, k2—5 sts.
Row 7 K1, k2tog, k2.
Row 9 [K2tog] twice. Bind off.

LEFT SLEEVE
Work as for right sleeve to top of cap shaping.

Top of Cap Shaping
Row 1 (RS) Knit.
Row 2 (WS) Bind off 5 sts, p to end—9 sts.
Row 3 K2, k2tog, k to end.
Row 4 Bind off 2 sts, p to end—6 sts.
Row 5 K2, ssk, k2—5 sts.
Row 6 P2tog, p to end—4 sts.
Row 7 Knit.
Row 8 P2tog, p2—3 sts.
Row 9 K1, ssk—2 sts.
Bind off.

FINISHING
Block lightly to measurements. Sew raglan sleeves into raglan armholes.

Neckband
With RS facing and circular needle, pick up and k 48 sts from back neck, 10 sts from top of sleeve, 30 sts along one side of front neck, 3 sts from center front neck, 30 sts along other side of front neck, and 10 sts from top of sleeve—131 sts.
Join to work in rnds and pm to mark beg of rnd.
Purl 2 rnds. Bind off purlwise.

Sew side and sleeve seams. ●

FRONT CHART

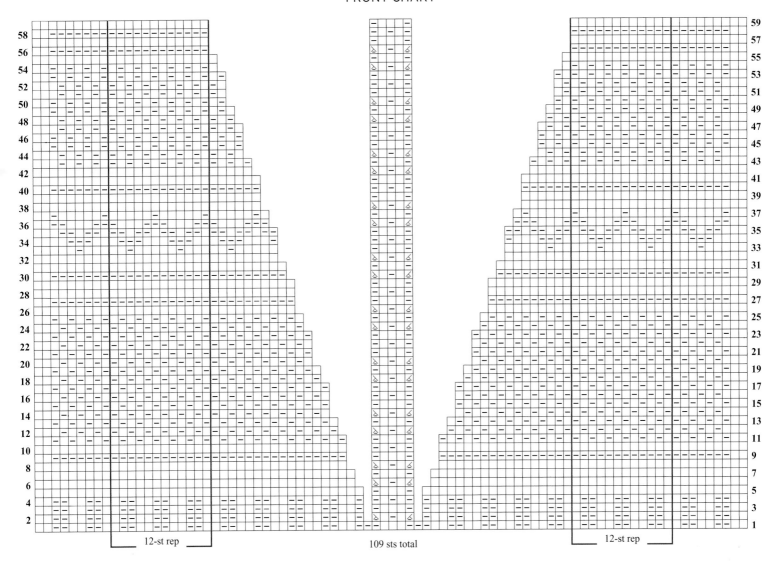

109 sts total

12-st rep

Stitch Key

☐ k on RS, p on WS

— p on RS, k on WS

◿ k2tog on WS

◺ ssk on WS

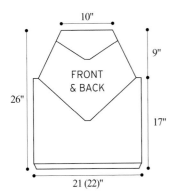

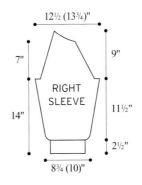

BACK CHART

Stitch Key

☐	k on RS, p on WS
⊟	p on RS, k on WS
◩	k2tog
◪	ssk

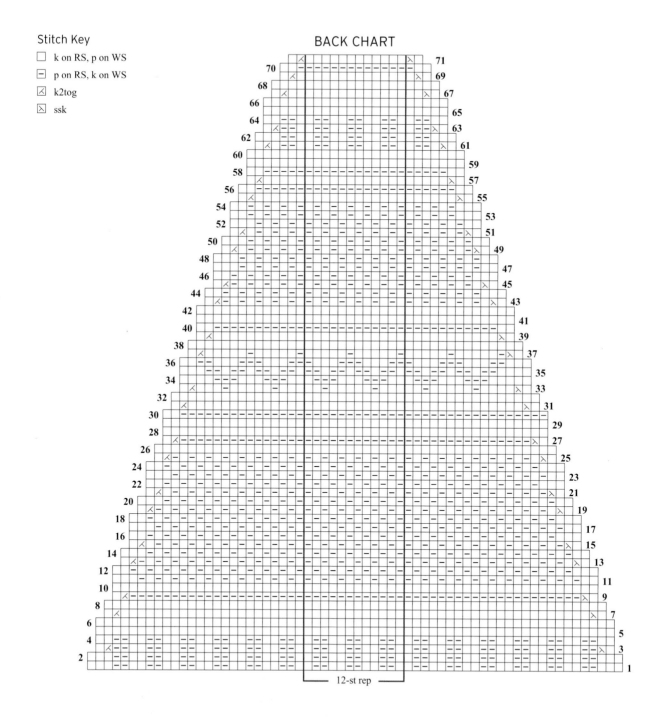

12-st rep

CABLED CARDIGAN

Labyrinthine panels of braids and traveling cables adorn the cardigan fronts, which are worked from the bottom up, decreasing into ribbed and braided bands that wrap around the neck and join to form a high back neckband. The same stunning panel courses down the center back. Designed with loads of overlap in the front, it works well in movement and flatters a variety of figures.

◼◼◼▭

SIZES
Small (Medium, Large, X-Large, 2X-Large). Shown in size Small.

KNITTED MEASUREMENTS
Bust (closed with approx 6"/15.5cm overlap) 40 (44, 48, 52, 56)"/101.5 (111.5, 122, 132, 142)cm
Length 27¼ (27¾, 28¼, 28¾, 29¼)"/69 (70.5, 71.5, 73, 74)cm
Upper Arm 11½ (12, 13, 14½, 16)"/29 (30.5, 33, 37, 40.5)cm

MATERIALS
• 14 (16, 18, 20, 22) 1¾oz/50g balls (each approx 145yd/130m) of **Brooklyn Tweed** Arbor (Targhee wool) in Heron (**3**)
• One pair size 5 (3.75mm) needles, OR SIZE TO OBTAIN GAUGES
• Cable needle (cn)
• Stitch markers
• Stitch holders

GAUGES
• 23 sts and 34 rows to 4"/10cm over St st using size 5 (3.75mm) needles.
• 64 sts of chart 1 = 7½"/19cm using size 5 (3.75mm) needles.
TAKE TIME TO CHECK GAUGES.

STITCH GLOSSARY
4-st RC Sl 2 sts to cn, hold to back, k2, k2 from cn.
4-st LC Sl 2 sts to cn, hold to front, k2, k2 from cn.
4-st RPC Sl 2 sts to cn, hold to back, k2, p2 from cn.
4-st LPC Sl 2 sts to cn, hold to front, p2, k2 from cn.
4-st RC-dec Sl 2 sts to cn, hold to back, k2, k2tog from cn.
4-st LC-dec Sl 2 sts to cn, hold to front, k2tog, k2 from cn.
4-st RPC-dec Sl 2 sts to cn, hold to back, k2, p2tog from cn.
4-st LPC-dec Sl 2 sts to cn, hold to front, p2tog, k2 from cn.
M1R Insert LH needle from back to front under strand between last st worked and next st on LH needle, knit strand through front loop.
M1L Insert LH needle from front to back under strand between last st worked and next st on LH needle, knit strand through back loop.

BACK
Cast on 164 (176, 188, 200, 212) sts.

Begin Rib and Chart 1
Set-up row (WS) [P1, k1] 25 (28, 31, 34, 37) times, pm, work row 1 of chart 1 over 64 sts, pm, [k1, p1] 25 (28, 31, 34, 37) times.
Next row (RS) [K1, p1] 25 (28, 31, 34, 37) times, sm, work next row of chart, sm, [p1, k1] 25 (28, 31, 34, 37) times.
Next row (WS) [P1, k1] 25 (28, 31, 34, 37) times, sm, work next row of chart, sm, [k1, p1] 25 (28, 31, 34, 37) times.
Rep last 2 rows, rep rows 1–4 of chart 1, until row 4 has been worked 6 times. Rib measures approx 3"/7.5cm.
Note Read instructions before cont'v to knit.
Dec row (WS) P2 (2, 2, 8, 4), [p2tog, p4 (4, 4, 4, 5)] 8 (9,10, 10, 10) times, sm, work row 5 of chart, sm, [p4 (4, 4, 4, 5), p2tog] 8 (9, 10, 10, 10) times, p2 (2, 2, 8, 4)—148 (158, 168, 180, 192) sts.
Cont chart, working though row 21 once, then rep rows 22–59, AT THE SAME TIME, work as foll:
Next row (RS) K to marker, sm, work next row of chart, sm, k to end.
Next row (WS) P to marker, sm, work next row of chart, sm, p to end.
Rep last 2 rows until piece measures 6"/15.5cm from beg, end with a WS row.

ROSE CALLAHAN

Side Shaping

Dec row (RS) K3, k2tog, k to marker, sm, work next row of chart, sm, k to last 5 sts, ssk, k3—2 sts dec'd.

Rep dec row every 26th row 4 times more—138 (148, 158, 170, 182) sts.

Work even in pats as established until piece measures 19"/48cm from beg, end with a RS row.

Armhole Shaping

Bind off 4 (4, 5, 6, 7) sts at beg of next 2 rows, 3 sts at beg of next 2 (4, 4, 4, 6) rows, then 2 sts at beg of next 2 (2, 4, 6, 6) rows.

Dec row (RS) K3, k2tog, sm, work next row of chart, sm, k to last 5 sts, ssk, k3.

Rep dec row every RS row 7 (7, 7, 8, 8) times more—104 (108, 112, 116, 120) sts.

Work even in pat as established until piece measures 7½ (8, 8½, 9, 9½)"/19 (20.5, 21.5, 23, 24)cm, end with a WS row.

Shoulder and Neck Shaping

Mark center 48 sts.

Next row (RS) Bind off 4 (6, 6, 6, 8) sts, work to center marked sts, join 2nd ball of yarn and bind off center 48 sts, work to end. Working both sides at once, bind off 4 (6, 6, 6, 8) sts at beg of next WS row, then cont to bind off 5 (5, 6, 7, 7) sts from each shoulder twice, AT THE SAME TIME, bind off from each neck edge 5 sts twice, then 4 sts once.

LEFT FRONT

Cast on 106 (112, 118, 124, 130) sts.

Begin Rib and Chart 1

Set-up row (WS) Sl 2 wyif, work row 1 of chart 1, pm, [k1, p1] 20 times.

Next row (RS) [K1, p1] 20 (23, 26, 29, 32) times, sm, work next row of chart, k2.

Next row (WS) Sl 2 wyif, work next row of chart, sm, [k1, p1] 20 (23, 26, 29, 32) times.

Rep last 2 rows, rep rows 1–4 of chart 1, until row 4 has been worked 6 times. Rib measures approx 3"/7.5cm.

Note Read instructions before cont to knit.

Dec row (WS) Sl 2 wyif, work row 5 of chart, sm, [p6 (6, 7, 7, 8)], p2tog] 4 (5, 5, 6, 6) times, p8 (6, 7, 4, 4)—102 (107, 113, 118, 124) sts. Cont chart, working though row 21 once, then rep rows 22–59 three times, then rows 22–51 once more, AT THE SAME TIME, work as foll:

Next row (RS) K to marker, sm, work next row of chart, k2.

Next row (WS) Sl 2 wyif, work next row of chart, p to end.

Rep last 2 rows until piece measures 6"/15.5cm from beg, end with a WS row.

Side Shaping

Dec row (RS) K3, k2tog, k to marker, work next row of chart, k2—1 st dec'd.

Rep dec row every 26th row 4 times more—97 (102, 108, 113, 119) sts.

Work even in pat as established until piece measures 19"/48cm from beg, end with a WS row.

Armhole Shaping
Note When chart row 51 is complete, work chart 2. This may occur at the same time the armhole is being shaped.

Bind off 4 (4, 5, 6, 7) sts at beg of next RS row, 3 sts at beg of next 1 (2, 2, 2, 3) RS rows, then 2 sts at beg of next 1 (1, 2, 3, 3) RS rows. Work a WS row.

Dec row (RS) K3, k2tog, k to marker, work next row of chart, k2. Rep dec row every RS row 7 (7, 8, 8, 8) times more.

Cont working even along the armhole edge and work chart 2 through row 16—16 sts have been decreased—64 (66, 68, 70, 72) sts rem after all armhole and chart dec have been worked.

Work even and cont to rep rows 17–20 of chart 2 until armhole measures 7½ (8, 8½, 9, 9½)"/19 (20.5, 21.5, 23, 24), end with a WS row.

Shoulder Shaping
Bind off 4 (6, 6, 6, 8) sts at beg of next RS row, 5 (5, 6, 7, 7) sts at beg of next 2 RS rows—50 sts.

Collar Extension
Next row (WS) Sl 2, work next row of chart.
Next row (RS) Work next row of chart, k2.
Rep last 2 rows and cont to rep rows 17–20 of chart 2, until extension measures approx 5"/12.5cm, end with a WS row.

Dec row (RS) P1, k1, ssk, k2tog, *k2tog, [ssk] twice, [k2tog, ssk] 3 times, k2tog; rep from * once more, k2, p2—28 sts.

Knit 8 rows. Cut yarn, leaving a tail for finishing. Place sts on a holder.

RIGHT FRONT
Cast on 106 (112, 118, 124, 130) sts.

Beg Rib and Chart 1
Set-up row (WS) [P1, k1] 20 (23, 26, 29, 32) times, pm, work row 1 of chart, p2.
Next row (RS) Sl 2 wyib, work next row of chart, sm, [p1, k1] 20 (23, 26, 29, 32) times.
Next row (WS) [P1, k1] 20 (23, 26, 29, 32) times, pm, work next row of chart, p2.
Rep last 2 rows, rep rows 1–4 of chart 1, until row 4 has been worked 6 times. Rib measures approx 3"/7.5cm.
Note Read instructions before cont to knit.
Dec row (WS) P8 (6, 7, 4, 4), [p2tog, p6 (6, 7, 7, 8)] 4 (5, 5, 6, 6) times, sm, work row 5 of chart, p2—102 (107, 113, 118, 124) sts.

Cont chart, working though row 21 once, then rep rows 22–59 three times, then rows 22–51 once more, AT THE SAME TIME, work as foll:
Next row (RS) Sl 2, work next row of chart, sm, k to end.
Next row (WS) P to marker, sm, work next row of chart, p2.
Rep last 2 rows until piece measures 6"/15.5cm from beg, end with a WS row.

Side Shaping
Dec row (RS) Sl 2, work next row of chart, sm, k to last 5 sts, ssk, k3.

CHART 1

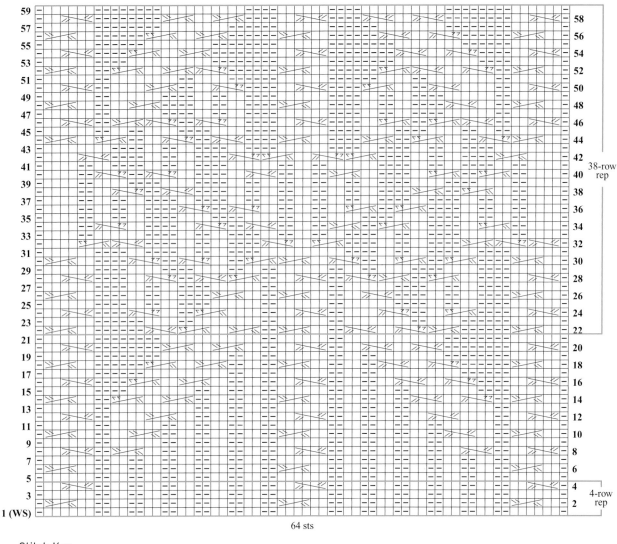

Left side row numbers (bottom to top): 1 (WS), 3, 5, 7, 9, 11, 13, 15, 17, 19, 21, 23, 25, 27, 29, 31, 33, 35, 37, 39, 41, 43, 45, 47, 49, 51, 53, 55, 57, 59

Right side row numbers (bottom to top): 2, 4, 6, 8, 10, 12, 14, 16, 18, 20, 22, 24, 26, 28, 30, 32, 34, 36, 38, 40, 42, 44, 46, 48, 50, 52, 54, 56, 58

4-row rep

38-row rep

64 sts

Stitch Key

☐ k on RS, p on WS   ⊟ p on RS, k on WS   4-st RC   4-st LC   4-st RPC   4-st LPC

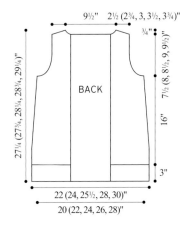

BACK

9½"   2½ (2¾, 3, 3½, 3¾)"
¾"
7½ (8, 8½, 9, 9½)"
16"
3"
27¼ (27¾, 28¼, 28¾, 29¼)"
22 (24, 25½, 28, 30)"
20 (22, 24, 26, 28)"

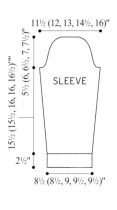

SLEEVE

11½ (12, 13, 14½, 16)"
5½ (6, 6½, 7, 7½)"
15½ (15½, 16, 16, 16½)"
2½"
8½ (8½, 9, 9½, 9½)"

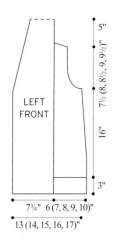

LEFT FRONT

5"
7½ (8, 8½, 9, 9½)"
16"
3"
7¾"   6 (7, 8, 9, 10)"
13 (14, 15, 16, 17)"

Rep dec row every 26th row 4 times more—97 (102, 108, 113, 119) sts. Work even in pat as established until piece measures 19"/48cm from beg, end with a RS row.

Armhole shaping
Note When chart row 51 is complete, work chart 2. This may occur at the same time the armhole is being shaped.
Bind off 4 (4, 5, 6, 7) sts at beg of next WS row, 3 sts at beg of next 1 (2, 2, 2, 3) WS rows, then 2 sts at beg of next 1 (1, 2, 3, 3) WS rows.
Dec row (RS) Sl 2, work next row of chart, sm, k to last 5 sts, ssk, k3.
Rep dec row every RS row 7 (7, 8, 8, 8) times more—80 (82, 84, 86, 88) sts.
Cont working even along armhole edge and work chart 2 through row 16—16 sts have been decreased, 64 (66, 68, 70, 72) sts rem. Work even and cont to rep rows 17–20 of chart until armhole measures 7½ (8, 8½, 9, 9½)"/19 (20.5, 21.5, 23, 24), end with a RS row.

Shoulder Shaping
Bind off 4 (6, 6, 6, 8) sts at beg of next WS row, then 5 (5, 6, 7, 7) sts at beg of next 2 WS rows—50 sts.

Collar Extension
Next row (RS) Sl 2, work next row of chart.
Next row (WS) Work next row of chart, p2.
Rep last 2 rows and cont to rep rows 17–20 of chart 2, until extension measures approx 5"/12.5cm, end with a WS row.
Dec row (RS) Sl 2, p1, k1, *k2tog, [ssk] twice, [k2tog, ssk] 3 times, k2tog; rep from * once more, k2tog, ssk, k1, p1—28 sts.
Knit 9 rows. Cut yarn, leaving a 24"/61cm tail. Place sts on a holder.

SLEEVES
Cast on 56 (56, 58, 60, 60) sts. Work in k1, p1 rib for 2 1/2"/6.5cm, end with a WS row.
Dec row (RS) [K6, k2tog] 6 times, k to end—50 (50, 52, 54, 54) sts.
Beg with a purl row, work in St st (k on RS, p on WS) for 7 rows.
Inc row (RS) K2, M1R, k to last 2 sts, M1L, k2—2 sts inc'd.
Work 7 rows even. Work inc row.
[Work 15 (11, 11, 7, 5) rows even, work inc row] 6 (8, 9, 13, 17) times—66 (70, 74, 84, 92) sts.
Work even until piece measures 18 (18, 18½, 18½, 19)"/46 (46, 47, 47, 48)cm from beg, end with a WS row.

Cap Shaping
Bind off 3 (3, 3, 4, 4) sts at beg of next 2 rows, then 2 sts at beg of next 2 (2, 2, 4, 4) rows.
Dec row (RS) K3, k2tog, k to last 5 sts, ssk, k3.
Rep dec row on next RS row, then every 4th row 8 (8, 9, 9, 9) times more.
Rep dec row on next RS row, then every other row 0 (2, 3, 3, 4) times more.
Bind off 2 sts at beg of next 2 (2, 4, 4) rows, then 3 sts at beg of next 2 (2, 2, 4) rows.
Bind off rem 24 sts.

FINISHING
Block pieces to measurements. Sew shoulder seams. Use Kitchener stitch (see page 174) to join front neck extensions tog. Sew sides of neck extensions along center back neck. Set in sleeves. Sew side and sleeve seams. ●

CHART 2

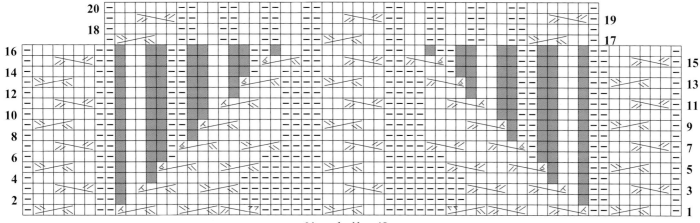

64 sts dec'd to 48 sts

Stitch Key

☐ k on RS, p on WS	4-st RC	4-st RPC	4-st RC-dec	4-st RPC-dec
⊟ p on RS, k on WS	4-st LC	4-st LPC	4-st LC-dec	4-st LPC-dec
▨ no stitch				

NATURE MADE

By Daryl Brower

NORAH GAUGHAN has always been a force of nature.
From the day she first picked up a set of needles as a teen, she's been fearlessly shaping yarn into breathtakingly beautiful objects. Her organic, unexpected designs have graced the pages of multiple magazines and made her a favorite on the teaching circuit.

With stints as design director at two major yarn houses (Reynolds JCA and Berroco) and two books, **Knitting Nature** and **Norah Gaughan's Knitted Cable Sourcebook**, under her belt (a third, **Framework: 10 Architectural Knits**, a collaboration with Quince & Co., is set to release this month), she's now reaching an ever-expanding audience as a member of the Brooklyn Tweed design team and as a contributor to a large number of magazines (both established and new) and small yarn companies.

You're pretty devoted to yarn and needles, and it seems it's been a lifelong love for you. Who taught you to knit?
I first picked up needles in 1975 (I was 14) and was instantly hooked. I'd been crocheting for a few years before I learned to knit, which I think made learning Continental easier. A close family friend, Grace Judson, who was about my age, taught me one summer during an extended visit. She started me off fearlessly with a two-color hat in fingering-weight yarn.

That's pretty ambitious. Your parents were both working artists. Do you think that had much influence on your own creativity?
My parents were both illustrators. My dad's specialty was science fiction, and he was pretty well known in his time. Mom [Phoebe Gaughan] illustrated all sorts of gardening and how-to publications. She's retired to making slab pottery in the last few years, but I believe the last thing she worked on was for the publisher of **Vogue Knitting**. My parents' creativity influenced me from all directions. It's impossible to separate which aspects came from nurture and which from nature.

How so?
On the nurture side, my brother Brian and I spent a lot of time making things. With Dad it was painting, printing from our own linoleum blocks, and playing drawing games. With Mom I made

Christmas ornaments and learned how to sew. I still miss decorating Easter eggs with both of them. We tried a different technique every year. One of the biggest influences from both of them was simply being aware that freelancing [as a career] existed. Plus, I'm not sure if I would have discovered the hand-knitting industry without Mom. My first published design was the direct result of her showing one of my sweaters to an editor she was doing illustrations for.

So let's put an end to the oft-stated rumor about your college years. You went to Brown University but you did not, in fact, study biochemistry.
I'm not sure where the biochemistry rumor came from—is that still on Wikipedia?

It is. You actually have a dual degree in biology and art, right?
Right. I studied biology at Brown—mostly evolution and ecology. I fulfilled the requirements for both a biology and an art degree, but it is only one degree. You save money that way!

So how did you end up working as a knitwear designer?
After graduation, I stayed on in Providence, and I found I was most passionate about knitting and designing. Biology was great to study. I still love learning about the subject, but working in the field didn't seem that appealing to me.

So you turned to knitting?
Providence was a good place for that! When [designers and longtime yarn-industry fixtures] Margery Winter and Deborah Newton advertised for knitters, I knew I had to meet them.

And they both encouraged your career?
Deborah advised me to submit [designs] to several magazines, which really added to my portfolio. Meanwhile, I started knitting [samples] for Margery and then designed for her when she became

an editor. She was an incredible mentor, amazingly supportive, and she pushed my artistic boundaries. I think of the time I spent working closely with her as graduate school. Years later we worked together again at Berroco.

Your designs have a lovely organic quality to them. Do you think that comes in part from your biology background?
I find that I most often combine a fashion influence with inspiration from somewhere else. When I wrote **Knitting Nature**, a layman's science book on patterns in nature became a fantastic jumping-off point. Nature's patterns influence my pattern stitches and the sweaters' structures, but I merge those inspirations with what I see happening in runway fashion at the time.

So you follow the fashion trends?
Keeping an eye on what's happening in the fashion world helps keep me out of a silhouette rut. I don't want to keep designing with the same proportions I used when I was in my twenties. It's way more interesting to me to use shapes I wouldn't have thought of if I stayed in my own little isolated bubble. I often get on a bit of a jag, exploring techniques thoroughly. For instance, one of the eponymous booklets I did for Berroco was directly influenced by a collection of crystals I saw at a museum in Florence. I used the vocabulary of polygons I learned when writing **Knitting Nature** in many of the pieces in that collection.

You mentioned earlier that your parents' experience taught you that you could freelance for a living. Do you think that helped you find the path to the knitting world?
I have never been one for a master plan. If I'd had one, I wouldn't have dreamed of this path.

So how did you become a designer?
It may be a silly thing to say, but one thing led to the next. I started as a knitter, became a freelance designer and then started developing my own patterns and stitches. My first "real" job was as design director

at JCA (Reynolds, Unger, Artful Yarns, Adrienne Vittadini and knitting Yarns). **Knitting Nature** came next, then my nine-year stint as design director at Berroco. The knitting world shifted drastically with the growth of the Internet. Now things I only dreamed of doing twenty-five years ago, like self-publishing, are easily achieved.

That's so amazing, isn't it? How do you think that's helped the design world grow?
Finally, the mechanism for matching designer and audience is in place. I've long held the theory that designers are best when they are being true to themselves, rather than trying to please the largest number of people at once. Success is a matter of finding your audience.

You've certainly found yours. You do a lot of traveling for teaching. What are your favorite projects to knit when you're on the go? Do you go for the complex or keep it simple?
Like most knitters, I think, I like to knit easy things on the road. Give me some stockinette stitch, garter, or an easily memorized texture pattern and I am happy. Teaching takes a lot of energy and brainpower. In the evening, I still want to knit, but it's best if I don't have to make decisions or follow a chart really carefully.

Your design for this issue is a little more complicated than your on-the-go pieces. What was the inspiration? Are there any special techniques that you used in creating the piece?
I was thinking about a cardigan shape that I like to wear and that I wished I had in my own wardrobe when I received an email from a knitter who said she wished she had a chart for a pattern stitch she saw in one of my classes. So I decided to combine the two—the silhouette and the stitch—in this design. I modified the cable so it decreases near the neckline, then morphs to ribbing and wraps around the back neck.

To see more of Norah Gaughan's designs and to view her teaching schedule, visit NorahGaughan.net.

NOTES FROM NORAH
TOP TIPS FOR BEAUTIFUL KNITTING

• **Use good yarn!** The process and the product are both important. We didn't have much money when I was a kid, but I have always been willing to spend twice as much money on yarn than I would for a ready-to-wear sweater.
• **There is no reason to stress out.** Don't be afraid—you can always rip out. Although many advise otherwise, I say don't read ahead. There's no need to get anxious about things that will be perfectly understandable once you get

there. So, yes, read ahead enough to see if you should be shaping several places at once, but don't try to deeply understand every aspect of the directions before you have even cast on.
• **When you're feeling like you want to, use the pattern as a starting point, but then make it your own. The designer won't mind (at least I don't).**

PERSIAN YOKE PULLOVER

With motifs inspired by Persian carpets, the bold and festive yoke is knit from the top down with no more than two colors in each row. Swiss darning, or duplicate stitch, is added later to add even more richness and complexity. With just a bit of striped ribbing, the stockinette body serves to highlight the gorgeous colorwork yoke.

SIZES
X-Small (Small, Medium, Large, X-Large). Shown in size X-Small.

KNITTED MEASUREMENTS
Bust 33 (37, 41, 45, 48)"/84 (94, 104, 114.5, 122)cm
Length (from center back) 21 (21½, 22½, 23, 24)"/53.5 (54.5, 57, 58.5, 61)cm
Upper Arm 10½ (12, 13, 14, 15)"/26.5 (30.5, 33, 35.5, 38)cm

MATERIALS
• 4 (5, 5, 6, 6) 1¾oz/50g hanks (each approx 137yd/125m) of **The Fibre Co.** Luma (merino wool/organic cotton/linen/silk) in Willow (MC) (⬤3)
• 1 (2, 2, 2, 3) hanks each in Sangria (C) and Aizome (E)
• 1 (1, 2, 2, 2) hanks each in Ciel (A), Kiwi (B), and Zinnia (D)
• 1 hank in Blanca (F)
• One each sizes 4 and 6 (3.5 and 4mm) circular needles, 16 and 32"/40 and 80cm long, OR SIZE TO OBTAIN GAUGES
• One set (5) each sizes 4 and 6 (3.5 and 4mm) double-pointed needles (dpn)
• Tapestry needle
• Stitch markers
• Scrap yarn

GAUGES
• 23 sts and 32 rnds to 4"/10cm over St st using larger needle.
• 23 sts and 30 rnds to 4"/10cm over St st and chart pats using larger needle.
TAKE TIME TO CHECK GAUGES.

NOTES
1) Body and sleeves are worked in the round from the top down to the underarm as one piece, then divided to work the body and sleeves separately.
2) Charts are worked in the round in St st. Read all rnds from right to left.
3) When changing colors, twist yarns on WS to prevent holes in work.
4) Some small areas in chart 1 are worked in duplicate stitch in finishing.

GERMAN SHORT ROW (GSR)

Work the number of sts stated in the pattern instructions, turn work. With yarn in front of work, slip 1 stitch purlwise. Take the yarn over the top of your needle (as if to yo), creating a "double stitch" on your right needle. Continue in pattern as instructed. To complete the GSR, the next time you encounter the "double stitch," work the two loops together.

YOKE

With larger 16"/40cm needle and C, cast on 126 (140, 140, 154, 154) sts. Join, taking care not to twist sts, and pm for beg of rnd. With C, knit 0 (2, 2, 3, 2) rnds.

For Sizes Medium (Large, X-Large) Only
Inc rnd With C, knit, inc 14 sts evenly around—154 (168, 168) sts.

For Size X-Large Only
With C, knit 3 rnds.
Inc rnd With C, knit, inc 14 sts evenly around—182 sts.

For All Sizes, Begin Chart 1
Note Change to longer size 6 (4mm) needle when sts no longer fit comfortably.
Rnd 1 (RS) Work 14-st rep 9 (10, 11, 12, 13) times around. Cont in chart pat as established through rnd 47—252 (280, 308, 336, 364) sts.

For Sizes Small (Medium, Large, X-Large) only
Inc rnd With MC, knit, inc 12 (10, 16, 18) sts evenly around—292 (318, 352, 382) sts.

For All Sizes
Cont with MC only as foll:
Place marker opposite beg of rnd marker at center of one rep for center front (see chart). Count over 42 (48, 52, 58, 62) sts each side of center marker and pm for right front and left front—84 (96, 104, 116, 124) front sts between markers. Remove original beg of rnd marker.

Begin Short Rows
Knit to right front marker, GSR, p to left front marker, *GSR, k to wrapped st, k wrap and st tog, k3, GSR, p to wrapped st, p wrap and st tog, p3, GSR; rep from * until 8 turns have been worked at each end. Turn, knit a rnd over all sts, knitting any wraps tog, end at left front marker.
Knit 0 (2, 5, 8, 10) rnds.
Inc rnd Knit, inc 10 sts evenly around, end rnd 1 st before left front marker—262 (302, 328, 362, 392) sts.

Divide for Body and Sleeves
Next rnd K1, place next 48 (56, 60, 66, 72) sts on scrap yarn (left sleeve), cast on 6 (6, 7, 7, 7) sts, pm (underarm), cast on 6 (6, 7, 7, 7) sts, k82 (94, 104, 114, 124) for back, place next 48 (56, 60, 66, 72) sts on scrap yarn (right sleeve), cast on 6 (6, 7, 7, 7) sts, pm (underarm), cast on 6 (6, 7, 7, 7) sts, k to first underarm marker, removing right and left front markers—190 (214, 236, 258, 276) sts on needle.

BODY
Note The first underarm marker is now the beg of rnd.
*Knit 9 rnds.
Dec rnd K2, k2tog, k to 4 sts before next marker, ssk, k2, sm, k2, k2tog, k to 2 sts before marker, ssk, k2—4 sts dec'd.
Rep from * 5 times more—166 (190, 212, 234, 252) sts.
Work even in St st (k every rnd) until piece measures 9 (9, 9½, 9½, 10)"/23 (23, 24, 24, 25.5)cm from underarm or 3½"/9cm

less than desired length.

Inc rnd Knit, inc 38 (38, 40, 42, 48) sts evenly around—204 (228, 252, 276, 300) sts.

Begin Chart 3
Rnd 1 (RS) Work 4-st rep 51 (57, 63, 69, 75) times around.
Cont in chart pat as established through rnd 8.
Change to smaller 32"/80cm needle.
With C, knit 1 rnd, then work in k2, p2 rib for 12 rnds.
With E, cont in rib for 5 rnds more. Bind off loosely in rib.

SLEEVES
With MC and larger dpn, starting at the center of the underarm, pick up and k 6 (6, 7, 7, 7) sts, k48 (56, 60, 66. 72) sts from holder, pick up and k 6 (6, 7, 7, 7) sts along armhole to center, pm for beg of rnd— 60 (68, 74, 80, 86) sts.
**Knit 13 (10, 7, 7, 5) rnds.
Dec rnd K2, k2tog, k to 4 sts before marker, ssk, k2.
Rep from ** 5 (7, 9, 10, 13) times more—48 (52, 54, 58, 58) sts.
Work even in St st until piece measures 12"/30.5cm from underarm, or 6"/15.5cm less than desired length.
Inc rnd Knit, inc 4 (4, 6, 6, 6) sts evenly around—52 (56, 60, 64, 64) sts.

Begin Chart 2
Rnd 1 (RS) Work 4-st rep 13 (14, 15, 16, 16) times around.
Cont in chart 2 pat as established through rnd 24, dec 8 sts evenly around on last rnd—44 (48, 52, 56, 56) sts.
Change to smaller dpn and B. Work 12 rnds in k2, p2 rib.
With D, cont in rib for 6 rnds more.
Bind off loosely in rib.

FINISHING
Work duplicate stitch foll chart.

Neckband
With smaller 16"/40cm circular needle and C, pick up and k 100 (112, 112, 124, 124) sts evenly around cast-on edge. Join and pm for beg of rnd.
Work in k2, p2 rib for 6 rnds.
With B, cont rib for 4 rnds.
With D, bind off as foll: K2tog, *[yo, pass st over yo] twice, k2tog, pass 2nd st over 1st st; rep from *around.
Block to measurements. ●

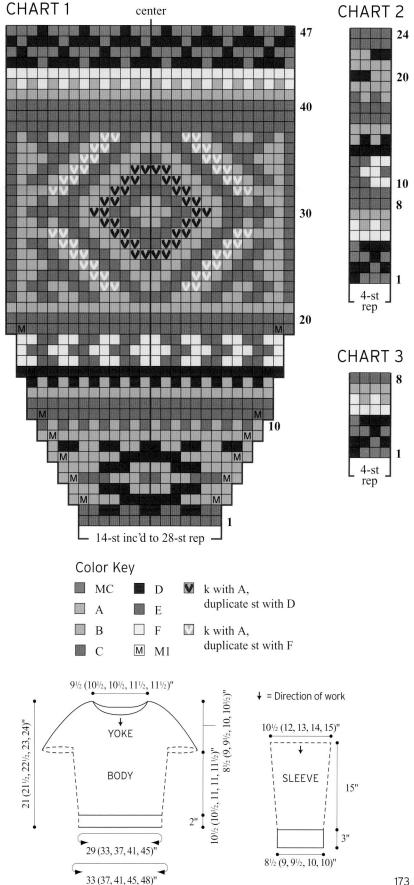

CHART 1

center

47

40

30

20

10

1

14-st inc'd to 28-st rep

CHART 2

24

20

10
8

1

4-st rep

CHART 3

8

1

4-st rep

Color Key

▨ MC	■ D	☑ k with A, duplicate st with D
▨ A	▨ E	
▨ B	☐ F	☑ k with A, duplicate st with F
▨ C	Ⓜ M1	

9½ (10½, 10½, 11½, 11½)"

YOKE

BODY

21 (21½, 22½, 23, 24)"

10½ (10½, 11, 11, 11½)"

8½ (9, 9½, 10, 10½)"

2"

29 (33, 37, 41, 45)"

33 (37, 41, 45, 48)"

↓ = Direction of work

10½ (12, 13, 14, 15)"

SLEEVE

15"

3"

8½ (9, 9½, 10, 10)"

ABBREVIATIONS

2nd	second
approx	approximately
beg	begin(ning)
CC	contrasting color
ch	chain
cm	centimeter(s)
cn	cable needle
cont	continu(e)(ing)
dc	double crochet
dec	decreas(e)(es)(ing)
dec'd	decreased
dpn	double-pointed needle(s)
foll	follow(s)(ing)
g	gram(s)
inc	increas(e)(es)(ing)
inc'd	increased
k	knit
kfb	knit into the front and back of a stitch—1 knit stitch increased
k2tog	knit 2 stitches together
LH	left-hand
lp(s)	loop(s)
m	meter(s)
M1(L)	Insert LH needle from front to back under strand between last st worked and next st on LH needle, knit strand through back loop—1 knit stitch increased.
M1 p-st	Insert LH needle from front to back under strand between last st worked and next st on LH needle, purl strand through back loop—1 purl stitch increased.
MC	main color
mm	millimeter(s)
oz	ounce(s)
p	purl
p2tog	purl 2 stitches together
pat(s)	pattern(s)
pm	place maker
psso	pass slip stitch(es) over
rem	remain(s)(ing)
rep	repeat
rev	reverse

RH	right-hand
rnd(s)	round(s)
RS	right side(s)
S2KP	slip 2 stitches together knitwise, knit 1, pass 2 slipped stitches over knit stitch
sc	single crochet
SKP	slip 1 stitch, knit 2 stitches, pass slipped stitch over
SK2P	slip 1 stitch, knit 2 stitches together, pass slipped stitch over 2 stitches knit together
sl	slip
sl st	slip stitch
sm	slip marker
ssk	slip next 2 stitches knitwise one at a time, return slipped stitches to left-hand needle, knit these 2 stitches together
ssp	slip next 2 stitches purlwise one at a time, return slipped stitches to left-hand needle, purl these 2 stitches together
sssk	slip next 3 stitches knitwise one at a time, insert tip of LH needle into fronts of these stitches and knit them together
st(s)	stitch(es)
St st	stockinette stitch
tbl	through back loop(s)
tog	together
w&t	wrap and turn
WS	wrong side(s)
wyib	with yarn in back
wyif	with yarn in front
yd	yard(s)
yo	yarn over
*	repeat directions following * as many times as indicated
[ ]	repeat directions inside brackets as many times as indicated

KITCHENER STITCH

Cut a tail at least 4 times the length of the edge that will be grafted together and thread through a tapestry needle. Hold needles together with right sides showing, making sure each has the same number of live stitches, and work as follows:

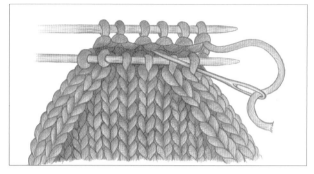

1) Insert tapestry needle purlwise through first stitch on front needle. Pull yarn through, leaving stitch on needle.

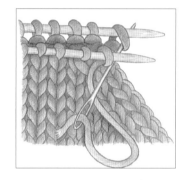

2) Insert tapestry needle knitwise through first stitch on back needle. Pull yarn through, leaving stitch on needle.

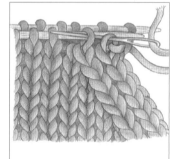

3) Insert tapestry needle knitwise through first stitch on front needle, pull yarn through, and slip stitch off needle. Then, insert tapestry needle purlwise through next stitch on front needle and pull yarn through, leaving this stitch on needle.

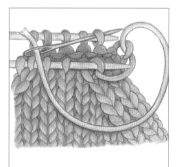

4) Insert tapestry needle purlwise through first stitch on back needle, pull yarn through, and slip stitch off needle. Then, insert tapestry needle knitwise through next stitch on back needle and pull yarn through, leaving this stitch on needle. Repeat steps 3 and 4 until all stitches on both front and back needles have been grafted.

KNITTING NEEDLE SIZES

US	Metric	US	Metric
0	2mm	9	5.5mm
1	2.25mm	10	6mm
2	2.75mm	10½	6.5mm
3	3.25mm	11	8mm
4	3.5mm	13	9mm
5	3.75mm	15	10mm
6	4mm	17	12.75mm
7	4.5mm	19	15mm
8	5mm	35	19mm

STANDARD YARN WEIGHT SYSTEM

Categories of yarn, gauge ranges, and recommended needle and hook sizes

Yarn Weight Symbol & Category	⓪ Lace	① Super Fine	② Fine	③ Light	④ Medium	⑤ Bulky	⑥ Super Bulky	⑦ Jumbo
Type of Yarns in Category	Fingering 10-count crochet thread	Sock, Fingering, Baby	Sport, Baby	DK, Light Worsted	Worsted, Afghan, Aran	Chunky, Craft, Rug	Super Bulky, Roving	Jumbo, Roving
Knit Gauge Range* in Stockinette Stitch to 4 inches	33–40** sts	27–32 sts	23–26 sts	21–24 sts	16–20 sts	12–15 sts	7–11 sts	6 sts and fewer
Recommended Needle in Metric Size Range	1.5–2.25 mm	2.25—3.25 mm	3.25—3.75 mm	3.75—4.5 mm	4.5—5.5 mm	5.5—8 mm	8—12.75 mm	12.75 mm and larger
Recommended Needle U.S. Size Range	000–1	1 to 3	3 to 5	5 to 7	7 to 9	9 to 11	11 to 17	17 and larger
Crochet Gauge* Ranges in Single Crochet to 4 inch	32–42 double crochets**	21–32 sts	16–20 sts	12–17 sts	11–14 sts	8–11 sts	6–9 sts	5 sts and fewer
Recommended Hook in Metric Size Range	Steel*** 1.6–1.4 mm	2.25—3.5 mm	3.5—4.5 mm	4.5—5.5 mm	5.5—6.5 mm	6.5—9 mm	9—16 mm	16 mm and larger
Recommended Hook U.S. Size Range	Steel*** 6, 7, 8 Regular hook B–1	B–1 to E–4	E–4 to 7	7 to I–9	I–9 to K–10 1/2	K–10 1/2 to M–13	M–13 to Q	Q and larger

* GUIDELINES ONLY: The above reflect the most commonly used gauges and needle or hook sizes for specific yarn categories.

** Lace weight yarns are usually knitted or crocheted on larger needles and hooks to create lacy, openwork patterns. Accordingly, a gauge range is difficult to determine. Always follow the gauge stated in your pattern.

*** Steel crochet hooks are sized differently from regular hooks—the higher the number, the smaller the hook, which is the reverse of regular hook sizing

This Standards & Guidelines booklet and downloadable symbol artwork are available at: **YarnStandards.com**

SKILL LEVELS

BEGINNER
Ideal first project.

EASY
Basic stitches, minimal shaping, and simple finishing.

INTERMEDIATE
For knitters with some experience. More intricate stitches, shaping, and finishing.

EXPERIENCED
For knitters able to work patterns with complicated shaping and finishing.

RESOURCES

Berroco
www.berroco.com

Briggs & Little
www.briggsandlittle.com

Brooklyn Tweed
www.brooklyntweed.com

Brown Sheep Company
www.brownsheep.com

Cascade Yarns
www.cascadeyarns.com

Classic Elite Yarns
www.classiceliteyarns.com

The Fibre Co.
www.thefibreco.com

Harrisville Designs
www.harrisville.com

Hikoo/Skacel Collection, Inc.
www.skacelknitting.com

Ístex
www.istex.is/english

Katia
www.katia.com

Malabrigo
www.malabrigoyarn.com

Plymouth Yarn Company
www.plymouthyarn.com

Quince & Co.
www.quinceandco.com

Rowan
www.knitrowan.com

Shibui
www.shibuiknits.com

Tahki Stacy Charles
www.tahkistacycharles.com

Trendsetter Yarns
www.trendsetteryarns.com

Universal Yarn
www.universalyarn.com

Valley Yarn
www.valleyyarn.com

Wool and the Gang
www.woolandthegang.com

INDEX